T0374140

# Reflections:
## *An Autobiography*

A STORY ABOUT FAMILY AND FRIENDS,
AND WYOMING'S SEVENTEENTH STATE AUDITOR

DAVE FERRARI

iUniverse LLC
Bloomington

**Reflections: An Autobiography**

**A STORY ABOUT FAMILY AND FRIENDS, AND WYOMING'S SEVENTEENTH STATE AUDITOR**



*iUniverse books may be ordered through booksellers or by contacting:*

*iUniverse*
*1663 Liberty Drive*
*Bloomington, IN 47403*
*www.iuniverse.com*
*1-800-Authors (1-800-288-4677)*



*ISBN: 978-1-4917-1304-4 (sc)*
*ISBN: 978-1-4917-1305-1 (e)*

*Library of Congress Control Number: 2013919554*

*Printed in the United States of America.*

*iUniverse rev. date: 11/8/2013*

# Contents

Prologue .......... ix

Chapter 1: Not Another Pissy-Assed Girl .......... 1
Chapter 2: Unsolicited Advice .......... 14
Chapter 3: Paths that Cross .......... 44
Chapter 4: "Dorm Chief, March these Hogs Back to the Barracks" .......... 49
Chapter 5: The Private Sector Experience .......... 57
Chapter 6: A Start in State Government .......... 62
Chapter 7: A Study in Government Efficiency .......... 94
Chapter 8: An Unlikely Politician .......... 117
Chapter 9: Which End Do You Put the Hay in? .......... 138
Chapter 10: The Second Term .......... 168
Chapter 11: "Trying to Look Ethical" .......... 203
Chapter 12: Time to Go .......... 217
Chapter 13: "Kiss My Ass" .......... 230
Chapter 14: Think About Living .......... 263

Epilogue .......... 271

# Contents

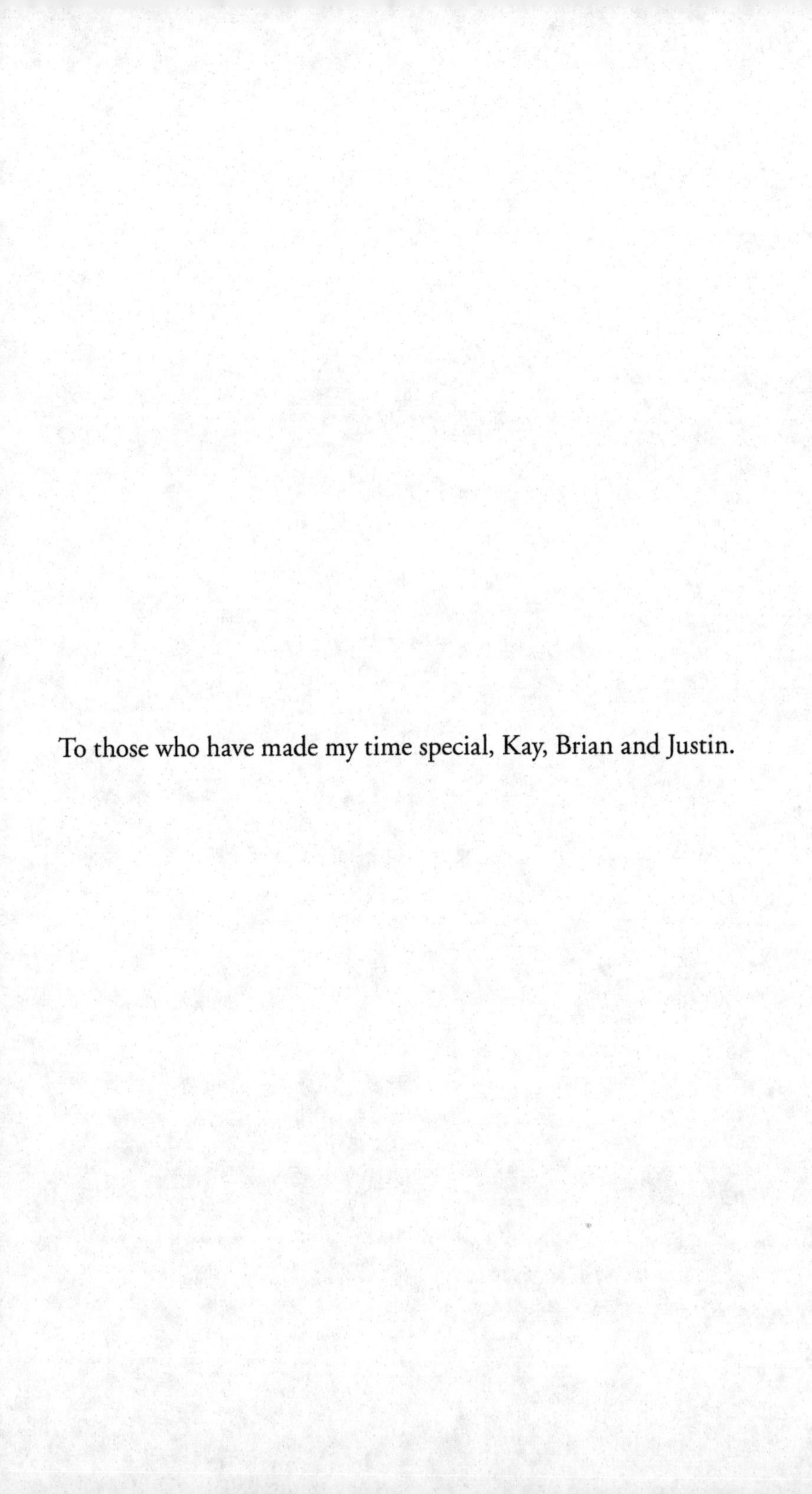

To those who have made my time special, Kay, Brian and Justin.

# Prologue

On Thanksgiving Day in 1985, I handed my dad, who was approaching his 76$^{th}$ birthday, a tape recorder and asked if he would tell his life's story. When I saw him a few weeks later, he said that he tried, but he couldn't "talk into that damn thing". So he decided to write his story. On January 12, 1986, he began. It was a difficult challenge for him but he stuck to it and over the next couple of years, he completed the effort. Not long after, on March 14, 1988, he died. Written in his own hand and housed in a spiral bound notebook, his story was fairly brief even though it covered some 77 years. It described experiences in his life that no one in our family had ever heard. He explained that when at age 12, he quit school to get a job in order to help support his parents and his five siblings. He reflected on his commitment to the family, as well as his loyalty to employers, and his dedication to meeting the responsibilities he faced and the challenges he overcame. His life was an example of the American Dream. He was the son of an Italian immigrant who started with nothing, but found success through devotion to a strong work ethic and honesty in dealing with others. His word was his bond. This approach to life enabled him to provide for his family, raise four children, own a modest but comfortable home, and retire with a few dollars saved and an adequate pension for his later years.

My wife, Kay, took his writings, supplemented them with pictures and graphics, and made copies for each of my siblings and their children. My family cherished this record of my father's life, and we all regretted that our mother hadn't told her own story before Alzheimer's robbed her of the ability to do so. Most of the people who lived during my parents' time are no longer with us, leaving a large void in the family history of that era. I thought that, even though lacking in comparable content and substance, I would someday prepare this story for my children and grandchildren. It was awkward to write these words in the first person, but somehow it seemed less clumsy. Though I am uncomfortable continually referring to me, my, mine and I, throughout, I am hopeful that future Ferraris will overlook this annoyance.

My story tells of some of the irrelevant happenings of childhood, high school pranks and foolishness, and less than impressive academic performances during my early years in college. Unfortunately, I didn't get serious until Kay and I married and I began that first professional job in my career. I worked my way up from entry-level to top management positions. These were important to me at the time, but pale in comparison to the responsibilities I had as one of Wyoming's five statewide elected officials.

My life has followed a path similar to that of most people, I suppose. I graduated from high school in 1961 and attended the University of Wyoming from 1961 through 1965. Kay and I both returned in 1970 and 1971 for Masters Degrees. Some of the highlights of my time so far, include when we were married in 1966, and when our first child was born in 1967, followed by our second in 1972. We have shared no greater thrill than when our own children married and began families of their own. We enjoyed a very close relationship with our parents during those early years. In 1979, I lost one of my brothers-in-law and one of my best friends, Ron Darnall, to a heart attack. He was only 49 years old. His death and funeral over thirty years ago, along with that of my dad some nine years later, remain as two of the more painful memories of my life.

I grew up in a very poor household. My parents were victims of the "great depression" and for many years my shirts were made from material my mother had salvaged from flour sacks. I was told of the cold Wyoming winters during which the only heating fuel my parents could afford was dry cow chips gathered from the droppings which occurred the previous summers. During my childhood years, meals frequently were made from cornbread and beans with an occasional fried chicken dinner. In the summers and early falls, the family garden provided much appreciated diversions from bean soup. It took me a long time to begin enjoying chicken again and to this day, I'm still not particularly fond of beans.

As I compiled information and began writing, it became obvious that the more disappointing memories involved my eight years in elected office and the resistance encountered in trying to bring honesty and integrity into the political process in Wyoming and ethics into the operations of the bureaucracy. My efforts were directed at getting legislation passed defining conflicts of interest, requiring financial disclosures, identifying gifts from lobbyists and special interests, and prohibiting unethical behavior on the part of government officials and employees and the people they do business with. The opposition was powerful, and, as recently proven, the opposition was wrong. According to a study[1] conducted in 2012 by the Center for Public Integrity, Public Radio International, and Global

---

1 http://www.foxnews.con/politics/2012/03/19/study-state-governments -at-hi...

Integrity, Wyoming's risk for corruption is, along with Georgia and South Dakota, the highest in the country. Wyoming ranked only 48th out of the 50 states because of our weak campaign finance laws, weak asset disclosure rules and weak lobbyist regulations. According to the study's authors, reporters in each of the states researched 330 corruption risk indicators across fourteen government categories[2]. Wyoming received an "F" grade in nine of the fourteen areas; a "D-" grade in one; a "C-" grade in two areas; and a grade of "A" in two categories. Overall, Wyoming's grade was a solid "F". According to the study's authors, Wyoming is not unique.

Their findings were summarized as follows: [3] "Not a single state – not one – earned an A grade from the months-long probe. That's the depressing bottom line that emerges from the *State Integrity Investigation*, a first-of-its-kind, data-driven assessment of transparency, accountability and anti-corruption mechanisms in all 50 states."

Outraged, the authors continued, "The stories go on and on. Open records laws with hundreds of exemptions. Crucial budgeting decisions made behind closed doors by a handful of power brokers. Citizen lawmakers voting on bills that would benefit them directly. Scores of legislators turning into lobbyists seemingly overnight. Disclosure laws without much disclosure. Ethics panels that haven't met in years."

"State Officials make lofty promises when it comes to ethics in government," the authors continued. "They tout the transparency of legislative processes, accessibility of records, and the openness of

---

2 http://www.stateintegrity.org/

3 IBID.

public meetings. But these efforts often fall short of providing any real transparency or legitimate hope of rooting out corruption."

In spite of these obvious shortcomings, legislators, lobbyists, and special interests, not only in Wyoming, but throughout the country, argue that no changes are necessary. "We're a small state," they would say; or "everyone knows each other; we're all friends; we can trust each other; we're unique; they don't understand our state; their information is wrong." These arguments were often intense and were always passionate. Consequently, getting effective legislation in place was impossible. Expectations that people ought to conduct their business with integrity and behave in an honorable way was often met with rejection and anger in the halls of government.

As we suffer through partisanship, incompetence, and absolute indifference from our elected officials, at both the state and federal levels, the questions that must be asked are: Where is the outrage? Why do we put up with this? Why do we continue to re-elect self-serving partisan opportunists? People are elected to serve the public not the lobbyists who constantly wine and dine them and not the special interests that seem to keep their campaign coffers full of cash and their own pockets lined.

I can't say I enjoyed taking on the special interests during my days in political office. Something in all of us wants to avoid conflict, be liked, and accepted. But avoiding conflict has been the pattern of many of our elected leaders for far too long. Some of the issues they neglected to deal with before statehood are still lingering today. Some of the actions I took during my time in office brought attention to many of these concerns. Some deficiencies were corrected but, as this new study proves, far more needs to be done.

One thing politicians at all levels of government need to learn is that there is life after politics. None of us, especially those who are elected to serve the public, are indispensible. Government goes on. Life goes on. Others will step up to take our place and although often unimaginable to those departing, the replacements may be even better at representing their constituents. Their new ideas and fresh approaches create opportunities for others in the bureaucracy.

Since leaving office in 1999, I haven't paid much attention to the performance of those who followed. Wyoming government seems to have gotten quieter during those years. Perhaps that is a good thing. Or maybe it simply means, as President John F. Kennedy once said, "If things are smooth and noncontroversial, there's probably not much going on." I suspect that to be the case.

# CHAPTER ONE

## Not Another Pissy-Assed Girl

My story began on January 12, 1944. I was my mother's third child and that day was a happy one for my dad, who wanted a son. Ten years earlier my sister Mae Belle was born and then on the day after Christmas in 1941, Jeanette Marie came along. My younger brother Kenneth followed me by nearly ten years, on September 24, 1953. The girls had always been perfect daughters, but there seems to be something in a man's nature requiring that he have a son, perhaps as proof of his own manhood. Or, in my dad's case, it was probably because of the fact that my Uncle Red and Aunt Louise had already had five children and all were girls. Poor Uncle Red, he didn't have it in him to produce a boy. When the last one, Helen, was born, he simply sat down, with tears rolling down his face and his head in his hands exclaimed, "Oh, Lord, not another pissy-assed girl." Nevertheless, it was exactly that- Five-out-of-five.

So, my dad had broken the spell. He was a proud father and named his first son after himself, calling him David Guy. I don't know where the name David came from, but the middle name, Guy, came from a name my dad chose for his own when he was twelve years old. He was born, Giuseppe Constantino Ferrari but hated the label so much that he would never use it. He signed all of his papers "Guy C." and when he became of age, he had his name legally changed. When I first heard this story, I assumed that the C. stood for Constantino. It was, of course, very Italian and, being proud of my heritage, I liked it even though I wouldn't want a name like that hung on me. But, "no," my dad said, "it wasn't short for Constantino." It wasn't short for anything. "It was simply C.," he declared. I always wondered if there was more to the story and to this day, suspect there was.

I was born in Scottsbluff, Nebraska, a town of about ten thousand people, situated approximately thirty miles east of Torrington where I was raised and attended school. I was never very proud of the fact that I had arrived by the way of Nebraska. Every true Wyomingite that I had ever known disliked Nebraskans, and I was no different. The guys from Nebraska drove nice cars, '55 Fords and '56 Chevys, riding low to the ground with V-8 engines, stick shifts, and dual glass-pac mufflers. The cars had a beautiful purr and they always outran the old six-cylinder junkers we drove. We never could understand what our girls saw in those guys.

When I was growing up, my family lived on several different farms in Goshen County, close to the town of Veteran, Wyoming, and we always had baby animals around. We raised chickens, pigs, lambs, and calves. Although we lived on the farm, my dad often worked at outside jobs besides his farming. When I was five years old, he worked on a large corporate farm, Paul Blood Farms, in Scottsbluff. It was a sheep or wool operation and the people in charge were quite fond of my dad. On many occasions, he would come home late from work in the dark of night with baby lambs in the back seat of his '39 Ford. He said that the little things were orphans and there was no way to care for them at Paul Blood's so they were simply given to him. Every year we built a small flock of sheep in this manner. It was my job to fill coke bottles with warm milk and feed the baby lambs until they were weaned. Looking back on the experience, it is clear that my dad loved his work and was rewarded for his dedication to the company. He was trying to teach me responsibility, but to me, it wasn't responsibility, it was a privilege being around those baby critters.

My first school was the little red school house in the heart of downtown Veteran, a town about fifteen miles southwest of Torrington with a population of twenty-five. In 1949, there wasn't any such thing as kindergarten, so every kid entered the first grade at age six except for me. For some reason, my folks thought I was ready when I was only five. School started in the middle of August, and I wouldn't turn six until the 12th of January, a full five months later. I was ok with that though because my best friend, Bruce Hatton, was starting school that year, too. Bruce and his family lived on a farm three and a half miles north of Veteran and my parents and his were good friends. They visited each others' homes frequently and when they did, usually Bruce and I got together as well.

There was only one classroom for first graders at Veteran, so we were all in the same room under the watchful eye of Miss Alkire, a frail, short, seventy-eight year old teacher of approximately eighty-five pounds with a very limited tolerance for boys who misbehaved. Miss Alkire had never married and had no children of her own. We thought there was a good reason for that, since she didn't seem to like kids. Besides her dislike for her students, she also had an aversion to dirt. In fact, she was absolutely obsessed with cleanliness and would spend the entire day carrying around a three-pound Maxwell House coffee can full of soapy water. She was also armed with tissue paper and Scott paper towels and refused to touch anything, including the classroom door knob, drinking fountain, desk drawers, her #2 pencils, or any other item without first washing and wiping it off with the soapy water. She would then grasp the item using the tissue or paper towel so her hands would never come in contact with anything. Needless to say, everyone except my parents thought this was very odd behavior.

One of the other disagreeable characteristics of this teacher that I and most of the other boys in the room noticed related to the way she handled chalk. Whenever anyone failed to listen or was talking when she hadn't called upon them or was, overall, not doing what she expected, she had this irritating habit of hitting them in the back of the head with a piece of chalk. She wouldn't just hit them lightly in the head. Apparently over the years, she found that it was more effective to drill the chalk, or drive it, by placing it in her closed fist with her thumb over one end while forcing the other end into the child's head. In all my years of education, Miss Alkire was the only teacher that used this particular technique.

In spite of my youth and Miss Alkire's peculiar behavior, first grade was a positive experience, as evidenced by my being asked to serve as master of ceremony for the first grade Easter program. This was a great honor, according to my parents, showing that I was one of Miss Alkire's leading students, and of course it was a good opportunity for me to display my leadership qualities. It would require considerable rehearsal and consequently enable me to spend extra time with Miss Alkire, gaining even further favor. I always thought that particular program turned out fine even if one of the other kids had to step up to host the affair since, at the last minute, I absolutely refused the part. Miss Alkire never did forgive me for selfishly and irresponsibly disappointing her and my parents.

I always figured I had suffered enough simply by showing up in that white bunny suit my mother made for me out of old sheets.

My parents' farm was only a half mile from the school house, which meant it was also only a half mile from Miss Alkire's home, which was two blocks east of the school. Although she lived in town, there weren't any sidewalks or paved streets and most of the residents also raised farm animals such as pigs and chickens. Miss Alkire's animals of choice were goats. She had eight or ten goats running around her place, climbing on top of old cars, firewood boxes and anything else they could find, and relieving themselves all over the yard. For some inexplicable reason, my classmate, Bruce Brownley, and I thought it would be interesting if we gathered up some of the goat droppings and smeared them on Miss Alkire's front step and door knob. It never occurred to us that someone might witness this senseless act, but within minutes, the school principal was in touch with my dad describing what vile behavior his son had been engaged in. My dad didn't like to give his kids a spanking, but when he did, it was usually of sufficient effectiveness that none of us forgot it in quite some time. This was one of the first times in my life that I remember being held accountable for my failings. I still remember the hurt in Miss Alkire's eyes and the disappointment in my parents' face as I apologized and tried to explain my unbelievable behavior.

I attended school in Veteran through the seventh grade. School was uneventful except for a couple of things. During those years, my dad was employed by the school as its janitor and school bus mechanic. This meant he always had keys to the facilities which included the school gym and while my dad was cleaning the classrooms, I was busy shooting hoops. Every night after school, my dad would unlock the coach's room so I could pick a ball and then spend the next hour or so preparing for my future NBA career.

Both Bruce Hatton and I played guard on the seventh grade team and between the two of us, usually dominated the scoring. This was partially due to all of the practices I got in at the gym but more than likely was because hardly anyone else on the team got to touch the ball. Our exasperated coach finally told us if we didn't start passing to our team mates we would both be sitting on the bench. It was at this very young age that I realized how important teamwork is and that when people work together they can usually always accomplish more than if going it alone. Bruce and I could score a lot of points, but it doesn't matter how many points you score if you and your team lose.

Veteran was probably a good place for a kid to grow up. It was a small community where everyone knew one another and people could be trusted to do what they said they were going to do. Until he bought the farm south of the school, my dad farmed for other farmers in the area and instead of paying rent, would share his crops with the landowner. He used to take pride in the fact that all of his agreements were based on a handshake, not a written contract, and in all of those years he never had a single disagreement over how much was owed after they harvested and took the crops to market. The first farm I have any recollection of where my folks were sharecropping was the Allen place. It was a small farm about a mile directly west of the town and my folks raised sugar beets, beans, and alfalfa. They ran a few milk cows and after keeping some whole milk for the family's use, separated the cream, bottled it, and sold it to friends and acquaintances in the area. They would then feed the skimmed milk, whether soured or not, to the pigs, who of course, would eat anything.

The Allen place turned out to be quite an interesting as well as dangerous place. When I was only three years old, my parents looked out of the kitchen window only to find that I was nowhere in sight. It didn't occur to them to look up in the sky, where they eventually found me perched on top of the windmill, some twenty-five feet in the air. I had managed to climb up the ladder on the side of the structure and once up there was too frightened to come back down. My dad had to climb up himself and retrieve me. He was afraid that I would either fall or the wind would come up and blow that big wheel around and knock me off. My folks were too thankful to be very angry so I escaped with just a light spanking and a stern lecture to never, ever play around the windmill again.

The first real beating I ever received from my dad occurred on the Allen place. He had a row of four, fifty-gallon drums lined up in the front yard, each mounted on a steel stand which held the barrels about three feet off the ground. Each had a faucet or spigot, similar to what you find at a filling or gasoline station today, so that the fuel could be drained from the barrels into a vehicle or container. Two of the barrels contained gasoline for his trucks and cars. One was used for diesel fuel for his tractors, and the fourth contained kerosene used for heating the home. There was an irrigation ditch about four feet from this row of barrels and at the time the ditch was filled with tumbleweeds and other debris from the previous year's growing season. My sister, Jeanette, and I were left alone in the front yard as my mother was off to town and my dad was out on a tractor plowing the field. Jeanette was seven years old at the time and since she was the oldest, she was in charge and responsible not only for her activities but also for mine. I usually paid no attention what-so-ever to her instructions and supervision and this day was no exception. For some reason, I thought it would be a good idea to drain a few gallons of gasoline into a five-gallon bucket, pour it on the weeds in the ditch, and light a match to them. Spilling gasoline from the barrels to the ditch, I managed to drag the can of gas, or what was left of it, to the weeds. There was a huge explosion when the match touched that gasoline and the fire and smoke could be seen for miles. I had no idea a 1939 Farmall tractor could travel that fast, but within seconds my dad roared into the yard and in what seemed absolute panic, grabbed a shovel and began furiously shoveling dirt on the fire and the trail of wet mud leading to the row of barrels. Miraculously, he managed to keep the barrels from going off, but once the fire was out and he laid down his shovel, the fireworks began for me and my innocent sister. I knew I deserved it, but I wasn't sure about her. However, she was supposed to be supervising. Because of my dad's swift action, we somehow escaped a disaster. Many more disasters would be averted today if we only learned that children can't be trusted in the care of other children.

The next year, in 1949, we moved to the Denny place. It was a four-room house consisting of two bedrooms, a kitchen, and living room. All of the rooms were small and it was very tight quarters for five people. I shared a bedroom with my sisters and the house had no bathroom and the only running water was from a hand pump which was mounted to the kitchen counter. Whenever it was time for a bath, my mother would drag a washtub into the living room, pour three or four gallons of hot water in it which she had heated on the stove, and instruct us not to watch the other one bathing. She didn't have to tell me more than once inasmuch as I would rather have died than have seen one of my sisters naked.

There was a huge trench going under the house beneath the kitchen area where my dad had installed a sewer line and the hand-pump for water. It was about four feet deep and three feet wide and extended out from the house's foundation about five feet. It was just large enough for my dad to be able to maneuver around in when he was working on the pipes. Months went by and my dad failed to fill in this hole. One day when everyone else was away, I heard a strange noise that sounded like it was coming from under the house. I rushed out of the house and around the corner and, sure enough, there was a noise coming from that hole. A small animal had fallen into the area and was trapped in the trench with no way to escape. At first, I thought it was a cat, but it wasn't really built like a cat. And, I had never seen a black cat with a solid white stripe running down the full length of its back and its tail. I didn't have a clue what to do about that creature and the only way I could think of to get the animal out was to scoop it out. It was squealing like a stuck hog when I stuck that shovel into the hole, but I did manage to lift it out of there. I don't know who was more frightened, me or that skunk, but fortunately, when it hit the ground, it tore off as fast as it could go. We never could figure out why that critter hadn't drenched everything in sight.

The Denny place had a water well out by the barnyard which was mounted on an eight- foot-by-eight-foot slab of concrete about two feet thick. Anchored to the concrete was the frame for a windmill that stood about twenty-five feet high. When the wind blew, the water would be pumped out of the ground and into a large stock tank that was twelve feet across and three feet deep. My mother raised chickens and she had my dad make her a "chicken-catcher" which was simply a steel wire not quite as big around as a pencil and six feet long. On one end was a handle curved in a half circle, and on the other, a hook about two-thirds the size of the top of a clothes hanger. To catch a chicken, she would merely sneak up behind one, hook it around the legs and feet with that rod, jerk its feet out from under it and then, drag it in. With its feet up in the air and back on the ground, there was no way for the bird to escape. Following this humiliating experience, my mother would then grasp the chicken by the neck and twirl it around rapidly in the air with its head in her hand. The chicken would be spinning like a top until such time as its head would come off in my mother's hand and its body would go tumbling through space, still flopping around as it hit the ground.

I discovered the effectiveness of this particular farmyard tool myself one day as I was playing on the concrete platform under the windmill. Because it was close to the chicken-coop, my mother kept this "catcher" hanging by the handle from a large nail on the windmill framework. The hook, which had been cut to a fairly sharp point, was about four feet above the surface of the concrete slab, unbeknownst to me. One time when I leaped from the platform to run to the house, I jumped directly into the hook which promptly sunk deeply into my right armpit. The steel wire was very strong and unfortunately didn't bend even slightly with what likely would be a sixty-pound carcass hanging from it. My momentum swung me out from the platform and over the ground below, but at the end of my swing, which was the exact distance of the length of the "chicken-catcher", my body abruptly stopped and then swung back the other way. When my feet again hit the concrete, I was able to extract this lethal contraption from my body and race to the house to receive medical attention. Following this incidence, I really never again had much sympathy for the chickens. Sometime later I realized that my pain from the chicken-catcher was pretty insignificant compared to the pain suffered by the chickens at the hands of my dear mother.

Most of the farm ground on the Denny place was supplied with water through irrigation ditches which were strung across the farm. About a quarter of a mile from the house there was a head-gate which was used to control the flow of water into the ditches that fed the fields. The head-gate was about three feet square and a half-a-dozen feet deep, constructed of concrete about six inches thick. One day, my Uncle Moses and Aunt Nadine came to visit. Moses Young was a good looking guy, about six-foot-four-inches tall, thin but muscular, with dark curly hair and brown eyes. You could tell by his looks and his actions that he was a tough guy who wasn't afraid of anything. For something to do we walked down to that head-gate and on that day it was full of not only water but also full of snakes. Water snakes. They were swimming and floating around on the surface of the water, and before we knew it Moses reached down in there. He snatched a snake by the tail, jerked it out of the concrete culvert, and promptly cracked it like a whip. The snake was instantly dead. I thought Moses was crazy to stick his hand down into that den of snakes and was lucky he wasn't bitten, but he proved it wasn't luck by retrieving every single snake and breaking their necks one after another. That was the first time I had ever met my Uncle Moses, and I was surprised by his boldness in dealing with those snakes. He made quite an impression on me that day, not by his words, but by his deeds. This very insignificant event, experienced at the age of six, remained with me for a lifetime. Young people are influenced by the actions of adults in their lives, which can be positive or negative. We have opportunities to make positive impressions on the young people around us and ought to engage in behavior more meaningful than snapping a snake's neck.

A group of my mother's friends met at someone's house every third Tuesday of each month. The women always had cookies and beverages ready for the big day and upon the last one's arrival, all of the kids were sent outdoors armed with a sack full of cookies, a half-dozen glass cups, and a pitcher of cool-aide. These gatherings were usually quite eventful for the youngsters. On one occasion when the club gathered at my mother's house, Mrs. Smith brought with her the family's ten-year-old Mexican Chiquaqu, a miniature dog which stood no higher than six inches from the floor and was no longer than a large rat. It was a cute little brown and white "puppy" that seemed innocent enough. I had no idea it would turn into a pit bull with a nasty disposition when lifted from the front seat of Mrs. Smith's car. In a ferocious attack, little Muffy tore half of my nose off before I could dispose of the little monster by throwing her half way across the front yard. In those days, plastic surgery was simply called "stitches" and after placing a dozen or so in my left nostril, the doctor explained that there would always be a small scar which hardly anyone would ever notice.

The next meeting was held at Mrs. Becker's house on the small farm ten miles west of Veteran. Mrs. Smith again showed up, this time without Muffy, but with her thirteen-year-old daughter who was a thin girl with light brown stringy hair and dark brown eyes. She was fairly attractive and was well enough endowed that she absolutely captivated Mrs. Becker's twelve- year-old son, Floyd. The feeling was apparently mutual, because in the middle of the ladies' meeting, Floyd and Mary were inside the barn playing house. The rest of the kids were banished to the barnyard where they watched the entire episode through the cracks of that old run-down weathered building.

My family moved from the Denny place to the farm my folks bought south of the Veteran school in the spring of 1951 when I was seven years old. It was a small operation, consisting of less than one hundred acres of irrigated crop land and pastures. It was bordered by the Veteran school on the north, the railroad tracks on the west, and a huge canal on the east and most of the south. There was also the local cemetery on the south border where Grandma Ferrari resided. My dad constructed an electric fence all along the canal and the cemetery to keep his milk cows off his mother's grave and a dozen others, whose families had abandoned years ago. The cattle were kept away from the steep banks which he said they wouldn't have sense enough to avoid. If they fell into the water, he explained, they would be quickly sucked under by the fierce current, drowned, and swept away. The fence served as an excellent deterrent and was particularly effective when it was wet. I don't know what voltage was running through that line, but during a rain it was sufficient to knock a three-hundred-pound cow flat, which seemed to concern my dad and was pretty alarming for a seven-year-old boy.

One of the teachers at the Veteran school, Mr. Youtz, claimed to have witnessed the start of World War III from the front bedroom window of his home which faced the north end of my dad's farm. I was never a particularly thoughtful or compassionate brother and sometimes could be downright mean and abusive to my ten-year-old sister. One morning, as we were getting ready for school, a fight broke out in the middle of the living room. I always figured I could lick my sister, but when she was really mad, there was always some question as to the outcome. On this particular occasion, I landed a pretty good blow. Unfortunately, it barely fazed her and I knew I needed to get out of there quick. I dashed out the front door and was running as fast as I could towards the school. Jeanette caught me about half way across the field, and it was one of those rare occasions when she showed little mercy for her victim. Later that morning, Mr. Youtz announced, not only that he had witnessed a battle in World War III, but he added to the humiliation by also describing the outcome to the entire class. I was the only kid in school who had ever been "licked" by his own sister. In reflection, the humiliation was short-lived, but the regret of having picked on my sister on that occasion and many others too numerous to mention has stayed with me all of these many years.

# CHAPTER TWO

# Unsolicited Advice

In 1956, my parents sold their farm and moved to Torrington, where both worked for Goshen County Hospital, my mother in the cafeteria and my father in maintenance. I enrolled in Torrington Jr. High School that fall, and although I hated leaving the familiar surroundings of Veteran, I quickly adjusted to my new school and the eighth grade. I signed up for football that year and was used as a backup punt returner and third-string quarterback by my new coaches. My career lasted only long enough for me to catch one punt on the five-yard-line and be tackled instantly in my tracks. I never did get to play quarterback as I left the team shortly after that game. The thing that contributed to my leaving, as much as anything, happened on the practice field to Waldo Moorhouse. He was a tall, skinny kid who played tight-end and most of the guys seemed to enjoy blocking and tackling him whenever they got the opportunity. They played like all-pros as they were hitting poor ole' Waldo and on one play managed to break his leg. Waldo was lying on the ground moaning and groaning with the bone sticking out through the skin. With fear and panic in his eyes, he was screaming out in pain when Coach Wiseman calmly and coldly exclaimed, "Aw, shut up

Waldo, we ain't never lost a player out here yet." "Yeah, but," Waldo howled, "there's a first time for everything." Waldo's football career ended that day and mine ended a short time later. Neither of us was ever missed, as near as I could tell. After quitting the team during the eighth-grade year, I never played organized football again. The coaches took a chance on me by trusting me to field that punt on the five-yard-line. It was probably blind luck that I caught that ball, or maybe it was simply good coaching. Either way, I should have trusted them to make a player out of me. I'll never know whether or not they would have succeeded. I suspect, given their love for and dedication to kids, they probably would have. Sometimes you have to believe in the ability of others even when you doubt your own.

Fortunately, basketball was a different story. I managed to make the team my first year in Torrington and, perhaps due to the NBA training in the Veteran gym, was proficient enough to make the starting five in the eighth grade and through most of high school. I played with some good players over the years and we had some pretty good teams, but we were never good enough to win the State championship. During my sophomore year nearly all of the juniors and seniors were kicked off the team for drinking. That enabled me and several other sophomores and a couple of freshmen to get some playing time, only to lose most of the games we played. But, as the coaches described it, we did get some "valuable experience." It must have been a valuable experience for the coaches as well because after losing all but two games, we had a new head coach by the start of the new season.

Bill Sharp was an all-star basketball player at the University of Wyoming in the mid-1950's and was clearly the most gifted athlete I had ever been around. He had a two-handed set shot that was as smooth as silk, and he rarely missed it from as far away as thirty to forty feet from the basket. In those days, there was no such thing as a three-point shot, but had there been, Coach Sharp would have likely set all of the three-point shooting records during his playing days. We were really excited about this new, young coach and he didn't disappoint, as there was never a dull moment during the two years I played for him. We had our share of victories on the court, but it wasn't so much the wins and losses that Coach Sharp was known for, but rather his antics both on the bench and in the locker room on game nights.

We were playing in Alliance, Nebraska, one night during my senior year and things weren't going well for the Torrington Trailblazers. Alliance had a reputation for hiring referees who were partial to the home team and that night was no exception. It was a game in which several of our players had fouled out, but the rest of our team was managing to keep the game close. There was a lot of tension and anger in the building. Coach Sharp was livid because of the obviously biased and poor officiating. The crowd was tense as the outcome was still in question until late in the contest, in spite of the fact that the referees had provided every opportunity for the home team to dominate. As the final seconds ticked off of the clock and yet another foul was whistled against the visitors, I looked down the bench just in time to see Coach Sharp flip the referees and the entire home crowd the "bird." This prompted half of the players on the bench to do likewise. Such effort apparently did not help our cause because, in the end, we lost. After the game as we were leaving the floor to go to our dressing room, Coach Sharp was confronted by a particularly irate spectator who happened to be the mother of one of the Alliance players. She called him and his team the most despicable people she had ever encountered. We were the poorest sports her son had ever competed against and we should be ashamed of ourselves for displaying such lack of good taste and sportsmanship. Coach Sharp should be fired, she said, as he obviously was a lousy coach who knew nothing about the game and lacked the character to lead young men. As she droned on and on, he became increasingly red in the face and the veins in his neck were bulging out. "Lady," he began, "I've played in more fucking games than you've ever seen. You don't know what the hell you're talking about; you don't know a damn thing about basketball. Now, get the fuck out of my face and don't tell me how to coach." With that, he brushed her aside and continued across the floor.

During my senior year there were several incidents involving Coach Sharp that to this day remain a topic of conversation at class reunions and other gatherings of members of the Class of '61. We were playing at home one night in Willie Gym against the Wheatland Bulldogs in a very close and exciting game. The score was seventy-nine to seventy-seven with ten seconds left in overtime and Torrington was to get the ball out under our own basket. We were behind by two points and Coach Sharp called a time out to outline the tying play. Our six-foot-three-inch center was to throw the ball in to one of our guards and then crash the boards for any possible rebound in the event the shot put up by the guard didn't go in. As the referee handed him the ball, it simply rolled out of his hands and onto the floor and was immediately snatched up by a Wheatland player. The ten seconds quickly ticked off of the clock and the game was over.

None of us knew what was going through our teammate's mind as that ball slipped out of his hands and along with it the game, but we suspected he had his thoughts on something else. Earlier in the week, his girlfriend informed him that he was going to become a daddy. Coach Sharp was convinced that was exactly what was distracting his starting center. As we entered the locker room following the defeat, a loud crash was heard as the coach's fist left a deep indentation in one of the metal lockers. "God dammit," he shouted, "when are you gonna learn that you can't build up your grip by pullin' titties?" That was the last game this great center played for the Torrington Trailblazers, but it wasn't the last incident involving Coach Sharp.

Later that season we were again playing at home, but the game wasn't going too well for the home team. One of our players was making mistake after mistake; and in spite of the fact that the home crowd was getting on the kid, the coach didn't take him out of the game. As we began to get further and further behind, the crowd became increasingly abusive. One of the spectators, Neal Walsh, was a junior in high school and secretary of his class. He was an all-state wrestler and a good, tough football player, but he had never played basketball. He was quite drunk in the stands and he began heckling the coach. After listening to this for half of the game, Coach Sharp finally had had enough and challenged the student to come down to the bench and "say that." To no one's surprise, Neal got up and began making his way to the bench. As he approached the coach behind the bench where the players were seated, he was abruptly greeted with a right-hand punch from the fist of Coach Sharp. The knockout blow propelled Neal backwards into the crowd and he had to be administered to by the school nurse. But, it did silence him for the rest of the game. Unfortunately for the coach, that punch also silenced his career at Torrington High School. The school board immediately suspended him and refused to renew his contract for the following year. The last I heard he was coaching in Salem, Oregon, where he had won several state championships. He was a great athlete who knew how to play basketball and how to compete. It wasn't until he got control of his emotions, however, that he became a great coach. I often thought that had he channeled his energy in a more constructive direction, perhaps we would have enjoyed those championships with him instead of the players in Oregon.

The disappointments of losing created the same frustrations for me as they did for Coach Sharp and after being eliminated, for the second straight year, at the State Tournament in Laramie, I thought I would never play basketball again. Don Woodley, who had been my freshman coach and who was now our high-school principal asked me not to make a quick decision. In the locker room following the game, he said the pain of losing would go away in time and I would want to return to the court. He had a friend coaching at Chadron State College in Chadron, Nebraska, who was offering full scholarships to both me and the other guard, Jerry Bullock. We had led the team in scoring that final season, Jerry with 344 points and me with seven more. Because of this and due to Mr. Woodley's influence, Jerry and I were also offered scholarships to Northeast Community College in Powell, Wyoming, where Jerry eventually accepted. I declined both and decided instead to attend the local college, Goshen County Community College, in Torrington.

When we first moved to Torrington and before settling in my final childhood home, my folks rented a house on East A Street, right next door to the Ellis-Chalmers Tractor dealership. The house had three bedrooms, and by this time my older sister Mae Belle lived in her own apartment, so I no longer had to share a room with my sisters. My little brother, Kenny, was now three years old, but he spent a lot of time living between my sister's house and my parents. For the first time in my life, our new home had an indoor bathroom with a door you could lock from the inside. It also had both hot and cold running water and a full-sized tub. The house had a front and a back porch which were enclosed with glass windows, and although the porches weren't heated like the rest of the house, they were reasonably comfortable if the weather wasn't too cold. I formed a basketball hoop out of a piece of copper pipe and made a net out of string to complete the six-inch basket and hung it on the wall over the back door. Other than the refrigerator, which my mother had my dad move from the kitchen, I had a 10-foot-by-12-foot gymnasium all to myself. I nearly drove my mother crazy running around that back porch, dribbling a miniature basketball and shooting jump shots for hours into the night.

It was also in this rented house where I nearly drove my sister, Jeanette, crazy as well. It was about this time that she had discovered boys, and telephones, and had connected the two. She would spend hours on end talking on the phone with her boyfriend, which in my mind was about the stupidest thing anyone could possibly do. To irritate her, I would make as much noise as humanly possible. I didn't realize that this was only making matters worse because, in order to be heard and not miss a single utterance, every word had to be repeated several times, dragging the conversation on for hours. Clearly, as was the case earlier, witnessed by Mr. Youtz, picking on my sister wasn't working out too well for me. I might have figured this out earlier had I been more thoughtful, but, that wasn't to be for many years.

We remained on East A Street for the next year during which time my dad bought on old house which was located out in the country and moved it to a lot on East F Street. Not surprisingly, the house needed to be completely renovated and had my mother known at the time that the project would last for the next twenty some years, I'm sure she wouldn't have stood for it. So, at six in the morning, on a clear spring day without any wind in the forecast, my dad and the house moving company he hired began the slow trek of moving the house from south of town. It took the entire day to move that old house eleven miles and when the trip was finished the house sat on a foundation which was exactly five blocks east of our current home and it didn't have a yard full of tractors parked next door.

The house had only one bedroom, but it would have a full basement when finished and my dad had plans to add a second bedroom and expand the bathroom upstairs by moving a one- room building he got from his son-in-law, Jim, and attaching it to the back of the place. By this time, my sister, Mae Belle, was married to Ron Darnall and living in Ft. Laramie, a little town some twenty miles northwest of Torrington. In her junior year of high school, Jeanette joined my little brother and lived with Mae Belle and my brother-in-law, Ron. She attended Ft. Laramie High School and apparently took enough time away from the telephone to meet and later marry Jim Pontarolo. Jim was a handsome, powerful, young man who grew up on a wheat farm south of Fort Laramie. He was about six feet tall and was a star basketball player at Fort Laramie High School. After finishing high school, Jim joined the United States Army and was shipped to Alaska, where Jeanette joined him. They were married in 1959.

The one-bedroom house would have never worked out had my two sisters not left home and taken my brother with them. My dad knocked out the wall that separated the front porch from the living room and turned this into a very large living room of over six hundred square feet, which, in itself, was bigger than the four-room Denny house we had spent so many years in. Before he did this, however, the front porch served as the home for the family dog, a black and white mutt we adopted after finding him wandering the streets. One day after returning from school, I entered the front door and found him lying in his basket next to the living room entrance. He was obviously not feeling well as evidenced by his hot nose and lack of enthusiasm for someone entering the house, but also by the intense aroma that was permeating throughout the entire place. I thought he surely must have relieved himself somewhere, but no evidence could be found. I had never smelled anything so debilitating in my life and it was hard to believe that such an unsavory smell so powerful could be produced by a little twenty-pound animal. But, it could, and it was, and by the next morning the little guy was gone. We never knew if it was from the illness or the odor, but his absence was felt for quite some time afterwards.

My dad finished the basement where my bedroom was located, along with a small bathroom and a tiny two-room apartment, consisting of a kitchen/dining room combination and a small bedroom. Each room was roughly ten feet wide and ten feet long, so the entire apartment was only about two hundred square feet. I don't know how my parents managed to do all of that work, while both holding full-time jobs. The place was always torn up and in some stage of construction, with dust everywhere. It was a huge project that lasted on and off for years and was accomplished without the help of outside contractors or construction workers. The only help my parents ever received was from their two sons-in-law, Jim and Ron. I was usually too busy with school, work, and other activities to be of any help and to this day regret that I didn't have the good sense to learn some of the carpentry skills my dad possessed and was anxious to teach me.

The first job I ever had was at the Elite Cleaners on East A Street when I was twelve years old. Bob Elders, the owner, needed someone to clean the lint from the dryer filters, empty the trash, and sweep the floors prior to opening. The one-hour task was something my parents thought would be a good experience and since we lived only a few blocks away, it would be ok to ride my bike to work. I would leave the house at 6:30 in the morning, clean for an hour, and then proceed on to school. I thought I was the only kid at Torrington Junior High with a real job because farm chores done at home, which some of the other kids did, simply didn't qualify as jobs. My boss was a kind, gentle man who obviously didn't expect much from a twelve year old, and it was this early experience that gave me the idea that work was a good thing. This job lasted for a couple of years and I enjoyed the early morning hours.

At age fourteen, I got my "learner's permit" so I could work at the Johnson Dairy north of town. This involved feeding corn silage to the dairy cattle before daybreak from a six-by twelve-foot trailer with two foot side boards. It took about an hour to scoop silage into the trailer and another hour to unload it into the feed troughs that were lined around the corral fences. At the time, I didn't think about the excitement and enthusiasm from that herd that greeted me at six o'clock in the morning, but have since come to realize that those dairy cows showed more appreciation and feelings than most people.

A couple of summers during the teenage years were spent on cattle ranches, but I quickly found that I didn't like the feeling of isolation that came with living several miles from town. I missed my friends and family and especially missed the contentment most of us feel from being in our own homes. After arriving at Jimmie and Betty O'Brien's ranch and wheat farm, located at the end of a forty-mile dirt road north of Fort Laramie, I stayed as long as I could before informing them it wasn't working out. This announcement was made more difficult by the fact that Ron and Mae Belle got me the job and the O'Briens were their best friends. It was also hard on

Marjorie, Irvin, and Harold, three adopted children of American-Indian heritage who followed me around from sunup until sundown and took turns riding with me on the ranch tractors. My departure was especially hard on Irvin, a five year old, who was by my side constantly. I don't know how long the sadness stayed in his eyes, but that in mine was gone by the time I completed that forty mile drive back to civilization and to my friends who were still cruising up and down Main. I have never forgotten Irvin and his sister and brother and often wonder what their lives would have been like had they not been adopted by the O'Briens. Born to alcoholic and abusive parents, they would have had no chance for happy and productive lives had it not been for the kindness and giving of the O'Briens who shared their home, lives, and love with their adopted children.

The next summer I took a job on Mrs. Jones' ranch near the Nebraska state line which was within commuting distance of my parent's home. Mrs. Jones was a widow whose husband had been gone for many years. With the help of a part-time hired hand, she ran an efficient operation. My job was to keep the fences repaired and to occasionally move cattle from one pasture to another. This was sometimes challenging for someone who didn't ride a horse very well. Mrs. Jones was a skilled rider and was none too sympathetic when my horse, Diamond, returned to the ranch-house one day without its rider. Diamond got spooked by nothing in particular and began racing across the pasture with a panic-stricken cowboy on its back. He was paying no attention whatsoever to attempts to slow him down or rein him in and a barbed-wire fence line was fast approaching. I figured he would slow down but when he didn't, I knew we were going to jump it. I was totally unprepared for the abrupt stop. After flipping me twenty-feet in the air over that fence, Diamond slowly galloped back to the barn. I knew he was through for the day and wasn't too surprised that Mrs. Jones was through with me. Losing the job didn't bother me much, because she didn't relate very well to a teenager who lacked ranching skills. She also had some strange behaviors which I couldn't get used to. I was uncomfortable when she bathed nude in the irrigation ditch that ran behind the house. She didn't seem the least bit embarrassed the first time I saw her crawling out of that ditch and although my eyes immediately focused on something other than that sixty-five-year-old body, it was a long time before the image left me.

After leaving her employ, I went to work on a survey crew hired by the Bureau of Land Management. My job was to go to a distant location with the survey rod, which was a one-inch-square wooden pole about eight feet tall with measurement indicators and other markings on it. The pole would be held with one end on the ground and the other straight up in the air. As the surveyor made his readings from a distance of up to a quarter of a mile, he would motion for the rod to be moved in one direction or another. The job went fine until one day I was spotted by a German shepherd which was about three hundred yards away. I could see him coming and assumed I was going to be greeted by the family's friendly house pet. It wasn't until the dog was within twenty yards that I could see the foam bubbling down his chin and the snarled lip turned up, revealing his razor sharp teeth. I kept the hundred pound beast at bay with the rod, but it was awkward trying to swing an eight-foot-long club at a charging angry dog. I was finally rescued by the dog's master who showed surprisingly little sympathy, demanding to know what I had done to provoke Shep, who wouldn't hurt a flea.

One of the shortest times ever spent on a job involved Mr. Lamphere's potato farm ten miles east and a little south of Lingle. He was in the process of harvesting his potatoes and needed someone to drive down the row of sacked spuds and load them on the flat bed truck. Several of my high school friends were hired and the plan was to take turns driving the truck while the others did the heavy lifting. When it was my turn to drive, somehow I inadvertently crossed over the row of sacks, knocking over each bag before running over it with the huge dual wheels. Several had fallen like dominoes and then been crushed before the vehicle was brought under control. Explaining that he had never seen anyone so worthless in his life, Mr. Lamphere immediately fired me with strict orders to get off of his property. This made a rather poor impression on my friends so as I hurried to comply, they made their exit as well. Having been on the job for less than an hour, after deducting the value of the damaged merchandise, the boss figured he didn't owe us anything. We were too frightened to argue the point.

I never considered myself to be a particularly good student, but managed to earn "A"s and "B"s during most of my high school years. I enjoyed school most of the time but was less focused than I could have been. I did exhibit some leadership qualities when elected vice president of the sophomore class for the 1958-59 school year and vice president of T-Club two years later. Looking back, I'm pretty sure I didn't give these leadership roles my best effort and often wonder where life would have taken me had I applied myself during those early years. Like most of my friends, my interests seemed to be more directed toward cars, girls, and basketball, and in no particular order.

When I was fifteen, my dad bought me a 1950 Chevrolet. After installing a brand new six-cylinder engine under the hood and putting new tires on the wheels that were covered by "moon" hubcaps, he had it painted a two-tone green. We finished it off by installing new seat covers on the front and back seats, and the car certainly didn't look like it was ten years old. It was a beautiful two-door coupe but with that small engine wouldn't go as fast as some of the cars around. After all of the money and labor my dad put into fixing up that car, he was extremely proud of it and continuously encouraged me to take good care of it. I promised that I would and kept it washed and shined. I should have paid more attention to his warnings not to drive it too fast or run it too hard. I hadn't had it very long before a carload of my friends and I were coming back from Henry, Nebraska, on Highway 26 east of town, when a 1950 Ford with Nebraska plates began passing us. It, too, was loaded with young boys and they were challenging us to a race. They were flipping us the bird, suggesting that none of us had fathers, and saying some unflattering things about our mothers. About five miles out of the city limits, my "green latrine," as it was referred to by my friends, was hitting ninety miles an hour and, for a while, managed to stay side by side with that white Ford coupe. Eventually, however, we became only a blur in its rearview mirror, and by the time we entered the city limits, there was a disturbing knocking sound coming from under the hood. I explained to my dad that the noise occurred for no apparent reason and wondered how long it would be before we could get it fixed. I knew I had made a grave mistake when he replied that it wouldn't be fixed. He sold what was left of the car to a mechanic he knew, and I had to resort to the humiliating practice of begging rides from my parents and friends. I was disappointed to be without a car, but worse, my parents were disappointed in me.

One of the great pastimes in Torrington and probably in every small town was to cruise up and down the streets with no purpose or destination. The main business section of the town ran north and south for about four blocks on Main Street. Businesses lined both sides of the street, most with huge picture windows to display their goods. Before blowing the engine in my car, a classmate, John Peterson, who was quite mechanically inclined, had discovered that somehow if you ran the vacuum tube, which was a little plastic hose about the size of a pencil, from the wind-shield wipers, to the engine block, the result would be a discharge of dense black smoke from the exhaust. The unbelievable amount of smog generated in this manner would settle on everything within twenty yards, leaving a thick film which was almost impossible to remove with normal window-washing solutions. In 1959, there were no environmental or clean air standards to violate, so when we were pulled over by the local police we were simply instructed to take the car into the local garage and have it repaired.

When we tired of cruising up and down Main Street, we would go out on Sheep Creek Road, a narrow two-lane paved highway that ran east from the north side of town towards Nebraska. Over the years, this became the favorite drag-racing strip and on any given weekend night there would be two cars lined up on the white line which had been spray painted across the highway to mark the starting point. Whoever was ahead at the end of the first quarter-mile was declared the winner and there was usually a large crowd there to witness the contest. One of the races that went absolutely no where was between Joe Bigner, who drove a beautiful 1956 Pontiac Chieftain, and Ray Wood, who was in his parents' black 1953 Ford. They were side by side; each revving and roaring their engines knowing that whoever got off of the line first would probably win. Joe had his gear in neutral and engine fully throttled while waiting for the drop of the flag to signal the race's start. Joe's strategy was to get the engine running at a good clip and then shift the transmission into drive. The resultant lunge would likely give him an early advantage which he would then try to maintain for the remainder of the race. In that particular make of Pontiac, the location of the transmission's gears was different than it is today in most vehicles. The sequence then was Park, Neutral, Drive, Drive 1, and Reverse, in that order. Joe had his vehicle in Neutral and when the flag dropped, the black Ford shot from the line. You could hear the clunk, clunk, clunk, as Joe shifted from neutral and failed to stop in any gear until he landed in reverse. There was a loud crash as the transmission exploded from its case. The Pontiac didn't move an inch. After towing the vehicle to town, Joe called his folks to explain that something had gone wrong with his car as he tried to pull away from the stop sign. Joe was a good person, as was his entire family, and I suspect it wasn't long before his mom and dad got the true story about what really happened that night. Eventually, he got the car repaired, but we never did see it out on Sheep Creek Road again.

Several months following my dad's disappointment of my blowing the engine in my 1950 Chevy, Eddie Stitts, who had dropped out of school to help on his father's sugar beet farm, had a beautiful 1955 Ford Victorian convertible he was wanting to sell. It was sparkling white, with a white canvass top, pink and white leather interior, and the label, "White Lightning" inscribed in two-inch-high pink lettering on the back rear fenders. The car was in perfect physical appearance without a scratch or flaw on it. Having seen Eddie gunning the car around town on numerous occasions, both my dad and I suspected that there may be some issues with the vehicle's performance and reliability. This, of course, didn't stop me from insisting that it was exactly the car I wanted and I would be forever indebted to my dad if he would help me acquire it. After several days, he succumbed to my constant pleading, and we went out and bought that magnificent machine. I don't know what Eddie had done to that car, but it had a "souped-up" V-8 engine with a stick shift. It was the only car I had ever seen that could hit 120 miles an hour in second gear before topping out at 160 in third. Not even the chief of police had ever seen anything like it.

Eddie, who had a reputation for hot cars and fast women, was five-feet-ten, handsome, muscular and known as one of the toughest guys in town. Even after dropping out of school, he still managed to be an irritant to our high school teachers and school officials. Mr. Stitt's farm sat on top of the hill north of the high school and the only way for Eddie to get from the farm to Holly Sugar Factory, where he hauled his dad's beets for harvest, was to drive down the hill on the street in front of the high school.

Eddie had his truck rigged with enormously loud mufflers that would thunder and roar as he would let off of the gas coming down that hill. The crackling and popping were so deafening that on each occasion the classroom windows would rattle and shake. The teachers and students could no longer hear each other and the noise was so loud and disruptive that the teachers would have to suspend all classroom activities until the beet truck had passed by. Completely exasperated on one occasion, after the noise subsided, Mr. Sieck, in the middle of one of his math classes, declared, "I'll be glad when that damn kid gets his beets hauled." This brought a snicker from the entire class, which was secretly enjoying Eddie's thunderous interruptions.

When Eddie wasn't hauling beets, he was cruising up and down the street in front of the school in "White Lightning." He had the car's springs clamped or pinched together so that it would ride low to the ground, with the front of the vehicle lower than the rear. With the springs compressed in this matter, their effectiveness was reduced, causing Eddie and the vehicle to bounce gracefully as he passed by. Every lunch hour, as the students were gathered in the front school yard, Eddie would drive by, slouched down low in the driver's seat, barely able to see over the steering wheel. With the top down and the car stereo blaring, he would turn to the girls with a cocky smile, wave, and then proceed on down the street. Being completely oblivious to everything but himself and the pretty girls in the school yard, on one occasion, he failed to notice that the highway patrol car in front of him had come to an abrupt stop. When he finally turned his eyes away from the girls, it was nearly too late. He slammed on the brakes and with a loud screech laid rubber for several feet. By less than an inch, Eddie avoided the sure collision, but not the embarrassment of an event witnessed by the entire student body. The patrolman turned on his flashing lights, got out of the car, and swiftly issued Eddie a ticket for careless driving. After that first beet harvest, Eddie joined the Navy and it was then that I became the proud new owner of Eddie's car.

It's important to be tough and rugged when you're sixteen years old and driving a dream car. Not all things turn out as they should, however, and one night my friends and I went to the drive-in theater. We had the top down on this warm summer night, enjoying the popcorn, cokes and star-filled sky. Alfred Hitchcock's *Psycho* was playing and becoming increasing horrifying as the night went on. A few moments into the movie, someone suggested we should roll up the windows. Sitting there with the windows up and the top still down provided only temporary comfort and after a few minutes we hurriedly put the top up, secured it firmly in place, and then locked our doors.

Cars were an important part of the lives of sixteen-and seventeen-year-old boys and most of my friends all drove at least one that instilled lasting memories for most of us. John Peterson, "Pete," liked his dad's 1955 Ford and when he could finally afford his own car, he chose a Ford as well. His was a 1953 Ford Fairlane, which was a red and white two-door coupe. It was a good looking car that quickly became the most important thing in his life. That is, except for Paul Mall cigarettes and Jan Feeser, who was a thin, dark-haired beauty in our class. Pete had a crush on Jan throughout high school. One night when we were out driving around town, we spotted the light blue 1959 Buick owned by Jan's dad. It was parked in an alley with the trunk lid open and several girls were climbing into the trunk. We made a quick phone call and then rushed over to the drive-in theater and waited for the results. Jan and Sherri Redding were the only ones inside the front of the car as they pulled up to the ticket-counter; and after paying for only two admissions, Jan was asked what she intended to do about paying for the girls in the trunk. "What girls," she asked in her most indignant voice. As the cars stacked up behind Jan's, the girls began to file out of the trunk one-by-one. Their embarrassment was exceeded only by our exhilaration at having pulled off such a clever trick. Pete was the only one among us who wasn't amused.

Pete had a reputation for being tough and a fighter, but to his friends he was, in fact, a gentle giant. However, when drinking he could become belligerent and uncontrollable. He occasionally showed off his strength by bear-hugging one of his friends or lifting him over his head. The victim would eventually recover with only minor injuries. The same could not be said, however, about one of our cars. Pete had a strong punch and pain was a feeling that he had apparently never experienced. After a few too many beers, for some peculiar reason, he would derive great satisfaction in putting the imprint of his fist in the surface of a car's dash. Each of our cars had the outline of Pete's fist clearly identified, except one. One night while riding in the front passenger seat of Tom Stricker's 1954 Ford, it occurred to Pete that he was sitting in front of a perfectly unaltered dash. Inasmuch as Tom had owned the car for several weeks, it seemed impossible that it did not carry Pete's mark. Nearly in tears, Tom pleaded with Pete to spare his car, but before the evening was over, the deed was done. That was the last time Pete was allowed in Tom's car.

During our senior year there was an incident involving two guys named Paul. Paul Walsh was a thin, wiry farm kid from out by Sheep Creek close to the Nebraska line. He played football and was on the wrestling squad in high school. Unfortunately, he was probably more interested in learning about Ardyce Hager than learning about anything in Mr. Paul Boucher's American History class. I knew Paul Walsh well because the previous summer the two of us had traveled to Jackson, Wyoming, together and worked on a haying crew run by Francis Warziniack's dad. Paul was a tough kid, probably as a result of all the work he did on the farm and from throwing those hundred-pound bales of hay around in Jackson. Combining his strength with his quickness, he was a formidable opponent for even the most skilled warrior.

Apparently, Mr. Boucher was unaware of the danger lurking in his classroom. During one particularly boring lecture, Paul, the student, was paying more attention to Ardyce than he was to anything else and his behavior was extremely annoying to the instructor. Having told him repeatedly to shut up, and being completely ignored, Mr. Boucher dashed to Paul's desk and grabbed him around the back of the neck. This didn't turn out too well for either one of them, because in a flash, Paul, the student, had Paul, the teacher, on his back on the classroom floor and appeared to be trying to bash his head in. In obvious pain and anguish, Mr. Boucher was screaming, "Help!"

"Help!" "Help!" and, "Hurry, someone go get the Principal!" Upon being summoned by one of the girls who ran to the Principal's office, Mr. Woodley quickly entered the room and helped pull Paul off of his teacher. He was immediately suspended for the remainder of the school year and the next thing I heard was working in a printing plant in Denver producing ticket stubs for movie theaters.

Mr. Boucher was an interesting man, but not because of his teaching. He had an unusual pet in his home. It was a pet monkey he called Sebastian. Seeing Sebastian was a reminder of all of our visits to the Scottsbluff zoo, which housed a monkey who would mimic everything we did. He would pick his nose, shake his fist, and even return the gesture when flipped the bird. Several of my classmates and I had been to Boucher's home and saw the animal when Paul Boucher decided he wanted a different pet. My cousin, Phyllis, also a student at the school, gladly became the proud new owner of the monkey. She didn't know why Boucher got rid of the pet, but soon found out. After owning it for only a few days, her mother insisted that she get "that damn thing" out of her house. Clueless, my sister, Mae Belle, and her husband, Ron, thought it would be fun to have a monkey. After being introduced to Sebastian, they knew they had to have that animal. They didn't know anything about raising a monkey and none of us had ever heard of anyone, other than Mr. Boucher, having one for a pet. But, they didn't let that stop them. So, they paid the $50 for the animal, his cage, and the remaining supply of food, and took him to his new home. To their shock and dismay, after they got him home, they discovered that, although he was kind of cute, he was also disgusting. He was filthy and had a foul odor about him. Sebastian hated water and refused to bathe. He would fly into a rage when anyone tried to get him near soap and water. They figured it would take him awhile to get used to them and his new environment and they probably just needed to be patient until such time as he came around. In the interim, they would keep him in the back bedroom.

One day when Mae Belle came home from work she found that somehow Sebastian had gotten out of his cage. Upon opening the front door, in complete shock, she entered the living room, which was in absolute shambles. There was trash and debris everywhere. He had gotten into the cupboards and removed everything in them. The household garbage was strung everywhere and Sebastian was perched on top of the curtain rods that held the shredded rags that once were curtains. He had urinated and defecated in every room of the house and seemed to be proud of the fact that he had completely destroyed their home. Mr. Boucher explained that he would love to take the animal back, but couldn't, and they should probably run an ad and try to sell the creature. They were pretty sure that no one would be stupid enough to buy the little monster so they promptly loaded him, his cage, and everything associated with him, in the car and transported him to Scottsbluff where they found a pet store that agreed to take him off their hands.

When I was a teenager, barely of driving age, according to legend, there was a house of ill-repute on the east side of town in Scottsbluff. Not surprising, about a half-dozen of my friends and I were curious. We left Torrington about midnight one night, arriving on the east side of Scottsbluff around one o'clock in the morning. There was very little traffic in the neighborhood at that hour, and sure enough, we found that infamous little house. The lights were on and my friends and I were scattered around the outside of the place trying to get a glimpse inside. Tom Christy and I were peeking in the living room window and could see a gentleman sitting on the couch thumbing through a magazine. He was obviously waiting for his turn.

There were bushes and shrubs in the front yard under that living room window, and it was a good thing, too, because we hadn't been there for two minutes when a set of headlights came roaring around the corner. We could see that, although not lit up, there were some red, orange, and blue lights strung across the roof of that car. About that time, a beam of light hit the house on the corner, then it moved to the house next door. In just a split second it landed on the house in front of us. The only thing that had kept our shadows from appearing on that wall was those bushes and shrubs, under which we had dived headfirst. As the light traveled on to the houses down the street, we both drew our first breath of air in what seemed like several minutes. Our relief was short lived, however; because suddenly, the police car stopped dead in its tracks. The reverse lights lit up and back it came down that street. For whatever reason, Christy discovered something humorous. At first, he was able to contain most of his chuckles under his breath. But, gradually, they became increasingly noticeable. Both of the car's front doors swung open and in a heartbeat, two police officers stepped out and were soon within fifteen yards of the very spot where we were lying. Inexplicably, this drew uncontrollable laughter from Christy which was followed instantly by the light from the officer's flashlight shining directly in Tom's face. In a split second it was also shining in mine. "You boys come out of there right now," one of them shouted. "What the hell are you doing down here? Are you crazy?" he asked. "We just had someone killed down here a couple of nights ago. This ain't no place for you boys," the other officer explained.

After a few minutes of lecturing, they could see that we lacked both the money and the courage to be paying customers of this business and were probably sufficiently scared that we would likely never return. They rounded up the rest of our friends and sent us on our way with strict orders to go straight home and never come back to Scottsbluff again after dark. Their comments were persuasive.

During my freshman year of school, the number one interest of all of my friends was girls. We thought about them constantly, but ironically none of us had a date the entire year, except Jack Prickett. Although he was in our grade, Jack was a couple of years older, having repeated a grade or two along the way. He was very experienced with the ladies probably due to his muscular build and good looks. Being one of the few guys in ninth grade with a car didn't hurt either. Jack lived with his parents across the street from Torrington High School. His bedroom, which had an outside entrance, was in the basement. He appeared to have complete discretion over his schedule and activities and entertained a lot of visitors at all hours of the day and night. The girls seemed to be especially intrigued with the coal-black, diamond-shaped birthmark which was about an inch long in the middle of his chest.

The high school football field across from Jack's house also served as our track facilities with the running lanes circling around the outside of the grassy area. As we were concluding our workout one afternoon, a couple of dozen athletes remained and were gathering their sweats and gear when they saw a young lady approaching them from the south end of the field. It was a cute little ninth grader with experience far beyond her fourteen years. Everyone froze in their tracks as she strolled to the middle of the field. It wasn't long before Jack, the girl, and a few of his closest buddies, disappeared down those stairs leading to Jack's room. Most of us had been welcomed to his house on several previous occasions, but not on this day.

Several years later, when I was a freshman in college, Sherri Palmer and I had been to the movies and before taking her home we stopped to have a coke at the Corner Café. Jack, who had recently been discharged from the Navy, and another ex-classmate, Dorland Smith, were concluding a night of drinking and had just finished an early breakfast. We left the restaurant at the same time and as we were getting into my dad's 1960 Chevrolet, Jack was crawling behind the wheel of his 1953 Olds. We were both heading north on Main Street when he pulled alongside and Dorland rolled down the passenger side window. They suggested that we have a contest to see which vehicle could first reach the top of the hill, about a mile away. At the end of that mile and in the middle of the hill, the street turned slightly to the east, made a half circle and then returned in a northerly direction. The half circle was necessary in order to avoid hitting a five-foot-high block-concrete wall and the home that it enclosed in the middle of Main Street. As Sherri and I rounded that corner, I looked in my rearview mirror just in time to see Jack and Dorland flying through the air after running head-on into that concrete wall. Upon contact, the vehicle did a spectacular somersault over the fence, landing upside down in the flower garden. Instead of stopping right there, horrified, we proceeded around the bend and returned to the site, approaching from the south. In spite of the time required to travel that three miles, we were still the first ones on the scene, which was littered with crumbled concrete, broken glass, parts from Jack's car, beer cans and whiskey bottles, some broken, some still full. Jack and Dorland were in the vehicle, moaning and groaning in obvious pain. Both were hurt but refused medical attention, insisting that the first priority was to gather and hide all of the evidence. I had retrieved the last beer and whiskey bottles as the police and ambulance arrived. It turned out that all of my efforts to clean up the scene were in vain because that 1953 Olds, now demolished, was itself full of other evidence. The next day the local radio station was reporting the news about a drunken crash that occurred up in Morehaven Heights, and the police were asking for anyone who might have information about the accident to get in touch with them. I wasn't tempted and neither Jack nor Dorland ever explained to the police what had actually happened.

Most of the guys in my class were in love, at one time or another, with three girls who shared a common first name. One was beautiful, having been selected court queen or attendant every basketball season. Another, our freshman class treasurer and representative on the student council her freshman and sophomore years was gorgeous, and the third, another homecoming queen and voted most witty her senior year, was cute with a bubbly personality. Every healthy young boy had fantasies involving the three ladies.

It was senior sneak-day and our entire class went to spend the night at Guernsey Lake, a recreation area thirty-five miles northwest of town. Somehow, I got hooked up with one of these beautiful girls for an uneventful night of hugging and hand holding. Inasmuch as she was madly in love with her boyfriend, a weightlifter who was three years older and the state high school heavy-weight wrestling champion, we both agreed it would probably be best if he didn't find out about the truly innocent activities that went on that night. The next day, after returning to Torrington, I received a call from my companion of the previous night, in which she gave me the unbelievable news that because she was feeling guilty, she found it comforting to discuss the entire matter with her future husband. A few nights later, while riding around town with my friends, we were pulled over and her boyfriend was delighted to discover me hiding under a jacket on the back floor board. After pulling me through the side window, we headed out to the country and upon our arrival, he showed me some of his favorite and most amazing wrestling maneuvers.

Torrington, a small town with a population of about five thousand people is separated from South Torrington by the Platte River which runs from west to east. South Torrington has a few hundred inhabitants, and as the name implies, is situated to the south of town. Except for a couple of classmates who lived there, most of us had only been to South Torrington a few times and after a terrifying experience there one night, had no plans to ever visit it again. It all began as we were cruising Main Street when we were flagged down by our buddies. They were agitated after having been harassed by some people in a car bearing Colorado plates. The vehicle was filled with several gentlemen from Mexico who spoke only broken, choppy English. Their language was sufficiently clear enough, however, to describe some "gringo chicken shits" whose own mothers had served as bed partners for the Colorado visitors. Upon making this unexpected announcement, the Coloradoans then fled to South Torrington where they apparently had an unlimited number of relatives living. It was suggested that we collect as many of our friends as we could find and go down there and teach those guys a lesson. After several minutes, a dozen or so of our friends had been rounded up and loaded into three vehicles, and we headed towards the Platte River Bridge. Whether due to slow traffic, delays resulting from red lights, or simply the need for more time for the occupants to gather their courage, as it turned out, none of our three cars arrived in South Torrington at the same time. This was a huge tactical mistake and there seemed to be no possible way to correct it.

My 1960 Chevrolet, which I had owned for only a short time, was the first to arrive in the neighborhood whose only street light was so far away it looked like a distant star. It was pitch black, but when my head lights fell on that car with Colorado plates, I slammed on the brakes and we skidded to a stop on that dark gravel street.

The Colorado car was sitting in the front yard of what appeared to be a rundown shack. The lights were on inside but there were no visible signs of any activity that could be seen through the tiny front window. However, we were sure that we had found the right car and figured the occupants had to be around somewhere close by. As we opened our doors to get out and investigate further, a huge army of men stormed from behind the house and into the street. They were swinging knives, tire irons, and chains and there was little doubt that we were in deep trouble. Seriously outnumbered, we couldn't believe our buddies had lost their nerve. What we didn't know was that one carload had already been there and left and the other was on its way, but would never arrive. At that moment, our only thoughts were of escape, but in the confusion and panic, we were no longer in the car, but were scattered about the street trying to avoid being killed. At one point in the melee, the only light provided was that from my car's headlights, and I looked up to see that I was surrounded by three opponents. Each had a chain and it obviously wasn't their first gang fight. They would converge on me, swinging their chains in unison. As they moved in, I would duck under as the wind and whistle from their weapons whipped by my ears. It was then my turn to swing my tire iron and as I was going for a home run, they would drift back far enough to avoid the hit. Ironically, the fear in their eyes suggested that they were as terrified as their prey. The swings and counter swings continued until I was able to break away and run to my car, which, surprisingly, was slowly idling down the street. As I went to get in behind the wheel, I found the driver's seat already occupied. Unfortunately, it wasn't one of our guys, but rather, one of theirs. To avoid capture, I ran completely around the car several times, when finally out of sheer panic, reached in and jerked the driver out by his hair. I jumped behind the wheel and with the engine still running and the doors half open, sped off. Fortunately, all of our guys were now in the car.

We didn't stop until we reached Main Street in Torrington where Chief Wonder and the rest of the night shift of the police force were waiting for us, along with the other two cars of our friends, who by now we were convinced were indeed "gringo chicken shits." The rear window glass of my car had been completely blown out by the force of the chain which had struck it as we left the battle zone and the imprint of each length in the chain remained imbedded in the leather at the top of the back seat until 1966 when I traded the car in on a new Chevy Impala. Blood from the wound suffered by our buddy Ray ran from his stomach down the front of the back seat and into the foot well. While treating our wounded at Goshen County Hospital, a couple of the killers themselves showed up in search of medical relief, which they were promptly given before being arrested and carted off to jail. Chief Wonder treated the entire incident as if somehow we were the victims, in spite of the fact that we had foolishly invaded their territory. It was unclear to Chief Wonder and my parents how anyone could display such a lack of intelligence to venture into South Torrington in the middle of the night, not knowing where they were going, who they were looking for, or what they would find once they had arrived. On the positive note, we never made that same mistake twice.

The only other South Torrington experience remaining in my memory was the car chase in Ken Stimson's nearly new, gold and white 1958 Chevy Impala. Several of the underclassmen were trying to avoid capture as we pursued them at a high rate of speed through the streets and alleys, finally culminating in that little town south of the bridge. It was dark and as Ken unexpectedly approached a sharp curve we began sliding out of control on that gravel road. A huge cottonwood tree was coming directly towards the passenger side of that beautiful Chevy coupe. Fearful of the impending crash, all of the occupants were frozen in time, unable to move a muscle. Except Max DeBolt, whose right elbow was hanging out of the window. In a flash, he jerked his arm inside the car and quickly rolled the window up, as the car slid to a stop just an inch short of the tree. Except for the tires on Max's side which had been drug off of the rims, Ken's car escaped being damaged. Capturing the low level underclassmen would have to wait for another day as it was several hours before a tow truck showed up to inflate the two tires that were completely flattened by the ordeal.

We spent an inordinate amount of time in our cars driving around town so it's a small wonder that a lot of things were discovered or experienced within the confines of one of our vehicles. One night while leaving the Out-or-In restaurant, Stimson passed gas. It was a quiet release that went completely unnoticed until such time as the odor instantly overwhelmed everyone. Without hesitation, DeBolt who was driving at the time, whipped over to the curb and in unison, three of the four car doors flew open and all but Ken bailed out. With the doors wide open and the passengers outside gasping for air, fanning their faces, and pointing at Ken inside the vehicle, it was obvious to all passing by what had transpired.

Reflecting on the incident some time later, someone wondered if a powerful gas of that nature would burn. Instantly, Billy Stout dropped his drawers, including his undershorts, propped both feet on the dash and with his cheeks spread, lit a match to a stream of vapor which was filling the car. To our amazement, it exploded like a blow-torch. He shrieked in pain as the flames reached his bare skin and the smell of burning hair filled the air.

# CHAPTER THREE

## Paths that Cross

Following those carefree high school days, most of my friends went their separate ways; some got jobs in the area, and others found work elsewhere, but, most went to Laramie to the University of Wyoming. I attended Goshen County Community College and at the end of the first year, I promptly left town to work for a pipeline construction company in South Dakota. The project was to begin at the Wyoming/South Dakota line near Edgemont, South Dakota, and run east to Hot Springs, then turn north and pass by Buffalo Gap, Fairburn, and Hermosa, before concluding in Rapid City.

I hoped to earn enough money during the summer and fall to pay for my enrollment at the University in the spring. I had never been around anyone in my life that could drink as much whiskey as the construction workers on that pipeline crew. It was absolutely unbelievable and very sad. One of the older guys on the crew couldn't even start work without first downing an entire pint of whiskey. After being on the job for a few months, something unexpected happened. One day, the Superintendent, Vince Johnson, asked me to jump in his truck and take a ride with him. He drove up to the top of a mountain and stopped at a point that overlooked the valley below. As we got out of the truck, I was expecting a lecture about some shortcoming I had been displaying on the job but instead was confronted with a passionate appeal to abandon my current construction career and get back in college. Life was too short to waste it with a gang of people who drank too much and would never amount to anything, Mr. Johnson, explained. He said I reminded him of his own son and he wanted far better for me than I apparently wanted for myself. I don't know why I was the one out of about two dozen men the boss took an interest in; perhaps it was because, at eighteen, I was the youngest. At any rate, our discussion made an impression on me and I soon realized that you can make a difference in someone else's life simply by caring about them. Thoughtful advice, even when unsolicited, can sometimes make all of the difference. Shortly following this discussion, I did return to the classroom.

Except for excelling in physical education, I had gotten by at the community college earning "average" grades in all other subjects. Most of the credit hours of courses taken during that year were accepted at the University of Wyoming. The difference in expectations between junior college instructors and those at a four-year university were unbelievable and became troublesome within the first several days at UW. My advisor, Dr. McDaniel, thought I was a good candidate for a non-credit course that taught students how to study, so the following semester, I signed up. Since I had no definite plans, it was Dr. McDaniel who steered me into the College of Commerce and Industry. He recommended the business college because it provided his students with marketable skills, enabling them to easily find employment when finished with their education.

After taking the self-improvement study course, my grades improved. My parents, instructors, and friends were all stunned when, my grades went from C's to straight A's, and I was named to the Dean's Honor Role. "I want to congratulate you and your son on this outstanding achievement," R. E. Kinder, Dean of Men, wrote to my mother. "His accomplishments reflect great credit on his parents, his home community, and the University of Wyoming, as well as on himself," Mr. Kinder concluded[4]. My parents' feelings of pride were only temporary, as I didn't return to the Dean's Honor role until several years later while working on my Master's Degree. I finished my undergraduate career with a disappointing overall GPA of 2.59.

While attending the University, I had taken a job at the Laramie Holiday Inn as a desk clerk/night auditor. The owner of the hotel was Todd Serman, a wealthy rancher who, in addition to the Inn, owned a huge ranch north of Laramie. He wore a handlebar mustache, cowboy hat, vest, and boots and, although very successful, looked more like a ranch hand than a business executive. I didn't see much of him because I worked mostly nights and he managed the bar during the day shift before returning to his ranch in early evening. However, he kept informed on the business by calling in several times every night. "How's it going?" he would ask about every thirty minutes. "Like it was the last time you called," I foolishly responded on one occasion. "You know what I mean," he shouted in to the phone. "How many damn rooms have you got rented, you idiot?" He would have fired me on the spot except he didn't have anyone else lined up to cover my shift, and he didn't want to drive back into town in the middle of the night. After he ended the call, I immediately called the general manager, Jerry McCue, who was also

---

[4] Letter from R.E. Kinder, Dean of Men, University of Wyoming, to Mrs. Guy C. Ferrari, June 22, 1964.

a business student at UW and by now a friend and told him I was about to be fired. "Don't worry about it," he said. "I'll call Todd and take care of it." Jerry was the only one who didn't shake in his shoes every time Todd or his wife Kay came around. In fact, it seemed that the Sermans feared Jerry far more than he feared them.

The Holiday Inn served as a perfect job while going to school because although it was nearly a full-time position, there were several hours between midnight and seven in the morning when it was quiet and I could get a lot of studying done. The day's business was closed out at mid-night and as soon as the cash was counted, the deposit prepared and placed in the safe, and everything was reconciled, which usually took about an hour or two, we were allowed to hit the books, interrupted only by an occasional late night arrival. I arranged my class schedule around the work schedule after that first year and remained in the job until leaving the University and Laramie two and a half years later.

A frequent patron of the Holiday Inn Lounge was my Principles of Insurance instructor. He had gone through an unsettling divorce and sought solace through advice and counsel from Taro, our bartender, who would keep his bar chair reserved and glass full. I first observed the results of Taro's expert counseling at two o'clock one morning when he asked my help in raising one of his customers from under the bar and transporting him to an awaiting taxi cab outside the barroom door. In the process of getting Taro's patron to his ride home, we neglected to notice his coat which was piled in the bar stool next to where he had spent the last several hours. The next night, a very embarrassed professor came to the front desk to inquire if anyone had turned in a beige three-quarter length overcoat with sheepskin lining. As I handed the coat over the counter, avoiding eye contact, he said, "Thanks, I'll see you in class." Following that encounter, I incorrectly thought that getting an "A" in Insurance 571D wouldn't be too difficult.

Insurance was the only class I had from this particular instructor during my college career, and it was in his classroom when I first heard the shocking and unbelievable news that our President, John F. Kennedy had been shot. Several years later, our paths would cross again after both teacher and student had left the University.

I enjoyed nearly all of my classes while studying at the University, but Business Law turned out to be my favorite subject. Both Business Law I and II were three-hour credit courses and both were required for a degree in Business. My instructor was Dr. James Wolf, and his usual approach was to present case studies from the textbook, involving actual contractual disputes, and then asking the students to identify and discuss the major legal elements of the disagreements. Following the discussions, the class would be assigned the task of researching similar court cases and in subsequent classes describe their findings. Actual rulings by the courts in resolving the conflicts would then be presented. The exams followed a similar pattern, inasmuch as actual cases would be presented and the students were required to discuss the probable court outcome and present legal justification for their arguments. I excelled in these classes and enjoyed a good rapport with the instructor. Several years later, Dr. Wolf and I came together again as government officials; he with the judiciary and me in the executive branch of Wyoming government.

# CHAPTER FOUR

## "Dorm Chief, March these Hogs Back to the Barracks"

My career in business, government, and politics did not begin until several months after graduation from the University of Wyoming. I, first, was to satisfy my military obligation.

During the height of the Viet Nam war, it seemed that Uncle Sam wanted everyone. Ken, Magoo, and I joined the Wyoming Air National Guard, headquartered directly north of the municipal airport in Cheyenne. We had been high school friends and college roommates and frequently discussed, with some trepidation, the situation in Southeast Asia and what our future role in the war might be.

I had known Ken Stimson since our freshman year. He had moved to Torrington to attend school because there was no high school where he came from. In fact there was no town where he came from. He grew up on a ranch in an area called Burgess, Wyoming, which was around thirty miles north of Torrington. Burgess had a one-room school house which housed all of the kids from the area in grades one through eight. Once they attained the ninth grade, however, they had to find another school to continue their education.

Most chose Torrington. Decked out in his ranch clothes, including boots, belt buckle, and cowboy hat, I first met Ken in front of the drug store on Main Street. He was about six feet tall, thin, and seemed somewhat restless as he milled around in front of the store. I had never really known a real cowboy as I grew up on a farm and most of my grade-school friends were farm kids, not ranch kids. The possibility of developing a friendship with this lanky young cowboy didn't occur to me during that brief encounter.

Ken lived in a basement apartment across town, about four blocks east of the high school. It was a lot bigger and nicer than the one in my folks' house, but after we became better acquainted during that first year of high school, for twenty-five dollars a month, he decided to live in my folks' basement apartment when the next school year came around. This was the beginning of a friendship that would last for the next fifty-five years.

I don't recall where or how I became acquainted with Bob Glover. His friends always affectionately referred to him as "Magoo"; a nickname that has also endured for the last fifty-five years. MaGoo, like his father, was tall, about six-feet-four, slender and soft spoken. During high school, he and his brother Jim shared a black and white 1953 Buick, two-door hard-top. In an attempt to make it louder, with a hammer and screwdriver, the boys poked holes in the glass-pack mufflers they had installed on the car. It did become louder, but there just wasn't any way to make this big box, with its Dyna-flow transmission and plush leather seats, sleek or sporty. The "Hog," as we called it, was a favorite among their friends, due mainly to the fact that the Glover boys were always driving around town and seemingly with unlimited gas money.

The Guard offered a number of opportunities in which a business degree could be utilized and we had our choice of assignments.

Both Magoo and Ken wisely chose their military career paths in personnel and office management. However, openings in these fields and others related to business would not be available until May of 1966. Since I was finishing classes in January, I anxiously, and as it turned out, foolishly, asked for the first opening in any field. I was assigned to a food service slot and was scheduled to be shipped out in February. I figured after finishing basic training and returning to Cheyenne I would request a transfer into a career field more compatible with my education and interests. This did not work out as hoped. The fact is, once you were assigned to food service there was simply no way to ever get transferred out of it. Because of an outbreak of meningitis at the base in San Antonio, Texas, my enlistment was delayed and it wasn't until June 12th that I was finally shipped off, not to San Antonio, but to Amarillo, Texas, for basic training. So, I left about the same time as Ken and Magoo, except I was in food service and they were in administration. That set the tone for the next six years of my life in the Guard.

Kay and I had been married only a couple of weeks and leaving our new apartment to live with a hundred guys in an open-bay dorm in a place far away wasn't exactly my idea of a honeymoon. The first order of business upon arriving at basic training was to get our heads shaved. I failed to see the humor, but all of the drill sergeants got a huge kick out of the new recruits with bald heads. The non-commissioned officers were career Air Force, most with twenty or thirty years of active duty, and without exception, they did not like National Guard troops. It was obvious that most of the instructors we encountered did not particularly like their jobs either. The training instructor for our flight was Sergeant Beaman, an obese, five-foot-six inch, two-hundred-and-fifty pound man. It was difficult to envision him as "one of America's finest." After every meal, our sergeant left the mess hall with a toothpick hanging out of his mouth, leaned against the side of the building, scratched himself, passed gas, belched, and then shouted: "Dorm Chief, march these fucking hogs back to the barracks!" I suppose maybe some of the troops qualified as hogs, but in comparison, the sergeant was a thoroughbred.

For six weeks, we encountered extensive verbal and physical difficulties and many recruits could not handle them. Surprisingly, some couldn't do a single push-up and fell victim to constant ridicule and harassment. John, a recruit from Cheyenne, sobbed and cried after each failure until the drill sergeant told "the fucking fat hog" he would be dishonorably discharged. His discharge was probably a lifesaver for Johnnie and was a relief to the rest of the squadron; he was physically unable to perform and the sergeant's constant abuse was demeaning and intolerable. Others, who couldn't complete the obstacle course, were forced to do pushups until they collapsed in exhaustion. Like Johnnie, many were also eliminated from the service.

The military at that time had a very strict rule against any of its members getting too much sun. In fact, if a sun burn was severe enough to prevent one from performing his duties, the offender was subject to court martial. This was bad news for David Stroud, a nineteen-year-old, slim, bespectacled recruit from Denver, who unfortunately subjected himself to that warm Amarillo sun and obtained a burn so severe that his back and legs, particularly behind the knees, were blistered. To avoid the intense pain, he attempted to march and walk without bending his knees. Resembling the stiffness of someone on stilts, he was quickly spotted by Sergeant Beaman. After slapping him repeatedly on the back to emphasize the seriousness of the offense, the sergeant marched Airman Basic

Stroud around the corner of the barracks and out of sight, never to be seen again. All assumed and hoped he had been discharged and sent home rather than executed.

We completed basic training on July 9, 1966, and were returned to Cheyenne where all food service recruits were promptly assigned to F. E. Warren Air Force Base for OJT (on the job training) for ninety days. I was the only airman with an apartment in Cheyenne. Prior to enlisting in the Guard, Michael Sara, a shy young man from Cheyenne, lived with his parents in their home on Cheshire Drive. All others in our training unit were from Colorado. Even though Mike and I had living quarters elsewhere, we were all assigned to the barracks at Warren and, being from the National Guard, were instantly unpopular with the full-time Air Force personnel. Many of the regular Air Force had never heard of the national guard or reserves and wanted to know how we "found out about it" and how they could get in and reduce their enlistment from four years to just six months. Of course, this wasn't possible and somehow Sara, I, and the other guardsmen, were personally responsible for the misery suffered by all full-time airmen on the Base. We were assigned rooms in the barracks, and inexplicably, each guardsman was placed in a room with a regular airman. My roommate was from Biloxi, Mississippi, and he readily admitted that he did not like "whities," especially those with only six months of active duty remaining.

Although I never spent a single night in the barracks, I was required to maintain a room there and keep a bed, closet, and all personal gear in perfect military condition. The rooms were inspected weekly and the first few inspections did not go well. My shoes lacked an adequate spit shine, the corners of my bed were incorrectly folded, the bed spread was rumpled, and the items in my closet were unclean, disorderly, and unkempt. Following receipt of the report and a reprimand from my commanding officer, upon returning to the room to assess the situation, everything looked to be in order. The violations cited weren't noticeable. In fact, my quarters looked far better than Airman Jackson's, my roommate.

After failing my second consecutive inspection, I needed to be present when the next inspection was to be conducted. I arrived at the barracks a few minutes before Lieutenant Anderson and immediately realized why my quarters did not measure up to military standards. To my surprise, Airman Jackson's name-plate was over my locker and my name-plate over his. My spit-shined shoes were under his bed and his dull, scuffed oxfords were under the foot of my bed. I quickly moved every item back to its proper place and easily passed the inspection. Airman Jackson wasn't so fortunate. He had absolutely no idea how our nametags and personal items got changed around.

Because I didn't sleep at the barracks, I only encountered my roommate a few times during the three months while stationed at Warren. I was always uncomfortable on Base, however, knowing how Airman Jackson felt about me and how seemingly all of the airmen felt about the guys in our guard unit. Several of the guardsmen were accosted at night and all, at one time or other, came out of the barracks in the morning to find their vehicles with tires slashed, side mirrors torn off, windows shattered, or paint scratched.

After six long years in the 153rd Support Squadron of the Wyoming National Guard, on the 29th day of November, 1971, I was honorably discharged after attaining the rank of Staff Sergeant. Looking back on the experience, it doesn't seem like much; but at the time, it was completely life altering. The Viet Nam War was in full force and guard units around the country were being activated and shipped to the war zone. Deployments in the sixties were not as common or as likely as they were with the Iraqi war and the war in Afghanistan, but we were constantly reminded by our superiors that we could be activated and we ought to be prepared for such an occurrence. And, we came close. On a Sunday afternoon at the National Guard base in Cheyenne, as we were finishing cleaning up the mess hall after serving over seven hundred hungry guardsmen, the radio was blaring out the names of guard units around the country which were being called to active duty. Our unit was not on that list but a companion unit in Pittsburg, Pennsylvania, with a similar airlift mission was. We found out later that the Cheyenne unit was originally selected for call up, but at the last minute was replaced by the Pennsylvania unit at the request of its commander. I have often wondered how my life would have been different had we been the ones to go to Viet Nam as originally planned. My concern for those who went in our place was certainly not misguided, as many of them never returned alive. Many who survived came back with less than what they had when they left.

Not everyone in the guard reacted to the uncertainty as I did. For the first few years, Kay and I were reluctant to buy a house or to incur much of any kind of debt because the ninety dollars a month I would earn if activated would be far less than sufficient to make house payments back in Cheyenne, Wyoming. Most of the men I worked with in food service worried about being called up because they really didn't like what they were doing. All were college educated and on the outside had professional positions with good salaries in the private sector. They could put up with the two-day-a-month duty assignments and fifteen days of annual active duty. But, the thought of a full-time job in a military mess hall for an extended period was simply not very appealing. In this regard, I shared their views.

There were other concerns that were more troublesome. I wondered whether or not the Cheyenne unit would have survived in a war zone. The Food Service Section was under the charge of an enormous man of about five-feet-eight-inches tall, who weighed around three hundred pounds. He was a Warrant Officer who was well known by the troops. Unfortunately, he appeared to be in very poor health. He kept his stash of Canadian Whiskey in his lower right-hand desk drawer and both he and the Base Commander enjoyed it several times during the day. I feared that this activity might have influenced our unit's readiness if deployed to Viet Nam. Fortunately, we never had to find out.

# CHAPTER FIVE

# The Private Sector Experience

After returning to Cheyenne from Basic training and while serving on active duty at Warren AFB, I had looked at several jobs in the Denver area. I had been invited for several interviews, but only two resulted in job offers. I didn't know what the position with Goodwill Industries would entail, but their recruitment material mentioned several qualifications and educational requirements that matched my background and training. When Kay and I arrived at their Denver offices, I was pretty sure that by the looks of things, it wasn't any place that I wanted to work. The lighting was poor and the building was dark and depressing. The floors were covered with dark colored linoleum, the walls were painted a dark grey, and it lacked warmth and appeal. The salary offered was competitive with those being offered in the private sector and the long-term opportunities described were appealing, but I knew I wasn't a good fit with Goodwill. Kay waited outside in the car while I interviewed. She wasn't disappointed to hear that the job wasn't going to work out. The dreariness of the facility had had a similar impact on her as well.

The Carnation Company was also looking for recent business graduates in the Denver area, and at the time one of my high school classmates, Larry Goddard, worked for the Company. Larry's job and the one being offered to me entailed going to grocery stores, writing orders for Carnation products, and arranging product displays. In other words, it was similar to a delivery man's job, the starting point in the company's management training program for recent college graduates. I traveled with Larry for a couple of days on his route and from this experience got a better idea of what the job would entail. Larry seemed to enjoy his work, but had no long-term career goals that included Carnation. In fact, he was anxious to leave the company and enter medical school, which he did, and for the next twenty years was my optometrist. He sold me my first set of contact lens and during the course of his career invented several products related to eye care and contact lens users.

At the time of the Carnation Company interview, I had also applied at the local offices of Burrough's Corporation in Cheyenne. The Company was one of the largest producers of mainframe computers in the world[5] and was one of the leading manufacturers and sellers of adding machines, typewriters and printers in the country at that time. Several years later, Burrough's merged with Sperry Univac and the name "Unisys" was adopted for the merged entities.

The company was located on West Lincolnway at the intersection of Missile Drive. The offices were not fancy, but they were bright and airy. Most of the people who worked there were seldom in but rather were out in the field on sales and service calls where the money is made. The company sold and serviced office machines, primarily those used in bookkeeping and accounting. Their big sellers, usually costing thousands of dollars, were what they called

---

[5] http://en.wikipedia.org/wiki/burroughs_corporation

"Posting Machines." The leading seller, the Burrough's Sensimatic, was a machine that could perform numerous business functions simultaneously. Utilizing a moving programmable carriage, it could maintain several ledgers, storing as many as twenty-seven different balances during the ledger posting process. This capability was nearly unheard of in those days. It was one of the few machines in the industry that could be programmed to perform specific bookkeeping and accounting functions unique to each business. Both the Burrough's salesman and the machine operator had to have some knowledge of programming, accounting and business applications. The salesman, or systems rep as we were called, needed to know how to program the equipment so that it would perform the desired functions, such as payroll, accounts payable, accounts receivable, etc. This was a position which would require applying the business training I had received in getting my Bachelor's degree, particularly in accounting. It also would require extensive training at the Corporate Headquarters in Detroit, Michigan, and periodic training around the country when new products were introduced. So, I accepted the position upon completing active duty with the Guard and became employed in October, 1966, joining the some 35,000 people employed by the Company. The starting salary was $525 per month which was guaranteed, regardless of my sales success. This was quite a boost from the $90 per month I had been receiving from the U.S. Air Force. My boss, Doug Moench, a thirty-year veteran of the Corporation, assured me that in a few years I would be making more money than any other company or employer in Cheyenne could pay.

I remained employed by Burrough's Corporation for about a year and saw some success in the sales field. Although I sold numerous small machines, the first and only accounting machine sale I landed occurred only a few weeks before leaving the company. The $10,000 sale was to the Chugwater Feed Company, a grain elevator in Chugwater, Wyoming. It was considered a fairly big sale by Burroughs and my boss was quite excited about it. He assured me that this was only the first of a long line of successes I would enjoy with the Company. In spite of his persuasion for me to stay, I was offered and accepted a position with the Wyoming Department of Education a short time later. I was very fond of Doug and hated to disappoint him, but I wasn't having much fun at the Company. I had attended numerous training programs with Burroughs, mostly in the Cheyenne office, but several were out of town as well. One session was in Detroit for four weeks and another in Dallas for two. Kay, who was six months along at the time, went with me to Detroit and while I was in training, she spent her days with her Aunt Mallie and Uncle Frank who lived in Dearborn, home to the Ford Motor Company, where Frank was an assembly-line worker. In spite of the fact that we barely knew them, they were very hospitable and I would join them on the weekends following a week of classes. This required travel by city bus on Friday nights and again on Monday mornings. I had no idea at the time that the Detroit riots would begin the week following my departure. There were no signs of racial unrest that I could see, but the riots took place in the very areas through which I traveled going to and from Uncle Frank's house. The racial mix in downtown Detroit at the time seemed to be about eighty to ninety percent black, and to a small-town boy from Wyoming, this was a little disconcerting. However, I was never hassled nor confronted in the bus system, which consisted almost exclusively of African American riders.

Another training program that I attended was in Dallas and it was during this meeting that I realized Burroughs would not remain in my long-term plans. The training classes themselves were interesting and helpful. However, I did not enjoy traveling or being away from home for extended periods. Doug assured me that, in time, I would grow accustomed to the travel and it wouldn't bother me, but it was too late. I left with mixed feelings as Doug Moench was a good boss and a friend, and I had learned a lot about all aspects of bookkeeping and accounting while I was there. During the 1960's, Burroughs was one of only eight computer manufacturers in the United States. The others included Control Data Corp., General Electric, Honeywell, IBM, NCR Corporation, RCA, and Univac. The employment opportunities afforded by these gigantic international corporations were unlimited, including the expectation of huge salaries, stock options, and national and international travel. These are perks that a small government operation, such as the State of Wyoming, simply cannot and should not provide.

The Wyoming Education Department job was the first in a long list of positions I would occupy over the next thirty-five years. I never regretted leaving Burrough's, and giving up the corporate opportunities to join government service. Over the next twenty years, I was fortunate to have had the opportunity to work for five different supervisors. They included Sid Werner and Dr. Dale Lucas at the Wyoming Department of Education; Terry Hanley, my finance instructor at the University of Wyoming and later my boss, in the State Budget Office; Governor Hathaway, who appointed me State Budget Director in 1973; and finally, Jim Griffith, Wyoming State Auditor, for whom I worked between 1975 and 1986.

# CHAPTER SIX

## A Start in State Government

My first position in State government evolved from a friendship which began when I was a sophomore at the University of Wyoming in Laramie where I had enrolled for the spring semester in 1963. I shared an apartment with Ray Wood, one of my friends from high school, following a year of study at the local community college in Torrington and after spending several months on a construction gang in South Dakota. It was a one-room apartment in the Knotty Pine Apartment house. It consisted of a small kitchen which you entered from the hallway and on the other end of the room was just enough space for the two single beds which stood about three feet apart. There was barely room for two desks at the foot of the beds, and there was no back door, which of course today would result in condemnation procedures because of a fire hazard. As the name implies, the unit was knotty pine throughout, with paneled walls and ceilings, all finished in a dark-brown stain. The apartment was somewhat cramped for two students and some occupants escaped the confinement by moving their beds up into the attic which was completely unfinished but did have three-quarter-inch thick sheets of plywood lying over the rafters serving as a floor on which a bed, a nightstand, clock radio, and reading light could be placed.

I got to know Ray fairly well in the spring following my seventeenth birthday when high school came to an end for the Class of '61. Both Ray and I took jobs with the local Coca Cola bottling plant. One aspect of these jobs was to deliver the product to the local retail outlets, including filling stations, restaurants, and grocery stores in Goshen and Platte counties. When not on my routes I would help Dave and Ron Murphy, whose mother actually owned the operation, with the manufacturing and bottling of various soft-drink flavors. My primary responsibility in this role was to prevent any dirt and crud from going undetected after bottles were washed and placed on the assembly line for refilling. The conveyer belts moved the empty bottles in front of bright lights where those bottles containing foreign objects were removed and sent back to be re-washed. This could be a pretty disgusting assignment as there might be the remains of bugs, spiders, and an occasional rodent in the bottom or lodged in the neck of a bottle. It didn't take much imagination to picture oneself choking on an undetected item while chugging down a coke.

Another aspect of my work involved delivering pop to Mom's Cafe on First Street in Wheatland, Wyoming. Mom was usually good for eight to ten cases of a variety of flavors and this would involve stacking them on a dolly and moving them into the restaurant through the back door which led to the kitchen. Once inside it was necessary to transport them through the kitchen to the storage area in the northeast corner. Throughout the entire delivery, food was being prepared, including meat which was being trimmed and cut on the prep table in the middle of the kitchen area. The cook was a chunky man about fifty years old, who had lost his left arm about an inch below the elbow. To facilitate his work, the left arm sleeve of his shirt had been removed. When cutting and carving the meat, he would of course take the butcher knife in his right hand which would necessitate holding the item firmly with his left. Having no left hand, he would lean down over the table and bury the stump of what remained of his arm in the meat, where it would immediately become covered in blood and beef remnants. At the time, I did not appreciate the commitment he made to his work nor his ability to do the job under very difficult circumstances. Instead, I was thinking about finding another place to have lunch.

The thoughtlessness I felt in the Wheatland delivery did not hamper my ability to succeed in the Coca Cola business; for at the end of the summer, Dave Murphy wanted to know if I would manage the Torrington plant while he and his brother moved to Gering, Nebraska, to take over the bottling and distribution operation there. This came as somewhat of a surprise to me because it hadn't been but a couple of weeks earlier when I nearly killed his mother. I was sent to pick her up in one of the company pickups, a maroon 1953 International half-ton truck with a stick-shift transmission and Coca-Cola emblem in the center of both doors. I was waiting behind the wheel with the engine running, the clutch depressed, and the transmission still engaged when Mrs. Murphy came out of her home. As she was walking in front of the truck to get to the passenger side, I thought I'd be a gentleman and open her door. I reached across the cab and grabbed the door handle. As I was about to swing the door open, my foot slipped off of the clutch and the truck lunged forward. Fortunately, the pickup killed its own engine just in time to avoid hitting a very big bump in Mrs. Murphy's driveway.

I decided not to accept the offer from the Murphys, choosing instead to work part time and attend college. Sharing an apartment in Laramie was convenient and more economical for both Ray Wood and me as we began our University studies. The first day after we moved in, I looked up to see a guy with a cast on his right hand standing in the doorway. Although he wasn't oriental, in his best Chinese impersonation, he shouted, "Yu oder fish?" "Who oder fish?" "I have twenty-pound oder fish for you." We, of course, thought the guy was a little weird as we explained that we hadn't ordered any fish, but it could have been one of the other students in the house. With that, a grin broke out on his face. This was not a Chinese fish salesman, but rather was Clyde Gerrard, a business-education major from Evanston.

Clyde was a stocky kid. He was five-foot-nine, weighing about one hundred seventy-five pounds. He was a graduate of Evanston High School where he played guard on the basketball team and was an all-conference center on the offensive line for the Evanston Red Devils. Clyde's apartment was the last unit at the end of the hall on the west side, which meant if he parked in the front lot at the north end of the building, he would have to walk by our apartment to get to his. In an attempt to relieve the phobic nature of the small apartments, most residents left the doors to their apartments open, enabling everyone passing by to see what was happening inside.

Clyde had a couple of roommates during the year we lived at the Knotty Pine. Roy Bennett, a tall, pleasant, brown-haired twenty-one-year old cowboy and Evanston native roomed with him during the first semester; but unfortunately, lost his life in a car accident one weekend on his way home. Roy was followed by Ed Stala, an all-state wrestler from Kimball, Nebraska, but the relationship got off to a shaky start and never did recover. The first time Ed visited his parents in Kimball, he came back to Laramie with the family's weekend leftover meals and demanded that Clyde pay for half whether he wanted any of it or not. Later, after Clyde left the University, he was pleased to hear that Ed got the crap beat out of himself by Ray Wood. I don't remember what caused the dispute, but the result was quite obvious. Ed's wrestling skills were no match for the Mohammad Ali type punches delivered by the six-four, two hundred pound Wood. Ray learned how to fight in elementary and junior high school out of necessity. Until college, he was always kind of a pudgy kid, with baby fat that he couldn't get rid of. Much of it settled in his chest area. P.E. classes were always tough on Ray, as was showering after football practices because the guys would enjoy poking fun at "Tits Wood." It wasn't until his senior year in high school that he went through a breast reduction surgery that literally changed his life.

Following our years at the University, Clyde and I remained friends and both ended up in Cheyenne. While I took the job with Burroughs Corporation, Clyde went to work as a Federal Funds Auditor with the Wyoming Department of Education. We were each having some success during our early years of employment, but Clyde was enjoying his work far more than I was enjoying mine. The daily pressure to produce was a constant at Burroughs and was measured by comparing sales to the sales goals established by management. We had a board posted in our office which listed each salesperson and beside the name was each individual's sales production for the month and year. Although salesmen with little or no sales were never ridiculed nor belittled by management, the self-imposed expectations were a source of constant stress and discomfort. Even when goals were met or exceeded, there was little time to celebrate because of concern as to where and how the next period's sales would be achieved. When Clyde called and asked if I wanted to apply for an opening in his office, I didn't hesitate.

During the presidency of Lyndon B. Johnson, a number of domestic programs were created and most remain to this day, nearly fifty years later. The Great Society[6] programs included such efforts as the Bilingual Education Act, the Civil Rights Act of 1964, the creation of Community Action Agencies, the Economic Opportunity Act of 1964, the Elementary and Secondary Education Act, the Food Stamp Program, Head Start, the Higher Education Act of 1965, Job Corps, Model Cities Program, NASA Art Program, the National Endowment for the Arts, the National Endowment for the Humanities, the National Teachers Corps, the Office of Economic Opportunity, Upward Bound, the Voting Rights Act, and the War on Poverty. There were others as well, but these are the more notable ones.

The Elementary and Secondary Education Act (ESEA) of 1965 contained several provisions that affected the Wyoming State Education Department (SDE) but the two that concerned Clyde and me were Title I and Title II. Title I provided federal financial assistance to local schools for the education of children of low income families. Not all schools in the state participated in the program because in order to do so required that approximately forty percent or more of its students come from families that qualify under the U.S. Census definition of low income. Title II provided federal financial assistance to schools for the purchase of school library resources, textbooks, and other instructional materials. This aid was not limited to low income schools; rather, all schools which applied qualified. Both Title I and II federal funds were administered by the SDE. Local schools had to comply with all of the requirements of the federal law and the rules and regulations formulated by the

6 Great Society-Wikipedia. http://en.wikipedia.org/wiki/Great_Society

U.S. Department of Education as well as the instructions developed by the State (SDE) for keeping track of receipts and expenditures at the local level. Most of these rules and regulations were designed to show what was purchased with the money and when, so that the schools could be reimbursed. Clyde and I designed the reporting forms for the schools to fill out and instructed the business office personnel in completing the forms. Later, we traveled to the school to audit the program and verify that the expenditures reported by the entity were accurate and qualified for reimbursement. All of this activity was under the direction of our boss, Sid Werner. Clyde and I both enjoyed working for Sid. He established reasonable time frames and we were given complete freedom to design the work flow, work schedules, on-site audits, and other aspects of the job. He trusted us completely. Government work under Sid certainly was kinder and gentler than work at Burroughs Corporation. And, it was fun.

Clyde and I shared an office in the northeast corner of the basement of the State Capitol Building, right next door to Sid's. I continued to work for Sid and with Clyde for a couple of years. Then, in 1971, Wyoming elected a new State Superintendent of Public Instruction, Dr. Robert Schrader. His deputy, Dr. Dale Lucas, had been employed in the department for several years and he was eager to make some changes. Sid was in charge of all financial matters concerning the department and the school foundation program which involved hundreds of millions of dollars and all of the school districts in Wyoming. He, for years, was the sole "expert" on school finance; and educational professionals, legislators, school superintendents, and others who needed information had to work with him to get financial information. Through the budgets, Sid indirectly controlled even their programs. Dr. Lucas was determined to make financial information more readily available and thought the best way to do it was to move some of Sid's duties to others in the department. He separated "internal" finances from "external" and asked Jim Sheehan to take over the school foundation program and he asked me to manage and supervise the department's budgeting, financing and accounting functions. He left Sid in charge of the State's school lunch program and federal program auditing. After the shakeup, Sid's staff included himself and five people; his personal secretary, Clyde, Clyde's secretary, and the school lunch staff including the nutritionist, Imelda Little, and the accountant, Bob LeGoff.

This was my first management job. It was the first time in my career involving the supervision of employees. I had no idea what I was getting into, but happily accepted the challenge as it was what I wanted to do. My degrees were in business administration and management so I believed that I was prepared for such an assignment. But in college, any college, they don't teach you how to deal with troubled employees. One member of the staff had worked in budget and finance for as long as anyone could remember. She didn't like the idea of having a new boss, particularly one who was half her age and had only been employed by the department for a couple of years. She knew how to handle Sid. She wasn't sure about me. Frankly, I had feared her from the minute I met her estranged husband. He lived across the street from Kay and me on Fremont Street in an apartment. When he heard that I worked in the same agency as his wife, he came over and introduced himself. The day before, he had survived an unfortunate encounter with her. Her capacity to inflict physical and mental harm was quite evident. His eyes were both black and his face was marked with bruises and scratches. His arms were showing signs of teeth marks as well as cuts and abrasions. He insisted "the bitch is crazy" and I feared as much.

My experiences over the next couple of years validated his argument. They were divorced a short time later and to no one's surprise, she got everything the two of them owned, including two chocolate-colored poodles. He was too frightened to fight for anything in the divorce and said later that he was thrilled to simply escape with his life. Fortunately, no children were created by the union. The fate of the two poodles was never known.

State government was entering a stage of change and uncertainty in the mid-seventies. Governor Stan Hathaway, a very popular and capable politician, had pushed for legislation to create the Department of Administration and Fiscal Control (DAFC). The objective was to consolidate all administrative and financial activities, which at the time were scattered around in separate agencies and departments, under the central management, control, and direction of the Governor. The director of the new department would be appointed by and report directly to the Governor. Each division within the new department including research and statistics, statewide budgeting, personnel, purchasing, data processing and two new centralized activities, printing and motor pool, would be managed by a division director, each appointed by the Governor, but reporting to the department director. Shortly after creating the new budget division, Terry Hanley, the division director, offered both Clyde and me budget analyst positions in the new agency. He was recruiting several employees to work with all of the operating departments in the State, including the legislative and judicial branches of government. These were newly created positions in Wyoming and we would fill two of six new slots. We were to learn everything we could about the agencies assigned to us and would serve as a liaison between them, the governor, and the legislature. Our jobs included advocating for their programs and budgetary needs with both the governor and legislature and, conversely, advocating the governor's position regarding the agency to that agency and to the legislature. We were either the best or the worst thing that could happen to the agency. Recommending for them could help them; recommending against them usually killed whatever they were seeking if it needed either the governor's or legislature's approval.

I had known Hanley for several years, having first encountered him as one of my instructors at the University of Wyoming. He taught insurance in the College of Business and Industry for several years and later moved to Cheyenne where he became employed by the State. Kay and I occasionally socialized with Terry and his wife Sue who taught with Kay in the Business Department at East High School. Over the years, we became friends and frequented each others' homes from time to time. I remember one night when most of the budget division staff was out on the town and concluded the evening by calling Hanley's house at 2:00 o'clock in the morning. He was asked to serve breakfast to the hungry crowd and for some reason he complied. He entered the kitchen wearing only his house coat and as he strolled into the room, the family cat was right underfoot, curiously peering up under Hanley's coat. When Terry stopped in front of the kitchen sink, to his absolute horror, the cat sprang into the air and with claws outstretched, snagged something under Terry's coat. Terry's shrieks and screams frightened the cat and it quickly released and darted into the other room. He survived and went on to become one of the best budget officers the State had ever had.

Working with the agencies was an interesting and exciting challenge. We learned as much as we could about each agency's programs, activities, and spending needs. We helped them prepare their budget requests and sat at the table when they presented their requests to the governor and appropriations committee of the legislature. We prepared written analyses of each agency and presented these reports to the governor and committee. The relationship between the analysts and the agencies was not always a friendly one. Disagreements on the amount of funds needed to operate their programs and departments were very common inasmuch as the agencies frequently overstated these needs. Our jobs were to conserve state funds; their jobs were to spend them, advancing whatever cause they were assigned by law or which they created by their own design. This often led to a declaration by the agency that the budget analyst "didn't understand," or was simply "unqualified" to make a judgment. But, since we worked directly for the governor and were an extension of him, we usually prevailed.

The budget division staff was a very close-knit group. The ten-member staff, under Hanley's supervision excelled and was generally considered a competent, knowledgeable group. It was the best working environment I had ever encountered in my career and has not been equaled since. For the most part, the people were very professional and avoided pettiness, gossip, innuendo, and the politics of personal destruction which are prevalent in most organizations. When the governor moved Terry over to be director of the Department of Health and appointed me as his replacement, I was blessed with a great opportunity and good people to work with. I was 29 years old at the time, and according to the Personnel Department, was the youngest to ever serve as the State's chief budget officer. Governor Hathaway was in the latter stages of his final term so I enjoyed working with him through his final budget submission to the legislature. On the final day of his term, my phone rang with him on the other end of the line. He beckoned me to his office and when I let myself in, he rose from his desk with a smile on his face and a partially smoked, unlit cigar dangling from his lips. "Davey," he began, "I want to thank you for everything you've done for me and for the State." He continued, "This isn't much, but it is the only thanks anyone will ever give you." He was right. That moment stuck with me for the rest of my career. It seems there isn't much thanks offered to government workers. I was young and working with the Governor was exciting and challenging. Getting to know the personal side of him was especially meaningful.

On December 2, 1974, as we were preparing to leave Office, he sent me a letter which I regard as one of the more meaningful memorials of my government service.[7] "It has been my pleasure to work with you during some trying times, which probably gave us both a great deal of perspective," he said. "When you look at the budget after the smoke clears after the next legislative session, some people may think that the two fellows from Goshen County didn't do a bad job," he concluded.

Governor Hathaway's service to Wyoming and to our Country is well documented.[8] He enlisted in the U.S. Army Air Corps in 1942, trained as a radio operator and gunner, and as a member of the Eighth Air Force's 401st Bomb Group, flying B-17 Bombers from England participated in 35 combat missions over France and Germany. One of his missions ended in a crash-landing in France. Another also nearly ended in disaster when a bomb got stuck in the bomb bay preventing his plane from landing. He was the one selected to stand on the bay and kick the bomb off into the English Channel.

---

7 Letter from Governor Stan Hathaway to David G. Ferrari, dated December 2, 1974.

8 Robin Beaver, "Wyoming's Favorite Son", Made in Wyoming: Our Legacy of Success, http://www.madeinwyoming.net/profiles/hathaway.php;stanhathaway

In spite of this, he refused to admit he was a hero, insisting instead that he merely was doing what he had to do and God would take care of things. His eight years serving as Wyoming's chief executive are noted for equally courageous acts, even if on a less life-threatening scale. He is probably best known for creating the State's first mineral severance tax in 1969, followed by a constitutional amendment creating the Permanent Mineral Trust Fund in 1974.[9] He proposed and got approved a senior citizen tax relief measure during the 1973 Legislative Session and got the Environmental Quality Act passed, creating the state Department of Environmental Quality. He saw the enactment of air-and water-quality standards and surface mining regulations. He was also known for creation of the Department of Recreation for the management of state parks and promotion of the tourism industry. And, he was responsible for creation of the Department of Economic Planning and Development to promote economic growth in Wyoming. His last budget for the 1973-1975 biennium totaled $329 million.[10] It was the one built while I served as his budget director and after we put the final touches to it and the legislature finalized the appropriations act, he summarized it like this: "Davey," he said, "this is the last conservative budget this State will ever see." It was during his first term that the State's general fund had run completely out of money and there was a cash balance of a meager eighty dollars. If you were governor during those days, you had no choice but to be conservative.

Most governors are honored, revered, and occasionally feared. They are not super-humans although are often thought to be by their adoring constituents, advisors, and employees. We forget that

---

[9] http://en.wikipedia.org/wiki/stanley_k._hathaway

[10] "1973: Wyoming/As They Saw It", http://astheysawit.com/11536-1973-wyoming.html

they put their pants on one leg at a time, the same as everyone else. This was evidenced by a couple of incidents during the time that I worked for Stan. The first happened during a discussion of education issues while putting together the State Budget one evening in his conference room. It had been a long day and everyone was tired. He was slightly irritable. Lee Galeotos, Director of DAFC, mentioned something about ESEA, assuming everyone in the room knew what he was referring to. The Governor turned to Lee, with a snarl on his lips and disgust in his face and said, "God dammit, Lee, what the fuck is ESEA?"

The Governor's personal side was also displayed when he was counseling one of our staff who was considering a divorce after many years. "Son," he said, "you need to do everything you can to salvage this marriage. The grass isn't always greener. You'll never regret holding this marriage together, but you will always regret it if you let it fall apart." His advice was persuasive, as the marriage was saved for years. It wasn't until long after Governor Hathaway left the Capitol Building that his friend and employee proceeded with the divorce. The marriage ended amicably and I often thought it was probably because of the kindness and thoughtfulness expressed by the Governor during those discussions.

I held that budget officer position until Stan's term ended on January 5, 1975, following the election of Ed Herschler in the general election of 1974. After defeating John Ostlund, the republican nominee, Gov Ed didn't move into the governor's office until the 6$^{th}$ day of January, but he began work on his transition immediately following the November elections. Two of his first tasks were to find people to work in his new administration and to get his budget recommendations ready for presentation to the legislature which would be meeting in January. He was a democrat, following twelve years of republican rule. Most of Stan Hathaway's appointees didn't expect to be reappointed by the new governor. I was surprised to glance up from my desk one early Monday morning and find Gov Ed standing there looking down on me. With a grin on his face and an outreached hand, he asked me to continue as budget director. I loved that budget job and would have liked nothing more than to accept the offer, but, I had already accepted the position of Deputy State Auditor with the new State Auditor, Jim Griffith. In an effort to enable me to stay on, he called my new boss to see if there was some way Jim could find another deputy. He said he would "give two democrats for that one republican," but Jim wouldn't go for it, so on January 6, 1975, I moved up to the first floor of the capitol building and assumed my new duties. Between November and January, however, I spent all of my time working with Gov Ed on his new budget recommendations and writing his "Budget Message" to the legislature. I also served with his transition team which involved defining his goals and objectives for all areas of the executive branch of government. He was very decisive in what he wanted to accomplish and the entire staff enjoyed working with him. One example of this had to do with the Federal-State Information Exchange System (FIXS). The program was funded with federal funds and involved compiling financial information on federal programs in the state. The system was under the direction of a life-long republican who had been appointed to the position by Governor Hathaway. It was rumored in the budget office that the individual was a dedicated party loyalist who was receiving a pay-back for being active in politics. Someone casually mentioned to Gov Ed that he ought to just do away with the program as it was full of errors, involved a lot of effort to compile, and the information was of no value. "Abolish the damn thing," he replied. Jerry Bryant, the analyst assigned to the agency offered to go over and tell the director that his program and thus, his job, had been abolished. "No," said the Governor with a twinkle in his eye and a smile on his face, "This is one job I want to do myself." And, he did, first thing the next morning.

One night, a few days before Christmas, we were having a holiday party at my house on Yucca Road when at about ten o'clock the door bell rang. There was a blizzard outside and I was surprised to find the new Governor standing in a foot of snow on the front step. He spent the next three hours sitting around the fireplace telling stories and visiting with the staff. He recalled being at a political dinner/dance when the then Secretary of State spotted him from across the room and began moving toward him. He said he was "scared to death she was going to come over and ask me to dance. I'd rather have my fingernails pulled out one at a time," he said, "than dance with that woman."

I really liked this new Governor and wished I hadn't been so hasty in accepting another position. But, there was no way to know he would offer me the job. He was the first governor in Wyoming to serve three full terms and although I never worked directly for him, over those twelve years there were many opportunities to work with him. It began as soon as I started my new job in the Auditor's Office. The Auditor's Office was a small office consisting of eight employees whose jobs were to keep track of appropriations and pre-audit all of the State's bills before they were paid. Over the years, the staff had grown old on the job and suffered from a lack of management and direction. Much of the activity in the office was being duplicated elsewhere in various other agencies. My first task as Deputy was to write a plan to eliminate duplication and consolidate these activities under the supervision of the State Auditor. I had discussed this with the Governor during the transition and the new State Auditor was enthusiastic about the proposal, so the office was expanded and reorganized following legislative approval of the plan during the 1975 Legislative Session. We went from an eight person office to twenty-one positions with statewide responsibilities for the state's centralized accounting, payroll, pre-auditing of all bills before being paid, and appropriations control. Every payment required our prior review and approval before a state warrant could be written. We also became responsible for all payroll functions in the State, excluding the Highway Department and University of Wyoming. This entailed writing payroll checks for over seven thousand state employees in dozens of agencies located throughout the state.

The State Auditor's Office, which previously was often ignored by the other agencies of government, was transformed into a true comptrollership function. Following the governor, the state auditor, because he controlled the purse strings, became the second most powerful office in State government. Not all agencies accepted this expanded role and power of the auditor and some rebelled or protested when their spending was questioned or forbidden. When this occurred, their only recourse was to go to the Governor and ask him to overrule the auditor's office. In the twelve years that Gov Ed served and Griffith was auditor, I can't recall an instance when the Governor disagreed with the Auditor's decision. The Governor trusted our judgment and supported our decisions. This was an amazingly effective relationship, considering we were operating with a democrat Governor and a republican Auditor. Partisan bickering, which today is a common impediment to government functioning, was very rare in those days. Government actually worked then.

There were a number of other incidents during my time as Deputy State Auditor when I had the opportunity to work with

Gov Ed. One involved the State Training School in Lander which at the time was the State's program for the mentally disabled. There had been a mysterious death at the institution and some had alleged that the patient had been murdered, either by other patients or by employees of the agency. The Board of Charities and Reform, under our Constitution, had responsibility for management and oversight of the institution. Chaired by the Governor, the Board voted to create a committee to investigate the deaths. Three people were appointed to the committee, including the late Joe Meyer, who, at the time was employed by the Legislative Service Office, but who would later serve as both Wyoming's Secretary of State and State Treasurer. The other two members were the late Pete Mulvaney, Deputy Wyoming Attorney General, and me. We spent a week in Lander interviewing the Superintendent and employees of the institution, along with a few patients who were communicable. After reviewing the circumstances of the death and visiting the site of the incident, we could find no evidence of foul play. The patient had died from drowning in a pond on the institution's grounds. The pond was fenced so access to it was confined to staff members with keys to the gate. The patient would have had to climb over the eight foot fence or been given access by a staff member with a key. No one witnessed the drowning and no employee would admit to giving the victim access to the pond. We concluded that the patient scaled the fence, fell into the pond, and drown. As chairman of the committee, I drafted the report with Joe's help and the three of us met with the Board in executive session and presented our findings. Our report silenced the critics temporarily.

Prior to serving on the investigative committee, I had visited the Lander facility several times while I was in the budget office. In order to better understand the agencies' programs and functions, our budget analysts often went to the site of the department to get a firsthand look at its operations. To me, the Training School was by far the most shocking operation in State government. Staff members at the facility referred to the residents as "our kids," but in fact, most were very elderly and severely impaired intellectually. Several impressions have stuck with me since those days and will remain with me for the rest of my life. I recall them now with a great deal of confusion and aversion. One area which housed numerous elderly women was a large open room or dorm which was portioned into dozens of spaces of about six-by-eight feet in size, separated by partitions which were about three feet high. Each contained a single bed and a rocking chair. Nearly every bed had a doll of some kind laying on it. Some were covered with blankets; others weren't. Some residents were in the cubicle sitting in a rocking chair holding a doll. All residents seemed convinced that the dolls were alive and were their babies. Many of the women referred to me and the men visitors accompanying me as "daddy." Many of the residents hurried to the visitors to grab onto them wanting to be embraced, hugged, and kissed. They were very loving and showed a strong desire for intimacy with their visitors. It was a very sad and uncomfortable encounter. Looking back on the experience, it is obvious now that they suffered from Alzheimer's. I'm not sure that at the time anyone knew what the disease was.

Caring for the mentally ill in the sixties and early seventies was entirely different than it is today. When we entered the severely impaired boys' or men's quarters, it was appalling to see the manner in which patients were bathed and toileted. The patients were not clothed and all of the toilet seats had been removed in the restrooms. The showers were open rooms with multiple faucets and no walls or curtains. Shower heads were replaced by hoses. Residents were literally hosed down like animals being prepared for auction. Nothing was done in private. Instead, several were bathed at the same time. Some were crying and screaming while running around the area trying to avoid the spray from the hoses. Others seemed to enjoy the experience. Toilets were not surrounded by walls but instead were lined up on the open walls. Some residents were perched on stools; all were naked, with their private parts dangling down. They appeared more like birds perched on a ledge than like human beings using the toilet. It was very shocking and sad. They could not communicate with the staff or the visitors, but it was obvious that many were frightened or uncomfortable with the experience. Feeding times at the institution were also repugnant. In order to keep the residents from hurting themselves or others, many were not given forks, knives, or spoons. Many were strapped into chairs like babies and fed by staff. Others fed themselves with their hands. Food was smeared all over the tables and chairs and on the residents themselves. It was very similar to infants, six to twelve months old, playing with their food.

Not all of the residents were in this condition. Some, in fact, were somewhat self-sufficient, providing personal care for themselves, such as personal hygiene, personal bathing, and feeding themselves. One, affectionately nick-named "Bingo," had free access to the entire grounds and assumed the responsibility of managing waste and trash pick up for the institution. He used a horse and wagon to load and haul trash. Bingo dressed up like a cowboy, complete with neck scarf, chaps, hat, toy guns, and holsters. One day when the Training School was hosting a conference attended by law enforcement officers from around the state, Bingo startled everyone by jumping off of the wagon, confronting the officers with his guns drawn. Not knowing for sure that Bingo was using toy pistols, the shocked officers hit the ground with their guns drawn as well. Luckily, no shots were fired and only Bingo was amused.

The administrator of the facility, Dr. Fred Heryford, was trying to move the facility from a warehouse type of operation to one where the patients were given individual attention. Progress was slow, however, due to the reluctance on the part of the State to provide enormous increases in funding which would be necessary to enable such services. The State was pushed in this direction during the nineteen seventies by lawsuits filed by the Protection and Advocacy Group[11] which was created in 1977 "to establish, expand, protect, and enforce the human and civil rights of persons with disabilities through administrative, legal, and other appropriate remedies." It was a slow process, but gradually funding increased and services began to improve for our institutionalized citizens. They were initially moved into cottages inhabited by six to eight residents with live-in supervisors or caregivers. Later, as the litigants demanded and the courts agreed and ordered more and more individualized services for the residents, the institution was transformed into a program serving only the extremely disabled. The less impaired were transitioned into community-based programs and nursing homes throughout the state.

During the last dozen years of my own mother's life, as she languished away with Alzheimer's disease, first in Torrington, then in Cheyenne, then again in Torrington, and, finally, in a Casper nursing home with a specialized Alzheimer's wing, I was often reminded of these experiences in Lander. No matter how personalized or expensive the care is for these innocent victims, it

---

[11] Wyoming Protection & Advocacy System, Inc., "Mission and History", http://wypanda.com/mission.asp

is an indescribably miserable, disheartening existence which only God himself can imagine or explain. The best we can hope for is to lessen their pain and make them as comfortable as possible and hope that they don't suffer for years and years as my mother did. I also can reflect on those earlier days and understand the anger and frustration shown by the Protection and Advocacy Group and the families and loved ones of our institutionalized "children." In times of distress and hopelessness it is perhaps natural to look to someone else, for relief from or to blame for our miseries. The state served as the villain, but no amount of court judgments or money directed at the problem can erase the pain and horror of this terrible affliction.

In the mid-70s, a scandal broke out at our State institutions. During a routine examination of vouchers submitted by the Pioneer Home, Karl Eickbush, supervisor of our pre-audit unit, questioned several expenditures. There were numerous expensive personalized items, such as toiletries and monogrammed towels; unusual items to be bought by a state agency, even one serving residents in a retirement home. A more careful review revealed the purchase of expensive stereo systems and thirteen very costly wide-screen RCA XL-100 television sets. In examining the State's inventory records, it was apparent that none of the stereos or televisions was recorded. In addition, dozens of expensive gift packs of nuts, candies, snacks, and other items were bought with state funds. There were a sufficient number of questionable transactions to warrant a trip to Thermopolis to do an on-site audit. Our suspicions were quickly confirmed upon discovering that only two of the RCAs were at the home and both were being enjoyed by the Superintendent and his wife in their personal residence. The others had been given to friends and acquaintances. Two were given to the Superintendent's boss, Secretary of the Board of Charities and Reform, who gave one to his friend who was also his secretary in Cheyenne, and kept the second for his and his wife's enjoyment in their home. Others were given to the Superintendents of the State Park in Thermopolis and the Veteran's Home in Buffalo. Some were unaccounted for but none were being used by the residents of the facility. When word got out that an audit revealed missing television sets in Thermopolis, there was a statewide scramble to recover all of the units and return them to the home. But, for those people involved, it was too late.

Following a very intense meeting in the Governor's conference room with the Board of Charities and Reform, the State's Attorney General, and our office, in which the audit findings were disclosed, the officials were charged with misappropriation of funds. One member of the Board was very upset that the matter had become public and accused Griffith of "grandstanding" and being a "publicity hound". "I saw you on television last night holding up that can of nuts with your little smirk. You were enjoying every minute of that!" he exclaimed. He insisted that the Board should have kept the audit findings secret. He said it would be best if the public did not know that such an abuse occurred and argued that the public would "lose confidence in their government" once the information got out. The Governor sided with the State Auditor and the Attorney General and the findings were turned over to the District Attorney. I didn't know Ed Witzenberger, the State Treasurer, very well, but Jim had always spoken highly of him, partially because of his sterling military record, but also because he had worked on Jim's campaign when Jim first ran for Treasurer and then served as Jim's investment manager in the State Treasurer's Office. Ed was a good friend of Griffith's and, in 1993, at Jim's request, Governor Hathaway appointed Ed to fill out the unexpired term of State Auditor Everett Copenhaver who resigned for health reason. Following that, Ed ran for State Treasurer and won and served in that capacity from 1975 until 1979.

My impression of that particular member of the Board changed on that day. I completely disagreed with his view that the audit should be kept secret and the matter handled administratively. I was not disappointed some years later when he lost his bid to be Wyoming's lone representative in Congress. He finished third in the primary, in a three-person race, consisting of Jack Gage, a friend of mine and an attorney who later represented me in a contract dispute involving a fast food chain, and Dick Cheney, the eventual winner, who later became U. S. Secretary of Defense under President H.W. Bush and then Vice President of the United States, under President George W. Bush.

The Governor did the right thing in his handling of the scandal. He took responsibility for the misdeeds of his Secretary of the Board of Charities and Reform and the superintendents, even though all were appointed to their positions prior to his arrival as the state's chief executive. He knew the public wouldn't hold individual board members, such as the treasurer or the auditor, accountable for problems at the institutions. Whenever things go wrong in state government the governor is blamed. The public believes the governor is in charge--not the treasurer, auditor, nor anyone else. All of the perpetrators involved were charged. All resigned or were fired from state employment. None served any prison time. Some died prior to sentencing. Nothing was kept from the press.

Following that exchange in the governor's conference room, I had another experience with several of our statewide elected officials which I will never forget. It was around this same time period that we were flying in one of the State planes from Evanston to Cheyenne late one night. The passengers in that small twin-engine six-seat aircraft included the two pilots, Governor Herschler, State Auditor Griffith, Witzenberger, and me. It was about ten o'clock and the weather was bad; snow, rain, sleet, and wind, were creating a lot of turbulence. Both Ed and Jim were seated with their backs to the cockpit, Jim facing the Governor and Witzenberger facing me. All had our seat belts fastened and were in the middle of a conversation when the plane dramatically and unexpectedly plunged from the sky, falling several hundred feet in seconds. The drop was so sudden that the thrust of the fall caused everything in the cabin to fly from the floor to the ceiling. I had a checkbook and calendar planner in my suit coat vest pockets, along with pens, papers and other loose materials. These items instantly flew out of the pockets and rocketed through the air, banging and knocking on the plane's ceiling. During the free fall, I looked over at the Governor who in a flash jerked at his seatbelt making sure it was firmly secured. He said later that he nearly gave himself a hernia. Glancing at Witzenberger, I knew we were in serious trouble. He had flown hundreds of combat missions in Viet Nam and when he looked over his right shoulder at the instrument panel in the cockpit, he had a look of terror in his eyes. Then, he simply began shaking his head as if to say there was nothing that could be done. After several seconds, the plane hit the bottom of an air pocket with an enormous banging sound. The airborne items, including books, briefcases and bottled drinks, crashed to the floor, after which the plane leveled out and again became responsive to the actions of our capable pilots. I asked Ed what was going through his mind during those terrifying moments. He said he had seen similar incidents in the past and was afraid that when the plane hit the bottom of the pocket, its wings would simply snap. He thought we were dead. We were extremely lucky, he said, that that didn't happen. After the incident we continued to

Cheyenne, only to learn that the conditions were too severe to enable a safe landing. None of us wanted to take any more chances, so we turned back around to the west and eventually landed in Laramie, where two highway patrol cars were waiting to drive the four of us to Cheyenne.

Theft at the state institutions wasn't the first scandal that Gov Ed had to deal with during his tenure as governor. There were a number of others during his twelve years at the helm. Several involved him personally. During our audit of the institutions, we worked with the Division of Criminal Investigation (DCI) of the State's Attorney General's Office. Neil Compton, Director of the DCI, and a holdover from the Hathaway Administration, felt that the Attorney General, his boss, was blocking or postponing investigations of these allegations. He and a couple of his agents accompanied our staff on our on-site audits so they were intimately aware of all of the irregularities that were uncovered. At the same time, the DCI was investigating allegations of misconduct in Rock Springs involving the mayor and the state chairman of the Democratic party. The state party chair was a close friend and business partner of Gov Ed and Compton sincerely believed that he had close ties with the Mafia.

During this same period, the DCI had set up an undercover operation to buy drugs from the younger brother of one of the state's most prominent officials. The DCI drug buyers were to meet the seller at 10:00 a.m. in front of a vacant retail store. On the day of the scheduled transaction, the seller didn't show up. Compton was convinced the Attorney General had warned the alleged seller of the sting operation. He went ballistic and also went to the press. "The Governor's Attorney General is a crook," he declared at his hastily called press conference. He then went into a full-blown description of the institution's misuse of funds, the alleged Mafia ties in Rock Springs, and the aborted drug buy. The Attorney General denied all of Compton's allegations and he specifically denied any connection to the drug incident. Since the Governor was a close friend and business partner of some of those being accused, he was clearly tainted by all of these charges as well. Compton raised such a fuss and, given the credibility he enjoyed because of his position as the chief crime investigator in the State, a grand jury was called to conduct an investigation. No charges were ever filed, but the case drew national attention, including a fifteen-minute segment on CBS's *60 Minutes*. I was with Jim Griffith at his townhouse in north Cheyenne and tape recorded the entire two-hour interview with Dan Rather and his one-man crew. The camera was focused on Griffith while being questioned by Rather. Rather was receiving the questions from his cameraman, Paul Lowenworter. Basically, they wanted to know what Jim thought of the Governor and his Attorney General. Were they indeed crooks, as Compton had alleged? And, should the alleged situation in Rock Springs involving Mafia ties to the Governor be investigated? Jim apparently didn't add any insight into the scandal because he never even appeared on the program. Mr. Rather's only reference to his interview with Griffith was at the end of the program when he said that the State Auditor agreed that a grand jury should be called to investigate the allegations. We both thought the Governor was a victim of an over-zealous criminal investigator, who by his very nature believed everyone is guilty until they prove themselves innocent. The Attorney General was a decent man. Whether or not he told anyone to stay away from that vacant retail store on that day is a question that only he can answer.

Another scandal touching the governor occurred when, in September, 1985, he declared personal bankruptcy.[12] The bankruptcy stemmed from the 18,500 acre Yellowstone Ranch near Lander, Wyoming, he owned along with three other partners. They had purchased the ranch in 1977 for between $4.5 and $5 million. The operation went smoothly until 1981 when they sold 3,000 head of cattle and couldn't collect the $1.5 million payment they were to be given in the transaction. The Wyoming economy was going through a very difficult period during the early 1980's. Land values were dropping sharply and interest rates were going through the roof. Cattle prices were dropping dramatically during this period and as a result of this botched transaction, the Governor found himself having to borrow at these high rates to make debt payments. The ranch was foreclosed in April, 1985, for $1.9 million.[13]

In spite of these difficulties, a public opinion poll taken during his last year in Office in 1986, showed that he was the most popular politician in the State.[14] Most people at the time believed he could easily have been elected to a fourth term had he chosen to run again. I always thought his popularity was largely due to his sense of humor. He was known for his witty, sometimes hilarious comments. I recall in one of our meetings he was struggling with a decision when he explained, "I have mixed feelings on this issue. It's kind of like watching your mother-in-law drive off a cliff in your new Cadillac."

Governor Herschler finished his third term at the end of 1986. During the year, Mike Sullivan, a Democrat from Casper,

---

12 "Wyoming: Governor Goes Broke", *Time*, September 30, 1985. http.www.time.com/time/magazine/article/0,9171,959965,00.html.

13 Ibid.

14 Ibid.

Wyoming, and a lawyer, ran for governor and won in the November elections. He had run a good campaign, influenced largely by Dave Freudenthal, an advisor to Gov Ed. Dave served as the Wyoming state planning coordinator and in my mind was the leading public policy expert in Wyoming. He was also one of my best friends. I had known Dave since 1974 when he worked for the Department of Economic Planning and Development and I was budget director for Governor Hathaway. As a young lawyer, Dave joined the Herschler Administration as an aide to the Governor. His office was on the first floor of the capitol building, on the extreme opposite end of the hall from mine. Topics considered by the elected officials, including his boss, the Governor, and my boss, the State Auditor, often involved staff research and analysis. We would sometimes find ourselves working on the same issues, trying to find information or potential solutions for their use. One night when I was working late long after everyone else had gone home, I heard a visitor coming through the reception room. Looking up, I was surprised to see Dave entering my office. He was obviously troubled as he slowly slid into one of the visitor chairs in front of my desk. I figured he had some difficult state issue he was wrestling with, but on this occasion, it didn't involve the state. Rather, it pertained to him. He said he was going through a divorce, and it was obviously tearing him up. We talked for a couple of hours but I was mostly just listening. I really had no insight into what he should do or how he should handle the problem. I was surprised that he was sharing these very private emotions and feelings with me, as we didn't know each other well. Our friendship took on an increasing importance, I think for both of us, following that night.

During Sullivan's campaign, Dave often asked for information or analysis on some issue being considered. Because the Auditor was the comptroller of government, we had financial data on all programs and agencies and the staff was accustomed to and experienced in doing financial analyses. It was logical that we would be asked to run numbers on various proposals. Requests came from both parties and both candidates. It wasn't restricted to the Democrats. But, because Dave knew what we could do, I got far more requests from him than from anyone else. When Sullivan was finally elected in November, 1986, I was asked to serve on his transition team along with Joe Meyer, Phil Kiner, head of the state's research and statistics unit, and Dave. We prepared briefing books and papers on all issues that might be useful to a new governor. Phil worked up graphs and charts on the State's economy as well as governmental revenues and expenditures. We also put together explanations of all agencies, programs, and issues in government, and the source and amount of funding and problems associated with them. The team also wrote position papers on initiatives proposed by the Governor during the campaign, often requiring work on legislation with the involved agencies and staff from the Legislative Service Office.

This was a trying time for my boss, the State Auditor. Jim was preparing to leave and those last several months were tough on him. Politicians are treated somewhat like rock stars. The reality of politics is that once you are defeated or you decide not to run again you become a "has been." You are no longer sought after by the throngs of folks who hang around politicians. They have a new hero; a new friend. All of the attention is focused on the new face. Your opinion is no longer valued or important to them. Some politicians have a hard time giving up the spot light. Jim had a problem with my involvement with the new governor. Being a good Republican, he didn't feel right about me helping Sullivan, the new Democrat governor. Although normally non-partisan, he seemed quite angry about it, but he didn't insist that I stop. It wouldn't have mattered if he had. I, too, was preparing to leave office. I didn't know what I was going to do, but I knew that I enjoyed working on the transition team and with the new governor. I told Jim if he wanted me to resign I would. "No," he said, "that isn't necessary. Just keep me informed about what you guys are doing." I think he got everything off his chest in this discussion and I tried to keep him briefed on everything I could. Some items couldn't be disclosed without compromising the Governor's position and I was careful not to tell Jim anything that could be passed on to the Republicans which might jeopardize any proposals advanced by the new administration.

Mike Sullivan took office on January 5, 1987, and became Wyoming's 29th governor.[15] Jim Griffith, Wyoming's 15$^{th}$ State Auditor left office the morning of that same day. My employment with the state expired along with Griffith's, as mine was an appointed position, serving at the pleasure of the State Auditor.

I got to know the new governor while serving on his transition team and thought I might accept a position in his new administration. But, the timing wasn't right. Some eight years earlier, in 1979, I had founded a fast food restaurant operation and in the early 1980s had acquired the national franchising rights to the company. We had opened a total of thirteen stores between 1980 and 1985 in the states of Wyoming, Montana, and Colorado; but my company, Ferrari Management Corporation (FMC), was experiencing some challenges as a result of recently detected internal fraud and embezzlement. I needed to spend some time cleaning up the mess and getting the franchising program back on track, following the firing of our

---

[15] Wikipedia, List of Governors of Wyoming, http://en.wikipedia.org/wiki/List_of_Governors_of_Wyoming

director of operations. I joined the small corporate staff on the second floor of the Equality State Bank building immediately upon leaving the employ of the auditor's office. My full-time attention to this effort was short-lived, however, as by the end of the legislative session, I was summoned to the governor's office for a discussion about recently enacted legislation dealing with the government bureaucracy and the funding associated with it.

## CHAPTER SEVEN

# A Study in Government Efficiency

During the transition, Governor-elect Sullivan recognized that a fresh look at the bureaucracy was needed. He proposed several pieces of legislation for the legislature; one of which was a statewide study of current and historical revenues and expenditures of all public sectors in Wyoming. The proposal would be a joint executive-legislative effort funded with a $200,000 general fund appropriation. The law required an eight-member oversight committee, appointed jointly by the governor, president of the senate, and speaker of the house to work with a private sector contractor who would compile the information for presentation to the 1988 legislature. The legislation authorizing the project required a study of revenues and expenditures in elementary and secondary education, community colleges, the University of Wyoming, and municipal, county, and state governments. The Governor created six advisory committees, comprised of six to eight members each, to work with the contractor and the oversight committee in each of these public sectors. The law also required an analysis of state fund and account balances, the flow of state resources to state agencies and political subdivisions, and an assessment of the sharing of these resources. In addition, the law required that excessive costs in each of the public entities be identified. Obviously, this was a huge study, and the governor, at the urging of Dave Freudenthal, wanted me to undertake it. I created a consulting company and hired a three-member staff, including two professionals I had worked with in the Auditor's Office, Ruth Sommers and Jan Washburn. And so began a consulting company and project that lasted for the next four years. The work was intense, the hours were long, and the results for the state were enduring. Several years later, in fact, a headline in the *Casper Star-Tribune* on Tuesday, February 16, 1993, read: "Five years later, legislature still debating Ferrari report."[16] The article pointed out that the legislature was coming to the same conclusions as were outlined in the 1988 study.

"*WYOMING 1988, A Study of Revenue and Expenditures*," the three-volume set of navy-blue books with white lettering, consisted of over one thousand pages and was released on January 25, 1988. Volume I was a 128-page summary of the study's findings and recommendations. Volume II, consisting of 565 pages, was the "meat" of the study, going into detailed discussions of the state's economy, taxing structure, and revenue and expenditure patterns in each of Wyoming's public sectors. Volume III contained some four hundred pages of appendices, reflecting literally tens of thousands of data collected during the course of the study.

The study attracted considerable attention throughout the state, largely because of the number of state legislators serving on the oversight committee and the various advisory committees. It was well received by the legislature and the general public and many of the

---

16 "Five Years Later, Legislature Still Debating Ferrari Report," *Casper Star-Tribune*, February 16, 1993, Judith Kohler, Associated Press Writer, p.A4.

recommendations reported became law or were implemented. One of the major findings of the study highlighted the lack of efficiency in the bureaucracy due to the structure of state government. As a result, the governor and legislature decided to authorize a study in state government efficiency to be conducted during the following year, with the results to be presented to the legislature during the next legislative session. The Ferrari and Associates consulting group was again selected to conduct the study.

In reflection, 1988 was a very significant year in my life. The consulting work was generally recognized as a success with publication of "*WYOMING 1988*," The study was regarded as credible and a good investment of taxpayer funds; in fact the speaker of the house, Bill McIlvain, said, "This is one of the finest reports done in a number of years that looks at state government overall." [17] An editorial in the *Casper Star*, entitled "Excellent state study shows there is a way," described it as follows: "They took less than a year and not a lot of money to offer the best overview of state government finances we've yet seen. We are pretty amazed at the amount of quality work accomplished." And, the *Riverton Ranger* said, "What may be Wyoming's most significant study of the century is being completed by the joint legislative-executive efficiency study committee. . . The committee, with the help from a capable consulting firm, is recommending ways to make Wyoming state government more efficient, more responsive and less expensive."[18]

But, it wasn't the consulting work that made 1988 an important time for me. My dad had been in failing health for a number of years and I guess it all culminated in early 1988. On March 14th,

---

[17] "Laramie County Lawmakers Generally Like Efficiency Report," *Wyoming State Tribune-Eagle*, January 13, 1989.

[18] "Our Bright Future," *The Riverton Ranger*, December 2, 1988, P.4.

he passed away, after spending a couple of weeks in intensive care at the Torrington hospital. He died just ten days shy of his seventy-ninth birthday. Not a day goes by that I don't think of him. He was a great father and a good friend.

As one enters the twilight of your life, you realize that genuinely good friends are not that easy to accumulate. Most of us think we have dozens, or perhaps even hundreds, of friends. But, do we really? Acquaintances are not the same as friends. Many of those who were once close are no longer with us. They have either moved on and we have lost contact, or they have gone to that mysterious place of no return. As I get closer and closer to my seventieth year, I realize that out of the hundreds of people I have known during my lifetime only a few have remained in my life. Today, I have many close friends, but spend quality time with only a few of them; one I meet for coffee every weekday morning, a second, who lives halfway across the country, I meet in Vegas a couple of times a year. I meet another, a former governor, for lunch or dinner several times during the year. I exchange rather obnoxious, crudely worded, text messages with a fourth about every other month or so. A fifth, a CPA whom I have known for over forty years, I see about once a year and talk with on the phone every three or four months. So, these are my best friends. I have known thousands of people during my time and have become close to hundreds of them; but I can count all of my best friends on one hand. I suspect that the same can be said for most of the people we know. Friends, whether it's one or a dozen, are very special and, if real, remain with us throughout our lives. Too often we fail to recognize and respect these extraordinary people when we can and while they are able to understand the special place they have in our lives. They really ought to know how we feel about them.

Following the funeral and after taking care of a few of my dad's affairs and, along with my siblings, seeing to it that my mother was going to be all right following his death, I returned to Cheyenne and continued work on the state government efficiency study. It was in 1988 that I met an incredible man, Robert Pettigrew, Jr., from Casper. Bob was an acquaintance of the governor and he agreed to serve as chairman of the Joint Legislative Executive Committee, appointed to oversee the study. He was the CEO of a successful Casper enterprise, Western Oil and Tool Manufacturing Co. (WOTCO),[19] which specialized in the metal fabrication of heavy equipment for the mining and construction industries. The company is a worldwide manufacturer of this type of equipment with three manufacturing facilities within its parent company, Austin Engineering, LTD, in Australia.[20] The company fabricates gigantic trucks, ranging from twenty-five to four hundred ton bodies. It also constructs huge water tank trucks which can carry up to 38,000 gallons of liquid.[21] Bob was also a former mayor of the city of Casper and was well-known and well-respected throughout the state. I liked him instantly; it was one of those rare encounters in life when you meet someone and enjoy an instant chemistry with that person. This began a relationship which continues to this day, some twenty-five years later. We frequently exchange greetings and from time to time, he sends me his excellent writings, on a variety of subjects. He was twenty years my senior, but we became quite close as we worked on this project. He was an expert on management, with

---

19 Westech Custom Mining Equipment, Westech-Watco History, http://www.wstch.com/about_us.html.

20 Austin Engineering Ltd.(ANG)-Company Profile, http://www.investment.com.au/shares/asx/austin-engineering-ANG.asp.

21 Westech Custom Mining Equipment, http://www.wstch.com/

vast public-and private-sector experience, and was very passionate about the good that could come from a restructuring of the state bureaucracy, which had undergone relatively few changes in its one hundred-year history.

On my forty-fifth birthday, January 12, 1989, I presented our study report to a joint session of the Wyoming House and Senate. I stood at the front of the house chambers, before a packed house of senators and house members. The galleries were also full of spectators, including most members of the press corps in Wyoming. Other members of the committee, including Senators John Perry and Alvin Wiederspahn and Representatives Craig Thomas and Bill Rohrbach were seated at the front of the room, along with our chairman. The presentation went on for hours with many concerns, comments, and questions expressed by the legislative members. It was a very sensitive topic with many political ramifications that neither I nor, I suspect, the committee members fully grasped at that moment. Political fallout would surface frequently in the weeks and months that followed. I was fortunate to be surrounded by very capable and respected committee members who were able to effectively help answer questions and provide insights as to how a reorganization of government would better serve the people of Wyoming. The front page headline in the next morning's paper[22] read: "Ferrari Presents Report to Lawmakers." The article quoted both Bob and me throughout with less reference to the politicians on the committee. I didn't think too much about it at the time but was reminded later that I ought to take a lower profile and let the elected officials take more credit for the product. This suggestion came to me in very

---

22 "Ferrari Presents Report to Lawmakers," *Wyoming Tribune-Eagle*, Nanette Bulebosh, January 13, 1989.

clear terms from the late Representative Craig Thomas, who later served in both the United States House and in the U.S. Senate. In the months that followed, I tried to take his advice but with little success. The press seemed to navigate to either the chairman or to me. I wasn't seeking the publicity and I think in time Mr. Thomas realized this and accepted it. At least, the issue never came up again. Clearly, the lack of attention didn't stifle Craig's political career, as he went on to serve several terms in Congress and was a very popular and respected advocate for Wyoming in Washington. Our paths crossed many times in the years that followed. We were both Republican candidates for statewide office; he for Congress and me for Wyoming State Auditor. Along with candidates for other statewide offices, we often campaigned together as we crisscrossed the state frequently ending up at the same campaign events. I liked him and his wife, Susan. Kay and I look back on the relationship with great fondness and appreciation.

The remainder of the 1989 legislative session was spent running to the second and third floors of the Capitol for committee meetings and testifying on the various pieces of legislation introduced to implement the study's recommendations. Reorganization of the government was to be a multi-year effort of reshaping Wyoming's 79 executive branch agencies, boards, and commissions into only twelve, not counting the five elected officials, including the Governor, Auditor, Secretary of State and Treasurer. The process would begin by having three constitutional amendments appear on the general election ballot in November, 1990, and creating three new agencies to be operational no later than July 1, 1991. Because several of the existing agencies were originally created in the constitution, three constitutional amendments were needed in order to fully implement the plan. The most important one was directed at the State Superintendent of Public Instruction. The amendment would have abolished this as an elected position and replaced it with a director appointed by the Governor. Another amendment would have deleted the State Engineer, Board of Control, State Examiner, State Geologist and State Inspector of Mines from the state constitution.

Finally, a third amendment would eliminate the Board of Charities and Reform as the oversight body for the state's institutions which are located around the state, including the State Penitentiary, Women's Prison, State Hospital, Training School, Veterans' Home, Pioneer Home, State Park, Retirement Home, and Boy's and Girl's schools. The Board of Charities and Reform was made up of the state's five elected officials and had been in existence since statehood. This amendment was approved, but not without considerable fanfare. Initially, the bill failed in the house on a 42 to 21 vote. However, the house voted to reconsider the amendment later that night and voted 43 to 20 to send the proposal on to the voters.[23] Watching this vote from the back of the house floor, I thought at the time that many legislators took pleasure in seeing the power of the state's five elected officials diminished in this way. Nearly everyone believed that the five officials sat on far too many boards as it was. And, often the public had little faith in their oversight. For example, some people were amused when learning that for years when Jim Griffith was Auditor he attended meetings of the Board of Deposits,[24] voted and signed documents. It was later discovered after some research was conducted that Griffith, as State Auditor, wasn't even a member of

---

23 "House Passes Massive Reorganization Plan," *Casper Star-Tribune*, Matt Winters, February 24, 1989.

24 "Big Five Meeting For Charities Sake?" *Casper Star-Tribune*, Joan Barron, October 13, 1991.

the Board of Deposits. Only the Governor, Secretary of State, and State Treasurer were.

I wondered when the legislature was in the process of abolishing the Charities and Reform Board if they had perhaps heard some of the rumors that frequently swirled around the capitol about the officials meeting on some back road somewhere, loading gifts, such as turkeys, hams, roasts, liquor, and other institutionally purchased items into the trunks of their state vehicles to transport back to Cheyenne for their own personal consumption and enjoyment. I don't know if any of those stories were true. Nothing like that ever happened during the eight years that I served as State Auditor and I have never heard of anyone ever being formally accused of this kind of thing. But, it was obvious that the earlier scandal entangling the Pioneer Home and other state institutions with the theft of stereos, television sets, and gift canisters of nuts didn't help the plight of the Board of Charities and Reform.

Although the Senate passed the amendment dealing with the chief state school officer, and sent it on to the House, there was overwhelming opposition in the House to eliminating the State Superintendent as an elected official from the State's constitution. The bills creating the three new agencies, including audit, employment, and commerce, sailed through the legislature without much problem, but it was with the requirement that each agency would be refined with precision during the coming year based on further study and broad statewide public input. Following a year of public input, the legislature would finalize each agency.

I spent the next couple of years studying Wyoming state government and the bureaucratic structures in place in most of the other states; writing reports; giving briefings to our committee and to various legislative committees; and working with the press and making presentations at public meetings. The work went well and many of our recommendations were implemented by both the legislative and executive branches of government. There were a number of disagreements, however, and a lot of contentious moments and confrontations. A major disagreement and very public conflict occurred with State Treasurer Stan Smith. Our report found that there really was no formal system of cash management in the state as reflected by the fact that agencies which collected the taxes, fees, and other receipts didn't transmit them to the treasury on a timely basis. Some collections, totaling tens of thousands of dollars, laid around in desk drawers for weeks and months before being forwarded to the treasurer for deposit. We suggested that with faster depositing, and with the help of professional management, the State could earn as much as $57 million more yearly on its investments.[25] We also questioned a plan by the treasurer to pay a brokerage firm ". . . as much as forty percent of the profits made from trading U.S. Treasury bonds and notes. Brokers at that time normally only charged a fraction of one percent of the total value of the bond or note traded, rather than a huge percentage of the profit from the trade."[26]

Stan, of course, did not like the conclusions and recommendations regarding his management of the investment program and publically condemned and criticized our work. Upon release of a draft copy of our report on investments, Stan said, "It's completely political and of very little value to the State."[27] He went on to say that he

25 "Committee Members Defend State Cash Management Study, Dispute Smith's Claim That Findings 'Political'," *Casper Star-Tribune*, Bill Lazarus, September 14, 1988.

26 Ibid.

27 Ibid.

already had "one of the best cash management set-ups of any state," and that our findings, which suggested that income on investments could be increased significantly, were "grossly overstated."[28] Stan was a popular politician who won re-election numerous times. I liked him personally, as did most members of our committee, but no one appreciated these public outcries.[29] When asked about the treasurer's comments, Representative Bill Rohrbach, a Republican from Park County and a member of our oversight committee, responded, "I refute that absolutely. We have been very, very cautious to be sure it was apolitical." He added that the committee "bent over backwards to make sure that Smith's concerns were included in the study. We didn't want to be unduly harsh." Another Republican, Rep. Craig Thomas, said he couldn't "fathom the meaning of Smith's remarks. I think it is an excellent report, and I feel it is going to be useful. When you deal with change, you get a lot of resistance. People feel threatened by change," he said. The senate gave final approval of our recommendations on a vote of 24-5. "Modern money management at last has a chance to catch up with Wyoming, through this vehicle," said Senator Tom Stroock, another Republican from Natrona County and future United States Ambassador to Guatemala. The House concurred.

During the next couple of years, reorganization continued down the general path that we had outlined in our reports. I continued to work with the legislative and the executive branches of government to implement the plans. As time passed, my vision of what the government structure ought to look like came under increasing criticism. We had originally hoped to create a total of

---

28 Ibid

29 Ibid.

ten departments out of the 79 we started with; but, in the end, sixteen agencies resulted. The easy changes were made early in the process. The more difficult ones, such as the Wyoming Game and Fish and the Highway Departments were suggested later. Some of the changes recommended were not made at all, as lobbyists and special interest groups became more organized and more persuasive in convincing lawmakers that the changes were without justification. As an example, employees and commissioners of the Game and Fish Department fiercely opposed all of the recommendations related to that agency.[30] "Over my dead body," was declared by Commissioner Denzel "Rebel" Coffey of Lusk. His actions reflected one of the very principles our reorganization efforts were designed to correct. No commissioner or official appointed by the governor ought to have the autonomy or the pretentiousness to refuse to cooperate with the governor. But, they often did. And, they did so without any serious consequences.

[30] "G&F Rips Efforts to Curb Independence, Tap Interest, 'Over My Dead Body,' Coffee Declares," *Casper Star-Tribune*, Dan Neal, December, 1988.

Helen Mae Hoyt Ferrari, 1879–1933, born in Massaschuetts. Parents were from England.

Liuge (Louis) Guiseppi Ferrari, born July, 1876, in Austria; died August 22, 1963, in Oregon; became a United States citizen on January 2, 1924, in Dysart, Pennsylvania.

These are the parents of Guy Ferrari

Dave's mother and dad, Waunita and Guy Ferrari in Torrington, Wyoming

Kay, Dave, Justin and Brian Ferrari. This picture was taken in 1990 as Dave was running for Wyoming State Auditor. The family was on the campaign trail that summer and traveled to every city and town in the State. We won the Republican Primary by less than 2,000 votes. In the General Election, we out distanced our opponent by a wide margin, 61% to 39%.

This picture was taken outside of my office door in the State Capitol on December 17, 1998.

Farewell, Diana and Dave. A farewell reception was given for Diana Ohman, Secretary of State, and me on December 17, 1998 as we were preparing to leave public office. The event took place in the west wing of the Capitol, outside of our two offices. Diana was a good friend and a dedicated public servant.

This is my good friend, Rich Lindsey, speaking at my retirement reception on December 17, 1998. We would later work together on Dave Freudenthal's successful run for Governor of Wyoming.

On December 17, 1998, Dick Sherman, father of my daughter-in-law, Cindy, attended my farewell reception in the State Capitol. Dick would retire a short time later and move to Arizona with his wife Jenny. We lost Dick to cancer in July of this year.

Fishing at Laramie Peak is great fun for Marcus and his grandpa. This was one of Marcus' first catches, a six-inch trout.

Brian, Kay and Justin at McCue Drive in Cheyenne. Laughter was abundant with these three.

No Shame. Marcus, Connor, and Payton Ferrari. Great fun was had in this miniature swimming pool.

Brian, Marcus, Connor, Payton (in front), Brooke, Justin and Cindy Ferrari. Taken on August 18, 2007 at Laramie Peak, outside of the church where Ken and Lynda were married.

Granddaughter Kaylan Ferrari. July 22, 2009. This was taken in Rhonda and Dennis Estes' back yard in Torrington on the day of Mom's funeral.

August 18, 2007. Kay and Dave in the church at Laramie Peak for Ken and Lynda's wedding. Granddaughter Brooke is to Kay's right.

July 22, 2009. Siblings and spouses. Front, Left to right, sisters Jeanette Pontarolo and Mae Belle Boyles and wife Kay Ferrari. Back, left to right, Dave, Gene Boyles, Jim Pontarolo, brother Ken and his wife, Lynda.

Siblings. Taken the day of Mom's funeral on July 22, 2009 in Torrington. Seated left to right, Jeanette and Mae Belle. Standing, Dave and Ken.

Celebrating Dave Freudenthal's victory in his run for Governor at the Hitching Post Inn on November 5, 2002. Left to right, Governor Dave Freudenthal, Rich Lindsey, Kim Floyd, Dave Ferrari and Al Minier.

We won! We loved winning. Left to right, Rich Lindsey, Kim Floyd and Dave Ferrari, election night, November, 2002, at the Freudenthal for Governor victory celebration.

July 22, 2009. Kay at Rhonda and Dennis Estes' back yard the day of Mom's funeral.

My good friend of over 55 years, Ken Stimson. We met on Main Street in Torrington when we were both fifteen years old and have kept in close contact for over a half century.

Clyde Gerrard. I met Clyde at the University of Wyoming when I was nineteen years old. We lived in the same apartment house in Laramie, later worked together at the Wyoming Department of Education, the State Budget Office and the State Auditor's Office, and we were partners in several investments and business ventures. We became close friends and remain so today, meeting frequently for morning coffee and conversation.

# CHAPTER EIGHT

## An Unlikely Politician

As my involvement in these consulting efforts wound down, I was faced with the decision of what to do next. I enjoyed some aspects of the consulting business and had been asked by the legislature in Arkansas to take a look at their government operations to see if we could help them improve their management and effectiveness. It was a small contract, and it was clear, following a presentation to that body in Little Rock, that Arkansas was not willing to commit enough funding for me to enter into any kind of a long-term agreement to conduct a full-fledged study there. In the meantime, the political season was heating up as candidates were beginning to file for public office in Wyoming. Dave Freudenthal and I had occasionally discussed the possibility of one of us running for statewide office. I always figured he would be the one to do it. Then one morning my phone rang. "Do you know what day it is?" he asked. "Yeah, it's Friday," I replied. "No, not that; it is the last day to file," he said. "Why don't you come over to my office and we'll talk about it?"

Before that day, I had never given the idea of running for statewide office serious consideration. "You can win this thing, and I'll help you. But I'll only help if you take the race seriously," Dave said. It seemed like an improbable idea, but I told him I would consider it and make a decision before the 5:00 p.m. deadline. That morning, Peggy, my corporate bookkeeper and secretary, went up to the Capitol to pick up the filing forms just in case we decided to do it, but I really didn't expect that would be our decision. Kay encouraged it. "You're only out a few dollars if you decide later you don't want to run," she said. So, I wrote out a check, filled out the form declaring my candidacy for Wyoming State Auditor, and at one minute until five that evening, the form and filing fee were filed with the Elections Division in the Secretary of State's office. Thus began my run for the statewide election.

Jack Sidi, the State Auditor at the time, had decided not to seek a second term. But his deputy, Tom Jones, had immediately filed his application for the office. Tom had served in that position for the past four years and was also a former chairman of the powerful Joint Appropriations Committee in the Wyoming legislature. Tom had been a prominent Republican legislator from Powell for over twenty years. He was well known in Cheyenne and, of course, in his home town and county. Clearly, he would have no trouble winning the election. Or, at least, that's what Mr. Sidi told the press that night when he saw my application. "Ferrari doesn't have a chance," he declared to anyone who would listen. I'm pretty sure everyone agreed.

But a funny thing happened throughout the campaign. In practically every community we visited, invariably, someone would come out of the crowd and ask how they could help in our campaign. The first time this occurred was in New Castle. When all of the speeches were finished, Dottie Thorson, a prominent local Republican came over to Kay and said she would do whatever she could to help us win. I don't know whether she liked me or not, but it was very clear she didn't want to see Tom become one of Wyoming's five statewide elected officials.

Kay and I spent the summer driving from one end of the state to the other, attending every campaign event we possibly could. Kay's friends, Don and Sue Riske, had a 1989 Chevrolet Suburban they had leased and they insisted we use the SUV in our travels. We loaded the back up with campaign signs, banners, brochures and other political material and stayed out in the field for weeks at a time. Our sons, Brian and Justin, accompanied us whenever they could, when it didn't interfere with their schooling. It was a lot of family time together on the trail and we learned a lot about each other, the state, politics, and the small towns and communities along the way. Most of the people we approached were gracious and open to consider our candidacy. This wasn't always the case, however, and to this day my boys still don't care for the town of Powell, Wyoming. Being Tom's home town, a lot of the folks we encountered were committed to helping Tom and had little time or patience to hear our story. We found Thermopolis to be less than friendly as well and attributed that to the fact that Tom's campaign chairman lived there. It was an exhausting campaign, but we had a lot of help throughout the state.

Bob Pettigrew served as my campaign chairman and his good friend, Art Volk, of Casper signed on as one of our major fund-raisers. One of Kay's best friends, Jan Stranigan of Cheyenne, agreed to serve as treasurer. Between Bob and Art, tens of thousands of dollars were raised for the campaign. And they worked relentlessly in Casper and Natrona County trying to get me elected. Their efforts paid off as we had a strong showing in that area and needed every vote they could muster. One of our biggest and most helpful supporters turned out to be the Wyoming Education Association

(WEA), with members living in every community in the state. The organization itself took no official position, but its members quietly supported our candidacy. They did not want to see my opponent elected. They believed that he, in his position of Chairman of the Appropriations Committee, year after year had been unsupportive of funding for education. Many of the WEA members felt passionately about it and worked very hard going door-to-door on my behalf.

Dave Freudenthal was also critical to our campaign, offering advice on all policy issues and along with his generous contributions, raising considerable money for the race through his contacts and through the Democrat Party faithful. It was surprising the amount of money that came in from Democrats, but they had no candidate running and had themselves encountered disagreements with my opponent in the past. We won the election by less than two thousand votes. Our victory was one of the last declared on election night due to the slim margin of victory.

Because no one had run on the Democrat ticket, unless there was a write-in candidate, I would have no opponent in the November general election. The primary victory, momentarily at least, meant that I would likely be the next State Auditor in Wyoming. However, during the primary, some in the Democrat party wanted a candidate to represent that party. Charlie Carroll, a Cheyenne attorney, received several write-in votes. He took all of the time he could before deciding to enter the general election race. I suspect he arrived at that decision knowing he probably wouldn't win but, at the same time, looking forward to all of the attention he would receive between then and general election day. It is always a difficult race to win for the Democrats, given the lop-sided number of registered voters, which favored the Republicans by about two to one. Since statehood in 1890, only three Democrats had ever been elected to the State Auditor's post, and collectively, they served a total of only twelve out of the past 123 years.[31]

The prospects for a Democrat being elected State Treasurer are even worse, inasmuch as only one has won that spot in our State's history--a discouraging fact, if you happen to be a Democrat in this State. That occurred in 1934 when the Democrats swept all of the statewide offices and Mr. J. Kirk Baldwin of Casper was elected.[32] He served a full four-year term.

So, we won. The race wasn't particularly close as the final vote tallies were: Ferrari, 91,811; Carroll, 58,655, which represented a 22-point margin of victory.[33] It would soon be time to serve. I finished up the consulting work between the general election and the first of the year and began preparations to get situated in the capitol. My offices on the corner of 19th Street and Thomes Avenue were closed, and all of the important documents were boxed and moved to a document storage facility.

The inaugural ceremony was held at noon on January 7, 1991, in the Rotunda of the State Capitol. I was sworn into office, along with Governor Mike Sullivan, Secretary of State Kathy Karpan, State Treasurer Stan Smith, and Diana Ohman, the new State Superintendent of Public Instruction. A reception was held immediately following the ceremony in the west wing of the first floor right outside of my office. Hundreds of people from around the State attended to meet and greet their newly elected officials. Mike and Kathy were both Democrats, beginning their second terms in

---

[31] Wyoming Department of State Parks and Cultural Resources, Cultural Resources Division, *Wyoming Blue Book, Volume V*, "History of Wyoming State Auditors", p.7.

[32] Ibid., pp. 1-11.

[33] Ibid.,p.36.

their respective positions. The rest of us were Republicans; Stan beginning his third term, and Diana and I both starting our first.

We appeared to be a fairly compatible group. Mike and Kathy were both lawyers and from every indication they were eager to cooperate with their new Republican colleagues. It seemed that Stan had forgiven me for disagreeing with him about the investment program during the efficiency study. And Diana and I had gotten to know each other pretty well, having campaigned together on several occasions during the months leading up to the general election. I was looking forward to working with this group on the various boards and commissions on which the five elected officials served, including the Farm Loan Board, State Land Commission, Capitol Building Commission, State Elections Commission, and the State Liquor Commission. Although the Board of Charities and Reform was to be eliminated during the reorganization process, it would be a year or two before a final plan was implemented, so we served together on that entity as well. Given such a variety of activities reflected in these diverse boards and commissions, no one is quite prepared to provide expertise or oversight when first assuming elected office. In time, knowledge is acquired and skills are developed which can benefit the departments that are under the supervision of this group. But, depending on a person's background, there is usually a fairly steep learning curve required before one becomes particularly effective. And even though I had been around government for years and had studied it extensively for the previous four, I didn't exactly hit the ground running. But I was prepared to take on the duties related to operations in the State Auditor's Office, and that is where the earliest impact was probably made.

I had campaigned on the premise that "State government should become more efficient and the state auditor could help." At the start of the 1991 legislature, working with Rick Miller, Director of the Legislative Service Office, I had four "good government" bills written which were designed to improve efficiency and accountability in state government.[34] One would have created a Grace Commission, patterned after the Peter Grace Commission at the federal level, to study and make recommendations to root out waste within governmental offices. A second would give the State Auditor subpoena power when investigating state payments. A third would give a newly elected state official the authority to review personnel transactions between the time of his election and when the official takes office. The fourth bill was a governmental disclosure act which would require executive branch employees to report any gift or benefit they receive to the Secretary of State. It was aimed at employees and officials who accept gifts from special interests groups during a decision-making period. I thought this would discourage government people from receiving gifts if they knew all would have to be reported. Surprisingly, each of these bills failed in our Republican dominated legislature. This was my first clue that my party perhaps wasn't really interested in an efficient and accountable state government?

While campaigning for office, I was approached by several state employees around the state who thought their group insurance program had become too expensive. The premiums were too high and the coverage was too low, they said. Was there anything the Auditor could do about it, they asked. At the time, the Auditor was one of seven members of the state's Group Insurance Board and I told the complaining employees that I would look into the program.

---

[34] "Ferrari Begins Settling in as State Auditor," *Wyoming Tribune-Eagle*, Kevin Lumsden, January 9,1991, p. 2.

When we examined what was occurring in other states, it became clear that Wyoming employees were paying more for their health insurance than what their counterparts in surrounding states were being charged. Claims in the Wyoming program, on a per capita basis, were much higher than in the other states examined. Were our employees, for some reason, sicker than employees in other states?

When the insurance report was released to the press it stirred up a hornet's nest. I made the mistake of discussing our findings in a speech at a Wyoming Employees Association meeting before discussing the report with the Board. Everyone involved in the program, including the executive director, insurance board chairman and other board members took the findings and recommendations personally. The State Treasurer, a member of the Insurance Board for over eight years, immediately became the spokesman for the program and the leading critic of the Auditor and the report. He, along with the board chairman and the program director, disputed nearly every finding contained in the report[35] and vehemently defended the program and their staff. They said that the information contained in my report was simply wrong; that I didn't understand insurance; I didn't understand the dynamics involved in our plan; and, I demonstrated "a lack of knowledge of state and federal laws governing group insurance plans, as well as a lack of knowledge of cost-savings techniques" previously attempted in the past. I was surprised by their attitudes. It didn't occur to me that they didn't know their program was in trouble and needed serious help. I thought they would welcome input from anyone who might shed some light on the problems. Their actions were characterized by

---

[35] "Employee's Board Won't Back Ferrari Cost Report," *Casper Star-Tribune*, July 9, 1991, p.A1.

the *Casper Star-Tribune* as, ". . . the Board went on the defensive with their backs up as if the study represented a personal attack on their abilities to oversee the health insurance program." The newspaper said one would have expected the Board to "welcome Ferrari's independent study and fresh outlook. It wasn't as if someone had wandered in off the street with a new idea. These were pros." [36]

We had compared Wyoming's program with those in Idaho, Montana and North Dakota. Such insurance plans are highly complex, with numerous factors that must be weighed carefully. In such an environment, there, of course, are some grey areas. But, facts don't lie. Premiums were higher in Wyoming and coverage was lower. The challenge was to figure out why. And, the answer was that our youngest, healthiest employees' family dependents were leaving the program because they could get better coverage elsewhere at less cost. What remained in the insurance pool were older employees with a higher incident of health problems. It was clear we needed to attract these healthier people back into the plan in an effort to spread the costs over additional employees and dependents, resulting in lower average costs for everyone. This would take time to correct, but the process needed to be started immediately.[37]

I gained a lot of support from state employees as a result of this effort, but there were a lot of hurt feelings among some members on the Board which made it difficult for them to work with me. It became obvious that in order for the Auditor to have the independence necessary to investigate the program, he should not be a member of the Board. In 1992, I had legislation drafted

---

[36] "Insurance Board Nixes Critical Study," *Casper Star-Tribune*, July 28, 1991, p.A1.

[37] "Cure Sought for State's Ailing Health Program," *Wyoming Tribune-Eagle*, Tad Segal, November 14, 1991, p.10.

removing the Auditor from the Board.[38] I also recommended to the legislature that an outside audit of the program be conducted. Perhaps the Board wouldn't be so defensive if someone other than the State Auditor offered an opinion on the program's performance. The board chairman, State Treasurer, and the program director were jubilant about the idea of getting me off the Board. With all of them enthusiastically testifying in favor of the bill, it passed easily. They hated the idea of an audit, however, but reacted more professionally when the Appropriations Committee asked that one be conducted.

Several years later, on October 9, 1994, there was an interesting headline[39] in the *Casper Star-Tribune:* "Ferrari right on group health," it declared. The article suggested that I must have found some solace in a Legislative Service Office (LSO) audit of the group insurance plan. It concluded many of the same things that we had some three years prior. The LSO report said that about one-third of the participants in our plan pay more than their counterparts in three other states; that our people pay higher out-of-pocket costs ($4,500 compared to only $2,000 in Utah and South Dakota); and, that even though the program is considerably better than it was, it could still stand more improvement. The article posed the question, "Wouldn't it be refreshing if government agencies would welcome outside views instead of trying to admonish the messenger?" Yes, it would, but that seemed to be the attitude of many government bureaucrats, during our studies of government efficiency and reorganization.

---

38 "Ferrari Requests Facelift for Health Insurance Board," *Wyoming Tribune-Eagle*, Tad Segal, January 31, 1992, p.16.

39 "Ferrari Right on Group Health," *Casper Star-Tribune*, Joan Barron, October 9, 1994, p.A1.

It was unpleasant to be criticized in such an unprofessional manner and to have my facts disputed by the Board in testimony before the Governor and legislative committees. I think it was obvious to almost every one especially our participants in the group insurance plan and members of the press, that the Board was simply being defensive in an attempt to make management of the program appear more effective. Conflicts of this nature are perhaps why most elected officials feel it just isn't worth the effort to try to make changes in the bureaucracy. I was surprised when one member of the Insurance Board said, "As an elected official, you shouldn't rock the boat."

We had another early success during the first several months in office. That was implementation of a credit card for use by state employees.[40] We negotiated with Diner's Club to provide a card to every state employee who applied which could be used to pay for the employee's travel, lodging, and meal expenses. It enabled our employees, traveling on state business, to receive an interest free cash advance, which was very helpful, especially to our lower-paid state travelers. Eventually, data gathered from use of the program served our office in negotiating discounts, ranging from 30 to 50 percent, with airlines, car rental companies, and hotels.

"Perpetrators of fraud are more likely to be a woman, more likely to be married, more likely to be active church members, more likely to be older, more likely to be heavier, more likely to be optimistic, less likely to abuse alcohol, more likely to have more children, almost always are a first time offender, have higher self-esteem, are more achieving, more socially conforming, have more

---

40 "State Workers to Get Credit," *Wyoming Tribune-Eagle*, Kurt J. Repanshek, May 14, 1991, p.10.

family harmony in their lives, and seem to be kinder and gentler people." These statements were made by the FBI and were part of my presentation at the June 19, 1991, Cheyenne Rotary Club meeting, in describing fraud in Wyoming.[41] Some three months earlier, we had installed a "fraud hot line" in the State Auditor's Office. The hot line was designed to serve as a deterrent to crime inasmuch as the perpetrator would know that people could call, remain anonymous, without fear of retribution, and report them for committing theft or engaging in corruption. Within the first couple of days, fifteen calls were received.

As one of the five statewide elected officials, there were a number of important issues considered during the first couple of years on the boards and commissions. Along with Diana, I cast a controversial vote against the construction of a new 350-bed medium-security prison to be built at Lovell. At the time, we had a prison population of over 700 men housed in our Rawlins facility, which was only built to hold 610 inmates. A prison needs study, conducted by Correctional Services Group, Inc., of Kansas City, MO, concluded Wyoming would need 1,001 beds by July of 1992, 1,041 beds by 1995 and 1,266 beds by 2001.[42] The ten-year percentage increase of this magnitude, over 80 percent, seemed exaggerated. The group used Wyoming employment forecasts largely for the basis of their projections, suggesting that future arrests would "mirror the gradual growth of employment." [43] The logic of such rationale for forecasting prison needs escaped me, and it seemed that other factors should

---

41 "Ferrari Touts Stop-Fraud Hotline," *Casper Star-Tribune*, David Hackett, August 13, 1991.

42 "Ferrari: New Prison Not Necessary Now," *Casper Star-Tribune*, Joan Barron, December 5, 1991, p. A1.

43 Ibid.

have greater influence on the incarceration rates in our State than simply the growth in the number of jobs. I wasn't convinced that we were helplessly destined for these consequences. I thought we could lessen future demands for prison beds by intervening in the lives of our troubled youth earlier and making sure services were in place to keep these troubled young people from becoming troubled adults. I also believed that our welfare system should be used to try to divert as many of these folks as possible from their likely prison destiny. The roles of Aid to Families with Dependent Children (AFDC) had increased by 131 percent in the past ten years and had increased by 25 percent in the last year alone. The State should be trying to impact the lives of these people in an attempt to make sure that prison is not an unavoidable part of their future. We were beginning to focus on "children at risk" in all of our youth service programs and this was to be a first step in getting young people on the right path earlier in their lives. I asked the Board of Charities and Reform to consider these possibilities before approving a new $30 million prison. Apparently, my arguments were unpersuasive, as the Board approved the new pen by a vote of 3 to 2.[44] However, after receiving another report from a Colorado consultant, and a member of the Colorado Corrections Commission, Roger Lauen,[45] in which he stated he didn't think we needed additional prison beds, the legislature decided to ignore the Board's recommendation and to delay further action on the prison for one year. This would provide additional time in order that alternatives to prison sentencing could be examined. The legislature was also cautious because our prison

[44] "BCR Votes 3-2 to Build Lovell Prison," *Wyoming Tribune-Eagle*, Kurt J. Repanshek, January 18, 1992.

[45] "Consultant: Lovell Pen Could Be Unnecessary," *Casper Star-Tribune*, Joan Barron, June 29, 1992.

population had recently been leveling off. It had peaked in September of 1990 at 738 inmates and had declined to only 695 on May 1 of 1992.[46] Lauen suggested that non-violent and less dangerous offenders should be given fines, community services, community corrections, probation, electronic monitoring or something other than prison. I asked Judy Uphoff, Director of the Department of Corrections, and State Lands Commissioner Howard Schrinar to use the one-year delay to evaluate Lauen's ideas, the impact of the State's increased emphasis and funding for the troubled youth program in the Department of Family Services would have, and the impact of additional federal funding being spent for drug-free schools.

It was noted that only 26 percent of new prison commitments were violent and 70 percent of the prison population was under the influence of either drugs or alcohol at the time of the offense. The Lovell prison never did get built, but nearly twenty years later, on January 6, 2010, the State opened a new penitentiary in Torrington, not far from my childhood home. It employs some 350 employees and can house up to 720 inmates. Given the fact that the Rawlins penitentiary holds some 500 inmates, the two facilities together now have the capacity to house around 1,200. It seems that the Kansas report back in 1991 which tied projected prison needs to employment growth really was lacking in logic, resulting in a huge over-statement of the number of prison beds which would be needed. Perhaps Wyoming's emphasis to provide services for troubled youth paid off. Had we ignored this possibility and gone with the Kansas consultant's assumptions and projections, there would have been prison space sitting empty in Lovell and probably elsewhere in Wyoming for some of the past twenty years.

---

[46] Ibid.

In early 1992, Wyoming got a dose of reality when the magazine, *Financial World*, named Wyoming as the worst managed state in the country.[47] We had dropped from 35th the previous year to the bottom in 1992, largely because we had poor employee and program performance evaluations, we didn't follow generally accepted accounting standards, and we had few outside financial audits performed. Most, if not all, of the bureaucrats in the executive branch disagreed with this ranking because the magazine failed to consider a number of factors that might have influenced the standings. For example, Wyoming was one of a few states in the country without any general obligation debt. Also, we had just spent the past five years moving towards a cabinet system of government, which was noted for its management efficiencies and was the system used by nine of the top ten states in the ranking. In addition, some of the agencies did follow generally accepted accounting principles, even if the State Auditor, which has responsibility for the state's controllership functions, didn't. But, *Financial World* failed to take any of this into consideration. As gloomy as the rankings made people feel, it did serve as a catalyst for improvement in the State's management. In fact, in May, a couple of weeks after the report came out, Governor Sullivan appointed a committee to study the issue. He asked Roger Dewey, Director of the Department of Audit, Phil Kiner, Director of the Department of Administration, Earl Kabeiseman, Director of the Department of Revenue, and me to serve on the Committee and report back to him within six weeks.[48]

---

47 "Magazine Names Wyoming the Worst-Managed State," *Wyoming Tribune-Eagle*, Kurt Moeller, April 24, 1992, p.10.

48 "Governor Appoints Committee to Study State Financial Rankings," *Wyoming Tribune-Eagle*, Kurt J. Repanshek, May, 1992.

During the 1993 legislative session, legislation was passed which required the state to adopt generally accepted accounting principles (GAAP) in its accounting and financial reporting. The GAAP Implementation Act also contained provisions for a performance measurement system to be used by each agency to track and report its progress in achieving objectives. As a result of this legislation, in 1993, *Financial World* improved Wyoming's position in the national rankings from last to 43rd.[49] Then, in 1995, we climbed to the thirty-first spot and were recognized as "one of the most improved states." I had drafted this legislation and pushed for passage, not to improve our image in the eyes of a New York based magazine, but to put in place a system of accounting and financial reporting that actually would improve our operations. We included in the bill requirements for an annual CPA audit of the state treasury and the state's financial statements as well as the requirements for strategic planning and performance measures. To explain the bill, I was invited to give presentations to the entire bodies of both the house and senate to discuss why the state should shift to generally accepted accounting principles and implement strategic planning, as well as outline the one-time windfall of funds the shift in accounting would bring.

During the previous year, in 1992, Wyoming native, W. Edwards Deming, the world famous author and management expert returned to his hometown of Powell and delivered several speeches on quality and efficiency.[50] Because of his development of efficiency measures which were used throughout Japanese industry, he was widely credited for Japan's exploding rise in its developing economy.

---

[49] "State Auditor Lauds Accounting Progress," *Casper Star-Tribune*, April 29, 1993.

[50] "Auditor: Let State Borrow Business Ideas," *The Billings Gazette*, Michael Milstein, January 26, 1993, P2c.

He was also the creator of Ford Motor Company's philosophy and motto that "Quality is Job 1." The legislature adopted the Deming approach to performance measurements which was contained in the GAAP legislation and the executive branch was given one year to come up with initial measurements and switch over to GAAP accounting. We recruited a governmental accounting expert and a CPA from Michigan, Peter Haufner, to help implement the conversion. Peter was influential with both legislative and executive branch people and this influence enabled implementation much quicker and more accurately. This conversion was a major development for management proponents and helped Wyoming overcome its reputation as a badly managed state in the nineties to become the nation's best managed state in 2010, during the second term of Governor Dave Freudenthal. There were other factors which helped, such as a balanced budget and excess reserves, but without compliance to good accounting principles and audited financial statements, a top rating would have been unattainable. I suspect we would not have been successful in passing this GAAP legislation, particularly the annual audit requirements and the adoption of performance measurements, had it not been for the fact that the accounting conversion freed up over $215 million, helping to wipe out a projected deficit of $150 to $160 million at that time.

Of all of the activities I was involved in during my elected years in office, I would rate the GAAP implementation program as one of the most rewarding and probably the most enduring. It is often difficult to get new legislation passed for a number of reasons. One, it creates risk; the Legislature is reluctant to make changes that might bring unexpected consequences. Second, there are always lobbyists who want to testify before a legislative committee whether or not they can bring anything of value to the discussion. After all, this is what they get paid to do. Typically, those opposed to a piece of legislation have more passion than those who favor it and negative comments, no matter how inconsequential, tend to cast doubt in the minds of the legislators. Additionally, some changes cost money. No one in elected office wants to go along with a bill that will require additional spending particularly one that has no constituents. Good government bills usually have few advocates especially those bills that aren't well understood. And this legislation was no different. People from my office, the Governor, and a few legislators were about the only ones favoring the bill. Most of those interested in it were opposed because they perceived its impact would provide little direct benefit to them or would be damaging to their operations.[51] For example, the University of Wyoming suggested the bill would negatively affect their bonding program. The Wyoming Association of Municipalities was opposed because of fear that cities might lose some funding if the accounting change was made. And, surprisingly, the Wyoming Society of Certified Public Accountants circulated a memo to all legislators outlining their many concerns.[52] They did not want the legislature spending the money that would result from the bill's passage. It seemed odd that CPAs would impede implementation of sound accounting practices. "We're not trying to kill the bill," a Cheyenne CPA told the committee. But, their actions were clearly having a negative impact on the bill's chances for passage. After much debate, the bill passed. The legislature couldn't resist a $215 million windfall which enabled them to avoid a politically unpopular tax hike or deep spending cuts.

---

[51] "Senate Committee Holds GAAP Bill Back," *Casper Star-Tribune*, Joan Barron, January 22, 1993.

[52] "Don't Spend GAAP Money, CPA's Say," *Casper Star-Tribune*, Joan Barron, February 10, 1993.

The accounting change was described in an article in the November 2, 1992, *City & State Magazine*,[53] and contained a picture of me with the slogan under it, that said: "Closing the GAAP." It quoted both Governor Sullivan and me. One of the quotes cited was: "What we're trying to do is give the public and the people of Wyoming a more accurate and clearer picture of revenues and expenditures in the same year." We were applauded by the Government Finance Officers Association and that international organization awarded Certificates of Excellence in Financial Reporting in both 1997 and 1998. The 1997 presentation was made in the rotunda of the capitol[54], and I accepted the award on behalf of the State.[55] This prestigious award would not have been attained without the efforts of Peter Haufner and his capable co-worker, Doug Hagenhour. Unfortunately, both of these great employees returned to Michigan a short time later, leaving a huge hole in our CPA staffing. I never felt quite the same about the state auditor's office after they left. They were good employees and good friends.

Shortly following the GAAP implementation, another program, the *Bond Guarantee Program,*[56] was crafted and gained legislative approval. This initiative was designed to reduce interest costs on local government capital construction projects which were funded using bond financing. I had learned of this program from the State of Texas and it looked like it could work well in Wyoming. The idea

---

53 "Wyoming Moves into Modern Times With GAAP, Auditor, Guv Join to Change Accounting," *City & State*, November 2, 1992, p.GM4.

54 "State Agencies Awarded for Accounting," *Wyoming Tribune-Eagle*, October 18, 1998, Rachel Keating, p.A6.

55 "State Auditor Receives Top Award," *Casper Star-Tribune*, October 18, 1998.

56 "Ferrari: Reduce School Construction Bond Costs with State Guarantee," *Casper Star-Tribune*, Joan Barron, August 10, 1993, p. A1.

was to use the State's permanent funds as a financial guarantee in the event that a local entity defaulted on its bond payments. Putting this guarantee on a bond issue would automatically raise the rating on the bonds from A, AA, and BAA to the highest level, AAA. This would result in lowering the interest rate by one-half to one percent over the life of the bond issue, which normally was thirty years. For every ten million dollars of bonds issued, a savings in interest costs of $50,000 to $100,000 per year is generated. Over a thirty-year period this would add up to an overall savings of $1.5 to $3 million. Dan Baxter, a representative of the bonding company, Kaiser and Co., and Mary Keating-Scott, a local bond attorney, helped design the program.[57] When I left office at the end of 1998, some $82 million was covered by the program. We estimated that, if fully implemented for the remaining $300 million to $400 million in outstanding school debt, the program could save as much as $72 million to $144 million in reduced interest costs over the life of the bond issues.

As is typical with new programs, not everyone thought it was a good idea. The State Treasurer suggested it would lessen the flexibility he currently enjoyed in investing the permanent funds. He argued that he would have to make investments of a shorter term in order to have the funds immediately available in the event of a local bond default, thus lowering his return on investment. He also argued that administrative costs would be incurred at the state level in reviewing and guaranteeing local bond issues but the savings in interest costs would be enjoyed by the local governments, thus, whatever savings accrued would not benefit the State. The idea was strongly endorsed by bonding companies, the Wyoming Education

---

[57] Ibid.

Association, the Wyoming Association of Municipalities, and the County Commissioners Association, so in spite of the arguments against it, we were able to get the legislation approved and the program operated successfully during the years I served as State Auditor. I was surprised to learn that shortly after I left the State the new State Treasurer asked the Legislature to kill the program. In spite of continuing support from the local bonding officials, and with little public discussion, they did. But it was good for Wyoming while it lasted. Unfortunately, often in politics, programs are judged, not on their own merit, but more on who gets the credit. My former boss, Jim Griffith, used to say we could get a whole lot more done in government if it didn't matter who got the credit. I have always thought that was the reason he and Governor Herschler worked so well together. Neither of them needed to take all of the credit.

# CHAPTER NINE

## Which End Do You Put the Hay in?

During my eight years in office, the most controversial issues involved management of our state school lands, some 3.6 million acres. The state constitution had been interpreted to require that the Land Board maximize income from these lands for the benefit of our public schools. Because of the special interest pressure applied, however, this had rarely happened. It seemed everyone wanted something for nothing, or nearly nothing. Those who use our lands for recreation, such as hunting and fishing, snowmobiling, hiking, camping and similar activities, don't want to pay much of a user fee for this privilege. Those who lease the land for agriculture grazing want to pay only a fraction of what they would be paying for the use of private lands. Leaseholders have a number of arguments supporting their position, including the fact that they have to maintain and manage those lands in much the same way as if they owned them. This includes such functions as maintaining fencing, providing a water supply, controlling weeds and other pests, cleaning up trash left by recreationists, and other costly, time-consuming responsibilities. And, of course, there are the energy companies, including oil, gas, coal, wind, and others, and their paid lobbyists, who have never seen a royalty, tax, deposit, or other fee that wasn't too high.

As an elected official you want to do the right thing for your constituents, but there are usually competing interests and you are often not dealing with all of the facts or with the truth. The facts presented by the State Land Office staff were often disputed or manipulated by the lobbyists or special interests. This was one of the few areas of debate where the arguments could get nasty and personal. If the powerful leaseholder, oil producer, or lobbyist disagreed, it wasn't unusual for them to call for the Commissioner of Public Lands to be fired. If not for strong support from members of the Land Board, especially the Governor, the Director could be replaced nearly any day for disagreeing with one of the land barons or prominent oil producers.

This isn't anything new. In the 1870s and early 1880s, large cattle companies were able to profit quite handsomely on Wyoming's open ranges where they could graze their cattle without the burden of providing water, paying taxes, or incurring other expenses which are associated with private land ownership. When homesteading threatened this activity, in order to maintain free use of the public lands, the ranchers would resort to a number of different strategies to discourage intruders from seeking these same advantages. One of the tactics was to illegally fence those sections of the land they wanted to control.[58] In 1879, Public Land Commissioner William A. J. Sparks asked the ranchers if they would like to own the land and what price they would be willing to pay for it. Not surprisingly, the answer was that they weren't willing to pay anything. They didn't want to own it since they were currently using it for nothing.

---

[58] Op. cit., *Wyoming Blue Book,* Volume V, p.250.

In response, Mr. Sparks asked for help from the federal government to remove the illegal fences. This action had an unfortunate impact on Spark's government career which came to an abrupt end.[59] The President and Congress responded to pressure from well-connected politicians.

In the early nineteen nineties there had been a number of issues regarding the management of state lands which were controversial and troublesome. The questions which were causing the most concern included several issues which related directly to our ability to maximize income from these lands: Should the lands be sold? Is the amount being charged to use the lands adequate? And, did giving current leaseholders a preferential right to buy or lease the lands diminish the amount of income that could be derived from them? These questions had been largely ignored prior to Howard Schrinar's appointment as State Lands Commissioner in 1984 by Governor Herschler. He was reappointed to the post in 1987 by Governor Sullivan and when Diana and I joined the Board in 1991 his recommendations for reforming the way our lands were managed and his attempts to generate more income from this management began to gain momentum. At that time, most everyone on the Board and in the Land Office accepted as fact that these trust lands should be managed exclusively for the benefit of the beneficiaries and that the trustees had a constitutional responsibility to maximize income[60].

---

[59] Ibid., p. 251.

[60] "Management of Wyoming's State Trust Lands From 1890-1990: A Running Battle Between Good Politics and the Law," *Land and Water Law Review,* Volume XXVI, Number 1, 1991, Clinton D. Beaver, Senior Assistant Attorney General for the State of Wyoming, Counsel to the Wyoming Board of Land Commissioners, p.70.

These questions and concerns were not unique to Wyoming by any means. Trust lands were granted to the State in 1890 upon entering statehood in a manner similar to those granted to twenty-four land grant states that preceded Wyoming, beginning in 1803 with the state of Ohio.[61] The constitutions and enabling acts of these early states, of course, were not identical and the number of acres involved varied considerably, ranging from as little as 2.7 million acres in Ohio and Nevada to as many as 24.2 million acres in Florida.[62] Including grants for schools, universities, penitentiaries, schools for the deaf and blind, public buildings, and similar public purposes, Wyoming received a total of 4,345,383 acres of which 3,472,872 were for public schools.[63] Except in the cases of New Mexico and Arizona, the requirement for these lands to be treated as "trust" lands and managed accordingly was not expressly written in the enabling acts of the 29 land grant states.[64] Nonetheless, courts which examined the issue in the majority of the states found that trust responsibilities were in fact created. Consequently, all of the states embraced the "trust" concept in the management of the trust lands, except the state of California which concluded that neither its enabling act nor its constitution imposed these trust responsibilities.[65] In 2003, several years after I left office, Wyoming's Supreme Court,

61 "History of Public Land Law Development," *History of State Land Grants in the United States*, Appendix C, Table 11(c), Paul W. Gates, 1968.

62 Ibid.

63 Ibid.

64 http://www.lincolninst.edu/subcenters/managing-state-trust-lands/publications/trustlands-doctrine.pdf.

65 Ibid.

in the case of *Reidel v. Anderson*, arrived at the same conclusion.[66] This decision came about as a result of a decision made when I was on the State Land Board. Many legal experts believe the Court's decision was wrong and it ought to be appealed to the United States Supreme Court.

In 1991, there were approximately 9,500 to 10,000 ranches in Wyoming and roughly 1,500 of them had grazing leases.[67] The lease holdings ranged from a few acres to tens of thousands of acres. The leases were held by both small and the very large operators. I was surprised that so many of our leases were held by out-of-state parties,[68] including entities such as Hunt Oil Co. of Dallas, Texas, with 24,000 acres under lease. Among the others were Exxon Coal Resources, Atlantic Richfield, Metropolitan Life, Colorado State University, and the Church of Jesus Christ of Latter-day Saints--entities you wouldn't normally think of as being in the cattle or sheep business. Altogether, some 307 out-of-state people or companies leased 532,253 acres of our lands, or fifteen percent of the total acreage.[69] The largest 116 grazing lease holders, which comprise less than one percent of all farmers and ranchers in the state, had over one-third of all of our school lands under lease. This group included the True family in Casper who had state leases totaling some 56,000 acres. The next largest 120 leaseholders controlled thirteen percent, or 450,235 acres. In other words, two-thirds of the state's total acres

---

66 Supreme Court of Wyoming, *Riedel v. Anderson*, 70 P.3d, 223, Nos. 02-60, 02-61, June 4, 2003.

67 "State Land Board Prepares for Debate on Grazing Fees," *Casper Star-Tribune*, Joan Barron, September 1, 1993, p.A1.

68 "Land Board between Rock and a Lease," *Casper Star-Tribune*, Joan Barron, November 7, 1993, p.A1.

69 "Battle Looms Over State Land Reform," *Wyoming Livestock Roundup*, Judith Kohler, November 29,1993, Volume 69, Number 134.

are controlled either by out-of-state lessees or by a very small number of the large operators within Wyoming.[70]

In the middle of 1992, the Board was examining lease rates, land management practices in other states, and state statutes that give leaseholders the preferential right to match the highest bid, both in situations where the land is sold and in instances where more than one party wants to lease the land. It was an especially timely review considering the level of controversy and contention that surrounded state land management during the past few years. For example, earlier in the year, the State conducted an auction for the sale of 27 acres of state land in Lincoln County.[71] The State received only one bid, from George Carollo, and it was in the amount of the appraised value for $13,800. Following the auction, the lease holder, Mr. Roy Hoffman, exercised his statutory right to purchase the land for the same amount. Mr. Carollo was upset. He thought he had merely opened the bidding and was waiting for the leaseholder to bid but, of course, the leaseholder never did. Another person at the auction said he was willing to pay $20,000 for the 27 acres or nearly 45 percent more than the State realized from the sale, but he knew he wouldn't get the land even if he was the high bidder because the leaseholder would simply exercise his right. The bidder said he, too, would have paid considerably more for the parcel in order to guarantee him access to his irrigation ditches and headgates. So, it was clear; the State received less than fair-market value for the land, the leaseholder got the land cheaper than he should have, and an innocent victim of the preferential right statute was denied the opportunity to buy

---

70 Ibid.

71 "Preferential Right Statute to be Reviewed by Commissioners, Schrinar: Lessees' Right Has Chilling Effect on Auctions," *Casper Star-Tribune*, Joan Barron, July 6, 1992.

a critical piece of property for his ranching operation. None of this seemed right, but as Mr. Schrinar said, "it's a hot political issue." He explained that the preferential right of a lessee "has a chilling effect on every auction," because it discourages others from bidding. Although we couldn't negate the sale, we were able to delay it long enough for the land office to negotiate an easement to the deed which would guarantee Mr. Carollo access to his ditches and head gates. Having accomplished this meant that the only real loser in this deal turned out to be the State, in other words, the taxpayers--the very people every elected official has sworn to protect.

Another hot topic for the Land Board was the 100-year-old preferential right of the lease holder to renew his lease at the end of the lease term. Many farmers and ranchers wanted to lease state lands but couldn't because their neighbors already had them under lease. In some cases they had waited for years for the lease to expire, but it was futile to bid on state lands because in Wyoming there is no competitive bidding process. In fact, the leaseholder doesn't even have to bid; they merely have to meet the highest bid. Knowing this fact, it is unusual for anyone to submit a bid on lands that are currently under lease by someone else. For example, in 1990, out of the 356 leases that expired during the year, all but one was renewed by the existing lessee without competition.[72]

In 1993, the land office proposed increasing the grazing fees for ranchers using state lands. Rates hadn't been changed since 1988. In fact, there had only been two increases in the previous twenty years.[73] Grazing fees on private lands usually are adjusted annually in response to market conditions. In other industries, rental rates are

---

72 Op. cit., Beaver, p82.

73 "State Land Board Prepares for Debate on Grazing Fees," *Casper Star-Tribune*, Joan Barron, September 1, 1993, p.A10.

adjusted frequently. For example, rates for apartments, housing, and other commercial uses are adjusted often to reflect current market conditions. At that time, the State grazing fee was set at $2.50 per AUM (animal unit month).[74] AUM being the amount of forage a cow and calf or five sheep consume per month. Private leases were going for between $8 and $22, and it seemed clear that the State's rate was seriously low. In fourteen western states, the average AUM for state lands was $6.08 and in the five surrounding states the average was $4.66 per AUM.[75] Comparatively, then, our grazing fee was indeed low. The Board was considering a proposal to raise the rate from $2.50 to $3.67 per AUM, representing a percentage increase of 46.8 percent, but far lower than our neighboring states. Keeping in mind that over half of our lands were taken by either out-of-state operators or very large corporations or ranchers, I supported the proposed increase in an effort to "level the playing field"[76] for our local operators who were small and who didn't currently have a state lease. Approximately 80 to 85 percent of the ranching operations in Wyoming did not have state leases. They were paying more for their private lands and complained that it was almost impossible to compete with ranchers who had state leases. One rancher told me he always got out-bid at cattle auctions by his neighbor who had state leases because his neighbor's land costs were so much lower.[77]

I was the only member of the Land Commission who supported this rate hike. As a result the proposed increase to $3.67 went nowhere. Instead, the Board voted to approve a rate hike, spread over

---

74 Ibid.

75 Ibid.

76 Ibid.

77 Conversation with rancher from Torrington, Wyoming.

two years. This action would result in an increase to $3.00 in 1994 and to $3.50 in 1995. According to the *1992 Wyoming Agricultural Statistic Report*, the average AUM fee on private lands in Wyoming in 1991 was $9.98.[78] But the influence of the Wyoming Stock Growers Association, the Wyoming Wool Growers Association, and the Wyoming Farm Bureau was too much to overcome. Several ranchers suggested that such an increase would run them out of business and the industry would collapse.[79] Following a public discussion of these fees, the Board was preparing to return to Cheyenne and was about to board the state aircraft at the Riverton airport when a group of ranchers entered the terminal. These ranchers expressed a fear that we were going to run them out of business, before boarding their private jets to return to their ranches. Was this argument perhaps a bit disingenuous?

The Board was also influenced by the actions of U. S. Senator Malcolm Wallop, who at the time was making political hay out of the Clinton administration's proposed doubling of federal grazing fees. The Senator suggested that any action by the State would undermine his efforts[80] to defeat what he called was Secretary of the Interior Bruce Babbitt's "*War on the West*" which he alleged was deliberately being conducted by the Clinton administration. Political rhetoric of this kind was nothing new in Wyoming. Hating the federal government over public land issues was a common emotion that could be traced back to the years prior to statehood. Senator Wallop managed to stir up a fair amount of animosity among the agricultural community for not only the federal government but

---

[78] "Land Board Hikes Grazing Fees, *Casper Star-Tribune*, Joan Barron, September 3, 1993, p. A1.

[79] Ibid., p. A10.

[80] Ibid., p. A10.

also for those of us at the State level trying to manage state lands. In hindsight, it is remarkable that other members of the Land Board supported any increase in fees. And, although I was criticized by the agricultural lobbyists and the large ranchers with state leases, the agriculture operators without state or federal grazing leases, the Wyoming Education Association, the Wyoming Wildlife Federation, the Outdoor Council, and the largest newspapers in the State supported an increase. The *Wyoming Tribune Eagle*[81] in its September 2, 1993, editorial entitled: "Land board should raise grazing fees," stated: "Ferrari's reasoning on this issue makes sense. There should be some leveling of the playing field so small ranching operators who must shell out big bucks for private land can reasonably compete with those who are able to obtain state leases."

The agricultural lobbyists, including the *Wyoming Livestock Roundup*, a small weekly self-described "newspaper for ranchers, farmers and agribusinessmen," stated that I held a "highly disputed interpretation of the Wyoming Constitution,"[82] which assumed that the state is "supposed to maximize the revenue from the lands." My understanding of the need to maximize income from the management, leasing, or sales of state lands evolved from studying historical interpretations of the constitutions in land grant states and from advice provided by previous officials serving as Wyoming's Attorney General. They had consistently said these lands were trust lands and the Board had trust responsibilities. Mr. Schrinar, an attorney, had studied these issues in great detail for years, and he certainly understood the law. He had no personal interest in the

---

[81] "Land Board Should Raise Grazing Fees," *Wyoming Tribune-Eagle* editorial, September 2, 1993.

[82] "State Lands Panel Holds First Meeting," *Wyoming Livestock Roundup*, Vol. 7, No.44, p.1, May 18, 1996.

outcome. His financial interests were unaffected. He was objective, intelligent, and informed. He was trained to understand the laws, and he was honest. I listened to these legal experts and looked at all of the facts brought to the Board. The Wyoming Act of Admission, in Article 4, declares that the lands were granted "for the support of common schools." The Constitution, in Article 18, Section 5, provides that "no law shall ever be passed by the legislature granting any privileges to persons who may have settled upon any of the school lands . . . . by which the amount to be derived by the sale or other disposition of such lands, shall be diminished directly or indirectly." There had previously never been any question as to the intent of this language.

I didn't ignore information presented to the Board by representatives of the agriculture industry, but I tried not to be overly persuaded by the hired guns brought into the argument by these special interests. What did influence me was the huge body of legal analysis that had been completed on the subject over the years. One example was an article written by Clinton D. Beaver, Senior Assistant Attorney General for Wyoming and counsel to the Wyoming Board of Land Commissioners since 1985, which appeared in the *Land and Water Law Review*, published by the University of Wyoming, College of Law in 1991.[83] In it Mr. Beaver acknowledged that management of these lands is difficult because they are trust lands. "It is difficult for elected officials to function as trustees. Good politics and the law often conflict," he wrote.[84] He discussed the difference between managing these trust assets and other government resources. He described these difficulties

[83] Op. cit., Beaver.

[84] Ibid., p. 72.

as follows: "Congress created an inherent management conflict between the interests of the public and the interests of the trust beneficiaries by granting the former federal lands to Wyoming in trust. Had the lands been granted unconditionally, state officials could manage them in the same manner as any other governmental resource." [85] He continues, ". . . because these lands were granted in trust, their management is limited by the terms of the grants. Management decisions must encourage the greatest financial return to the trust beneficiaries . . . ."[86]

In 1982, the Supreme Court of the state of Oklahoma ruled that the constitutionally created state land trust must be managed for the prime benefit of public schools.[87] Since the laws in Wyoming and Oklahoma are similar, even if not identical, it was thought by all legal scholars who had examined the issue as well as others who were familiar with state land management that the same ruling would apply in Wyoming. In a hearing back then, Oklahoma District Judge Joe Cannon said:[88] "I think what happened is that everybody forgot who the beneficiary of this thing is and that's the school kids of Oklahoma. It's not the farmers and ranchers, it's not the agricultural interest. And I think you ought to start also figuring out how to cancel every lease you've got all over the State of Oklahoma," he said. "I think you've been operating unconstitutional for 75 years. You violated the Federal Constitution, the Oklahoma Constitution and the Enabling Act. You violated all of them."

---

85 Ibid., p. 90.

86 Ibid., p. 90.

87 "Status Quo on State Trust Lands," *Casper Star-Tribune,* Joan Barron, October 20, 1996, p. A1.

88 Ibid.

During our discussions of the issue, Jean Hayek, president of the Wyoming Education Association, testified that courts in other states had ruled the lands cannot be used in any form of direct or indirect subsidy for a particular industry. She said the State constitution "is very clear and provides no wiggle room in the State's obligation to maximize revenue for the school foundation."[89] She noted that Arizona was prohibited from providing favorable mineral royalty terms for mineral development, Washington was not allowed to give favorable timber leases to encourage the timber harvest, and New Mexico was prohibited from using a small portion of the income from public lands to advertise to encourage tourism.[90] These rulings, along with the language contained in Article 18, Section 5 of the Wyoming constitution, greatly influenced my thoughts on our responsibilities to maximize income for our schools.

During the eight years that I served on the State Land Board, two different state land task forces were created to examine state land issues. The first, under Governor Sullivan, was created in 1992. At its first meeting in 1992, Wyoming Attorney General Joe Meyer informed the group that the preferential right given to leaseholders was unconstitutional.[91] At the conclusion of its work, the task force's report, accompanied by the Land Board's recommendations, was submitted to the Joint Committee on Agriculture, Public Lands and Water Resources in the legislature in 1993. The more significant recommendations of the task force included: removing the right of

---

[89] "Grazing Fees, Education Linked," *Casper Star-Tribune*, Kerry Drake, July 25, 1995, p. A1.

[90] "WEA Joins Calls against Grazing Cap," *Casper Star-Tribune,* Kerry Drake, July, 1995, p. A1.

[91] "WEA Hits Preferential Grazing Reversal," *Casper Star-Tribune*, Joan Barron, November 19, 1993, p.A1.

the leaseholder to meet the highest bid on grazing lease renewals and removing the right of the leaseholder to meet the highest bid in the auction of state lands.[92] Several members of the legislative committee were ranchers who were also leaseholders. I don't think anyone was surprised that these ideas went absolutely no where in the legislature. In spite of all of the time and effort expended by the task force members, the land office staff, the attorneys, and the board in dealing with these issues, the legislature took very little action on state land issues. Reflecting on this, Joan Barron in her November 7, 1993, column in the *Casper Star-Tribune*[93] described the situation as follows: "The lobbying and thrashing about on these issues makes clear why previous state boards have plowed on with the status quo, reluctant to examine their state land policies and laws." She added, "In light of all this turmoil, the idea to sell off much of the state lands makes more and more sense."

The Land Board persisted to struggle with land management issues throughout the remainder of my first term in office and Governor Sullivan's last, amid controversy and persistent pressure from the larger leaseholders and agricultural associations. Without success, I pressed for changes in our management practices which would provide more opportunities for our smaller Wyoming-based farmers and ranchers to obtain leases on state lands and, at the same time, generate greater income for the schools from the use of these lands. This prolonged public discourse only served to add fuel to the fire to get rid of Howard as the State's Land Commissioner and to create yet another state lands task force to re-visit the very issues that the previous task force examined.

92 "Battle Looms Over State Land Reform," Judith Kohler, Ibid.

93 "Status Quo on State Trust Lands," Joan Barron, Ibid.

Jim Geringer was elected governor in 1994. One of his first acts, even before he was sworn in, was to start the process of replacing Mr. Schrinar. Howard had been controversial; but in my opinion, he was one of the best directors the Land Office ever had. Prior to Howard's service, there had only been two other commissioners in the previous twenty years: Albert King from 1963 until 1979 and Oscar Swan from 1979 until Howard's appointment.

Folks who had been influencing state land decisions for years and, in some cases, generations, were finding their influence didn't weigh as heavily with Howard as it had with previous administrations. Howard's willingness to stand up to the special interests gave Wyoming its best opportunity in decades to improve management of the trust and enhance income for our public schools. But when the new governor fired Howard, he eliminated that opportunity completely, and I don't think to this day the Land Office has ever quite recovered from it. Not only was management of the State's land negatively impacted by this move, but this bizarre decision damaged the Governor's credibility and hindered his ability to work with three members of the Board during his initial term in office.

But the new Republican governor wasn't the only politician who wanted Schrinar gone. The largest single leaseholder in the State was True Ranches, owned by the family of Diemer True, who was chairman of the Wyoming Republican Party and a former president of the Wyoming Senate. He, along with his family, held roughly 56,000 acres of state land leases and, according to an article in the *Casper Star* on November 7, 1993, when he was in the Senate, he attempted unsuccessfully to get Howard fired.[94] Republican Senator Charlie Scott of Casper also thought Howard ought to go. He

[94] "Land Board between Rock and a Lease," Joan Barron, Ibid.

said he "fundamentally disagrees" with Howard's interpretation of the constitution that the state lands should be managed for the maximum benefit of schools. He said that Schrinar held extreme views, and if he were elected governor he would want someone else in that position.[95] Senator Scott lost the Republican primary race to Geringer later that year.

After firing Howard, Geringer hired Jim Magagna, the unsuccessful Republican candidate for U. S. House of Representatives, as the new state land director and the director of federal land policy in Wyoming. I, Diana, and Stan were shocked that the Governor would hire someone who had grazing leases on 9,101 acres of state lands[96] and 89,400 acres of federal land leased from the Bureau of Land Management (BLM). According to that agency he was one of the 150th largest leaseholders[97] of BLM land in the country. At the time of his appointment he was director of the Rock Springs Grazing Association and owner of 1.5 shares in the Association. Each share enabled the shareholder to run 3,500 head of livestock.[98] According to an article in the *Casper Star-Tribune*, "The association controls more than 1 million acres of federal, state, leased and private land east and west of Rock Springs along the Union Pacific Railroad checker-board."[99] The combined state and federal government lands were intermingled among his own private holdings. They were an

---

95 "Scott Hits Schrinar's Land Managing Plan," *Casper Star-Tribune*, Daniel Wiseman, February 15, 1994, p. A1.

96 "Counting Sheep Leases," *Casper Star-Tribune*, Joan Barron, June 11, 1995, p. A1.

97 "Magagna under Fire," *Wyoming Tribune-Eagle*, Brett Martel, August 11, 1995.

98 "Conflicts of Interest: Different Views," *Casper Star-Tribune*, Joan Barron, November 26, 1995, p. A1.

99 Ibid.

integral part of his ranching operation. Shortly after his appointment, Mr. Magagna made the unbelievable statement that there is no constitutional mandate to maximize revenue from state trust land leases.[100] I had been in state government for nearly thirty years and on the Board for over four years by then, and it was the first time I had ever heard anyone, who was even vaguely familiar with the state lands, make this argument. "There simply are no words to that effect in the constitution," Magagna said. "So when someone says it's unconstitutional to put a cap on grazing fees or we're not getting the maximum dollar, I don't find any basis for that."[101] These statements were contrary to everything the land office staff had presented prior to Mr. Magagna's arrival. He went on to say that, "If you were to give something away clearly totally below its reasonable value, then I think you've violated your responsibilities. On the other hand, you can look at it and determine what's a reasonable return to the schools as your first priority, but also what is reasonable to ensure that these lands contribute to the overall economic welfare of the state, which is also important to the schools. I think there is an opportunity for a balancing there," he added.[102] He appeared to be saying that you can make sure the agriculture operators with state leases are healthy by keeping state grazing fees low and this will contribute to a stronger economy overall, thereby also benefiting the schools. This contradicted every legal case I had ever seen and, of course, brought a new dimension to the discussions about state lands and the trust responsibilities of the Land Board. It added fuel to the fire of the special interests and the agriculture industry lobbyists. The huge

---

[100] "Grazing Fees, Education Linked," Kerry Drake, Ibid.

[101] Ibid.

[102] Ibid.

leaseholders were delighted with this turn of events. The problem I had with this was that such action would be inconsistent with a trust officer's fiduciary duties. It would also have a negative impact on the majority of the agriculture industry without state leases which would be harmed by such a policy.

It was clear that Mr. Magagna had a conflict of interest when discussing state or federal land issues. At the Governor's request, he attempted to resolve the conflict by placing his state leases in what he described as a "blind trust" with First Security Bank of Rock Springs.[103] However, the blind trust was ineffective because it violated the basic premise of a blind trust, which is that the trustee must be given complete discretion to manage the trust. According to the National Council of State Legislature's model legislation,[104] this means the trustee must have "the power to dispose of and acquire trust assets without consulting or notifying the filer." A preamble to this legislation says, "To be truly effective, blind trusts must not allow a public official or public employee to peek at the assets or to play even a minimal role in their management". Any recommendation Mr. Magagna made to the Board, if implemented, could affect his personal financial interests. Any decision the Board might make on state land issues directly affected Mr. Magagna's financial interests. Mr. Magagna claimed to be speaking, not in behalf of his self, but in behalf of the agriculture industry whose interests just happened to coincide with his own. I could not ignore the conflict, and it was awkward for me to question Mr. Magagna.

---

103 "Banking Official Puts Stock in Blind Trust," *Casper Star-Tribune*, Joan Barron, June 11, 1996, p. A1.

104 *Council on Governmental Ethics Laws (COGEL),* Council of State Legislators, September, 1991.

Some of the other Board members did ignore it, as did virtually all of the spokesmen and lobbyists for the agriculture industry.

But, the conflict of interest bothered a lot of people in the state. Walt Urbigkit, an attorney, former legislator, and former Wyoming Supreme Court judge, said "The rights that Magagna would have under his lease with the state and under the trustee are essentially the same. The economic interest of Magagna under the trust remains that the lower the grazing fees, the greater the benefit; there is a direct pecuniary interest in what happens to the land with or without the trust." [105] Tom Thorpe of the Wyoming Outdoor Council said that the fact that the blind trust Magagna set up did not resolve his financial interest was of considerable concern. "He has the largest holdings in the state, and having him manage these lands when he has such a large financial interest is really inappropriate,"[106] Thorpe said.

Governor Geringer also appointed a new Attorney General, William U. Hill. Hill had looked at the constitution and the statutes, but his interpretation was different than his predecessors. It was more in alignment with Magagna's thoughts. In a July 20, 1995, opinion[107] he said that the board, for 66 years, had operated under what he called the "discretionary clause" in Wyoming statutes 36-2-106. "This required that the grazing rentals be fixed on as near an equitable basis as possible from information available,"[108] he said. He didn't define the term "equitable basis," however, so the opinion itself was of little help to the Board. However, his views became very important later when the issue was considered by the Wyoming

---

[105] "Magagna under Fire," Brett Martel, Ibid.

[106] Ibid.

[107] "Land Board Sets '96 Grazing Fee," *Wyoming Livestock Roundup*, September 23, 1995.

[108] Ibid.

Supreme Court, of which he had become a member in 1998. In fact, he was serving as Chief Justice between 2002 and 2006, when the issue came before the court.[109]

The second state lands task force was named in March of 1996. It consisted of seven private citizens and four legislators. The Governor appointed members who he said "could represent a cross-section of interests and would not lobby for a specific agenda or cause."[110] His appointees included Rex Arney, attorney and former legislator; John Etchipare, rancher and current state land lessee; Liz Fassett, Wyoming Outdoor Council; Elizabeth Horsch, high school teacher; Dave Klym, independent oil and gas producer; Jim Thompson, professor at the University of Wyoming; and Dave Neary, associate director of the Nature Conservancy. The four legislators, appointed by the Legislative Management Council included Sens. Jerry Geis, R-Worland, and Rich Cathcart, D-Carpenter, and Reps. Sylvia Gams, R-Cowley and Joe Selby, R-Cheyenne.[111] So it appeared we were back where we started. The entire effort to study state land issues would be repeated with this newly elected governor, a new attorney general, a new land office director, and a new task force.

Following the suggestion advanced by Mr. Magagna in 1995 to establish a minimum fee per AUM as well as a maximum fee which could be charged for leases, Diana and I sent a memo to other members of the Board, as well as to Hill and Magagna asking that questions be submitted to the Court.[112] The land director was proposing policies

---

[109] Supreme Court of Wyoming, Riedel v. Anderson, June 4, 2003.

[110] "State Land Sales Moratorium Looks Dead," *Casper Star-Tribune*, March 31, 996, p. A8.

[111] Ibid.

[112] "Trust Obligations: Go to Court," *Casper Star-Tribune*, Joan Barron, September 24, 1995, p. A1.

which would clearly limit the amount of income which could be earned on grazing leases. In addition, since his arrival, many other concerns were being expressed by the leaseholders and their advocates. Given this increased level of controversy it was becoming almost impossible to manage these lands for the benefit of public schools. We needed judicial guidance and in our correspondence we asked specifically, "Can we compromise the financial benefits received by education in favor of other possible state considerations such as access (to state lands), beef prices, "war-on-the-west," droughts, preserving traditional family ranching operations, etc.?"[113] We further outlined five key questions for the courts:[114]

- Does the Wyoming constitution and other documents or law impose a trust obligation on the land commissioners with regard to state trust lands? If so, is that obligation identical to responsibility imposed on private trusts?
- Does the present practice of not charging recreationalists, hunters, and fishermen fees for use of trust lands violate the constitution or the commissioners' trust obligation?
- Would setting a maximum grazing fee at a level of anything less than the fee bid by the highest bidder violate the trust responsibilities of the state board?
- Does the present practice of leasing lands for grazing without open bidding violate the trust obligation or the constitution?
- Does the present practice of allowing the lessee the right to meet the high bid on the sale of trust lands violate the constitution and the board's trust obligation?

---

[113] Ibid.

[114] Ibid.

Our push for an answer from the courts, I believe, was one of the reasons the Governor wanted a new study on state lands to be conducted under the watchful eye of his new Republican administration. There was also a need to address the public's concern about the board's recent approval of land sales. There was a perception during that election year that a huge number of acres were being sold off. This misconception was fueled by exaggerations put forth by people who ought to have known better. For example, a reporter for the *Casper Star-Tribune* was apparently trying to enrage rather than inform his readers on November 21, 1993,[115] when he wrote that there had been a "spate of state land sales the past several months." He said the sale of these lands became controversial because they were being sold "at an alarming rate."[116] Perhaps his most offensive remark in that same article was: "Apparently, there are some members of the State Land Board who enjoy doing business in a daring, carefree way and who do not feel any particular need to know much of anything about the land they are going to sell."[117] The facts were, between July 1, 1990, and the end of 1993, a total of 32,360 acres had been sold, which were roughly eight-tens of one percent of the State's land holdings. At that rate of sales, it would take the Board 395 years to sell off all of the State land.[118] This was hardly a "spate," a fire sale, or an "alarming rate" of sales. These sales brought in a total of $10.9 million in revenue for the schools or an average of $336.84 an acre. Given the fact that the State at

115 "Yes, There is No Confidence in Land Board," *Casper Star-Tribune*, Tom Bishop, November 21, 1993.

116 Ibid.

117 Ibid.

118 "State Land Sales – Moratorium on State Land Sales Achieves HB 100 Intent," *Wyoming Tribune-Eagle*, April 11, 1994.

the time was receiving roughly $.70 per year on each acre from grazing and timber harvests, it would take approximately 480 years to collect $10.9 million from these uses. The economic benefits to the taxpayers of Wyoming were obvious and any responsible trust officer could not ignore them.

However, because of the concerns and emotions expressed over these sales, at least partially due to inaccurate reporting, legislation was passed by the 1994 legislature to place a two-year moratorium on state land sales. The bill, sponsored by Senator Charles Scott of Casper and Representative Bill Bensel of Sheridan[119] was needed, Scott argued, "until a change in the management can reverse the current policy of selling state lands."[120] He was referring to Howard Schrinar and Governor Sullivan, whose term as governor would expire at the end of the year. Scott, a rancher and also a state land lessee, said the State should not sell the lands because they were needed as a "hedge against inflation and for recreation, scientific and access purposes."[121] He further proclaimed that "it is a great mistake to sell our heritage and our future to solve short-term budget problems."[122] Although the Senator's intentions were probably pure, it appeared to me that he was wrong on a couple of counts. First, money from the sale of lands does not go into the budget to be spent but rather is deposited into the permanent land fund for investment. Earnings from these investments are what is spent, not the proceeds from the sale. Since the constitution requires that these proceeds be retained inviolate, this is a hedge against inflation. Second, it doesn't

---

119 Op. cit., "Scott Hits Schrinar's Land Managing Plan," Daniel Wiseman.

120 Ibid.

121 Ibid.

122 Ibid.

make sense to hold on to landlocked lands as a hedge if you are going to continue to lease them for a fraction of what they are worth. The public will never benefit from this kind of ownership and management. The hedge against inflation in these cases becomes counter-productive. At that time, the State was receiving about 70 cents in income per acre from grazing fees. Sixteen years later, in Fiscal Year 2010, the income was still only $1.48 per acre.[123]

Even though it is far more economical for the leaseholders to lease the lands than it is for them to buy them, there are nonetheless times when the leaseholder wants or needs to own the lands. If there is a moratorium in place, there is no possibility to buy the land. Since only three percent of the sales were instigated by the Board, and another four percent were nominated by third parties, over ninety percent of the lands we sold were nominated by the leaseholders.[124] The discontent about land sales was coming mostly from agricultural journalists, legislators with land leases, wildlife enthusiasts, and other outdoor users. What these critics were primarily concerned with was the loss of access to these lands if they were no longer owned by the State. What they failed to consider was the fact that a lot of these lands are land-locked by private lands, and there is little opportunity to access most of them anyway. At the time of statehood, sections 16 and 36 of every township were set aside for schools. They are surrounded obviously, by either private or federal land. Most people, including legislators, were not opposed to selling those parcels which would be used by cities, towns, or school districts, or which could be used to advance economic development. Largely, for this reason,

---

[123] Office of Wyoming State Lands & Investments, *2010 Annual Report*, Ed Grant, Director, p.7.

[124] "Officials Say No 'Fire Sale' on Lands," *Wyoming Livestock Roundup*, Judith Kohler, November 29, 1993, Volume 69, No. 134.

Governor Sullivan wisely vetoed the bill and the board continued its own moratorium[125] until such time as the land office staff could work through the some eighteen to twenty-four month backlog of nominations that were pending at the time.

Following Sullivan's departure and Geringer's entrance on the land board, the moratorium expired in the middle of 1996; but before it did, I made a motion[126] at the June, 1996, Land Board meeting to extend it. Having previously failed to get legal questions answered regarding state land issues, my motion contained three stipulations which were designed to remove the confusion regarding the Board's responsibilities in managing state lands. The first stipulation was that the 1997 legislature conform respective statutes to the State Constitution. Second, should the legislature fail to do so, any member of the Board could file for a declaratory judgment on the constitutionality of the statutes; and, third, if the Attorney General would not represent the Board, the Board would seek outside counsel.

The strategy was to get this issue into the courts, where an impartial body could examine it without the influence of powerful special interests. I was convinced then, and remain so today, that the State was not receiving adequate return from the leasing or sale of these school lands. I was also convinced that the courts would direct the State to abandon its current practice of protecting the interests of the current leaseholders at the expense of agricultural

---

125 "State Land Sales – Moratorium on State Land Sales Achieves HB100 Intent," *Wyoming Tribune-Eagle*, Ibid.

126 "State Land Board Favors Short-term Moratorium," *Casper Star-Tribune*, Kerry Drake, July 10, 1996, p. A1.

operators without state leases. My motion failed[127] on a vote of 3 to 2. Both Diana and I voted for the motion. Governor Geringer cast the final vote to table because he wasn't comfortable with these stipulations. I suspect he was influenced by his attorney general, who previously had refused to file the suit, saying that somehow it would be "unethical."[128] It was unclear to me how such action would be unethical, but it was becoming clearer that the only state officials wanting an answer to the question of constitutional trust responsibilities were Diana and me.

In reviewing Land Board actions nearly a year earlier, the *Casper Star* on September 24, 1995, observed: "Ohman and Ferrari have taken a lot of abuse over their positions on state lands issues–positions which are rooted in their loyalty to the Constitution and their trust obligations. They should be commended for pressing these critical questions."[129] Instead, we were criticized by the ranchers with state leases at the public hearings conducted to obtain the public's input. On numerous occasions, we were accused of having some kind of ulterior motive. "Is there some hidden agenda?" asked a rancher from Boulder, "Is this some kind of cultural cleansing of the hinterlands?"[130] One comment offered by an irate rancher: "Where is the problem that needs fixed? Why do things need changed

---

[127] "Ferrari Wants Land Sales Put on Hold," *Wyoming Tribune-Eagle*, Tony Monterastelli and Brett Martel, July 7, 1996.

[128] "Land Sales Issue Put Off," *Wyoming Tribune-Eagle*, Brett Martel, June 7, 1996.

[129] "Trust Obligations: Go to Court," *Casper Star-Tribune*, Ibid.

[130] "Ranchers: State has joined 'War on the West'; Land Board Taken to Task for Grazing Fee Hike Proposal," *Casper Star-Tribune*, Kerry Drake, September 16, 1995, p.A1.

at all?"[131] Another was, ". . . this is not an economic issue. There must be more behind it." One witness said it was beyond him how "somebody in Cheyenne who doesn't know which end you put the hay in can be telling us what grazing is worth."[132] Another said, "Some members of the State Land Board have set out to mislead and misinform the public of Wyoming. It is my belief that Ms. Ohman should remove herself (or be removed) from office because of the bias she so obviously holds and is so clearly attempting to propagate."[133] A rancher from Garrett said any attempt to increase grazing fees "is an out-and-out attack on the livestock industry." He continued by declaring, "It seems some members of the Land Board have joined Interior Secretary Bruce Babbitt and declared war on the West, with a Western headquarters."[134] These comments confirm some observations Mr. Beaver made in his 1991 article:[135] "State officials are on the front lines of this management conflict. When administering trust lands, state officials are required to function like private trustees. Yet the narrow focus of a trustee cannot accommodate the broad concerns public officials are accustomed to addressing. The state official is caught in the crossfire."

During the previous task force proceedings, Barbara Parsons, a member appointed to represent the interests of recreational users, called for the development of a land inventory. Both Diana and I

---

[131] "State Grazing Fee Controversy Unfolds at Hearings, in WEA and WASA Statements," *Wyoming Livestock Roundup*, Julie Bousman, September 9, 1995, p.14.

[132] Letters to the Editor, "State Land Board", *Casper Star-Tribune*, September 7, 1995.

[133] Ibid.

[134] Op. cit., "Ranchers: State has joined 'War on the West'; *Casper Star-Tribune*.

[135] Op. cit., Beaver, p.90.

supported the proposal.[136] Such an assessment would provide tools to determine over both the long and short-term, which lands have public access, which ones don't; which lands should be retained and which should be sold; and which had the best potential for the best uses, such as economic development, mineral extraction, recreation, hunting, fishing, grazing, timbering, etc. With an inventory of this nature, the state could develop a management and marketing plan which could serve to remove the controversy which has historically obstructed the effective management of this very valuable state resource.

Every parcel of land sold while I was on the Board was first studied and analyzed by the staff, and their findings and assessments were presented to the Board for consideration before a decision was made on the possible sale or retention of the parcel. But, an overall assessment and categorization of all of the State's land holdings has never been done. If the Land Board used such an inventory, it would not mean members of the Land Board would not continue to be accused of having a "highly disputed interpretation" of their trust responsibilities. You can probably never remove the politics from state land management or the conflicts of interests of those who both control state land leases and at the same time make decisions on state lands as part-time legislators, but you can at least counter these negatives by using factual information.

There were other controversial topics handled by the Land Board which did not involve ranchers with grazing leases. In our December, 1994, meeting, we were considering a request from Kenetech Windpower, Inc., for an easement to construct wind turbines on

136 "Ferrari, Ohman call for Wyoming Lands Inventory; Needed for Planning, They say," *Casper Star-Tribune*, October 14, 1993, p.A1.

state land along Interstate 80 in eastern Carbon County.[137] I was the only one to oppose. Having just returned from visiting a wind power project on Tehatchapi Pass in Kern County, California, I was concerned about the visual impact that some 1,400 turbines would have. In my view, the California project had completely ruined the aesthetics of the beautiful hill sides on both sides of Route 58. Of course, the project there was much larger, consisting of some 5,000 wind turbines. I suggested the Board conduct additional public hearings before proceeding with approval of the easement. Two public meetings had been held by the staff: one in Laramie and the other in Rawlins. Only 60 to 70 people had shown up, so there appeared to be little concern about the aesthetics of the project. I voted no anyway. I thought we needed more public input than that. In hindsight, I was probably wrong back then. The project was expected to create $600 million in economic development to Carbon County, and generate some 500 megawatts of power when fully operational. Environmental concerns are now commonly expressed regarding wind generation involving windmills standing hundreds of feet in the air with propellers spanning twenty-five feet. The viability of wind generated power is also now being questioned.

Sitting as one of the three-member State Canvassing Board, on an early morning in late November, 1994, Governor Sullivan convened a meeting of Secretary of State Kathy Karpan, and the State Auditor to begin at 6:00 a.m. at the State capitol building.[138] The meeting was held early so it could be broadcast live on NBC's morning news program, the *Today Show*. The purpose was to select

---

[137] "State Grants Easement for Wind Power Facility," *Casper Star-Tribune*, December 4, 1994, p.A1.

[138] "Luthi Wins Star Valley Seat in Ping-Pong Draw, *Casper Star-Tribune*, Kerry Drake, November, 1994, p.A1.

a winner to represent Wyoming House District 21 in the legislature, which had ended in a dead heat between Republican Randall Luthi and Independent Larry Call. Each had received 1,941 votes in the November 8 election. According to Wyoming law, the winner is picked by drawing a Ping-Pong ball. We decided to pull the ball out of Governor Sullivan's rumpled cowboy hat which contained two balls: one with Luthi's name on it, the other with Call's. The Governor held his hat high above his head so that no one could see in it and Kathy reached up and pulled out the winning ball. It was labeled, "Randall Luthi." Before his name was drawn, Luthi said if elected, he may take a look at changing that law, but after the drawing, he called Wyoming's system of breaking election ties "an excellent process." He then went on to serve several terms in the House before becoming Speaker. It was a "feel good" meeting and a "feel good" story in Wyoming. The NBC crew enjoyed the drawing and emphasized the fact that every vote really does count.

# CHAPTER TEN

## The Second Term

My second term in office began in much the same way as the first one ended, with continuing controversy over positions taken on the State Land Board. In preparation of running for a second term, on Thursday, April 21, 1994, as my first term was into its final year, State Superintendent of Public Instruction Diana Ohman introduced me before a crowd of a couple hundred supporters and announced my intent to run for a second term.[139] I highlighted what I felt were the accomplishments of the past four years and discussed the issues that would be dealt with in the years to come if re-elected. I promised to continue work on the state lands issues and to introduce an ethics bill in the 1995 legislative session which would make it unlawful for a public employee or official from any branch of government, state or local, including school districts, to accept anything more than a cup of coffee from a lobbyist or anyone doing business with or who is regulated by the government. Several months earlier, Joan Barron, a reporter for the *Casper Star-Tribune*, had asked me about

[139] "Ferrari Seeks Second Term," *Casper Star-Tribune*, Joan Barron, April 22, 1994. P.A1.

another term. In her reporting on Sunday, September 26, 1993,[140] she made the following observation: "Ferrari is the least political of politicians, a quiet, hard worker who keeps finding money for the state." When we later began preparations to run for a second term, all of our campaign materials contained this quotation.

Following the primary election, on October 9 of 1994, Joan wrote another article about my candidacy.[141] We had gone through the primary election unopposed and had no opponent in the general election as well. She called it a "free ride" and it was nearly that. She quoted one Democrat who said his fellow party members ". . . felt Ferrari was doing a good job and should be left alone." She added, "The Democrats could not have fielded a candidate who could beat Ferrari anyway." She began the article by referring to the group insurance study we had conducted during our first year in office:

> "Officials of the state's group health insurance board roasted and toasted Auditor Dave Ferrari three years ago. The reason was the white paper prepared by Ferrari, then a member of the board. The report pointed out shortcomings with the state's health insurance plan. Essentially, Ferrari's report said that employees in other states in the region were getting a better deal than Wyoming plan participants. Sadly and typically, the board and plan administrators took the report personally and lashed back at Ferrari. One response from

---

140 "Governor Runner Up in Mr. Frugal Race," *Casper Star-Tribune*, Joan Barron, September 26, 1993.

141 "Ferrari Right on Group Health," *Casper Star-Tribune*, Ibid.

> this group said, in effect, that Ferrari was talking through his hat and knew nothing about health insurance."

Joan went on to say that a recently conducted audit had concluded about the same things I had some three years earlier. She suggested I must have gotten some comfort out of the report and offered the following: "Given that backdrop . . . . Ferrari didn't wilt under the assault and has continued to poke and prod into government's dusty corners. . . If he makes some enemies along the way, it won't hurt his chance for re-election." She was right. We garnered over 98 percent of the vote. Other than a few write-in votes, the remaining two percent didn't vote for anyone. In fact, we officially collected 168,014 votes,[142] the highest vote total cast in history in the general election for any candidate running for state or national office in Wyoming. This total has never been exceeded. Candidates coming the closest before and since included Max Maxfield, who garnered 148,210 votes in winning the Secretary of State's race in 2006; Max Maxfield, winner of the State Auditor's race in 1998, with 139,441 votes; and, Cynthia Lummis winner of the State Treasurer's race in 2002, with 152,583 votes.[143]

I interpreted these election results as approval of the work performed as the state's chief financial officer as well as the positions taken as a member of the State Land Board. As our state lawmakers continued to vote on various issues in which they had a personal financial interest, it became increasingly obvious that ethics legislation was needed which, among other things, would

[142] Op. cit., *Wyoming Blue Book*, Volume V, p.36.

[143] Ibid., pp. 32, 36-37,43.

clearly define what a conflict of interest is and how it should be dealt with when one occurs. Year after year, legislators who held leases on state lands would vote on bills dealing with these lands without disclosing that they had a financial interest in the matter. The most memorable case occurred in 1997 when a state lands bill was being considered in a House-Senate conference committee which was working on a compromise version of House Bill 177a. In this case, several environmental lobbyists suggested two members of the committee had violated the Wyoming constitution and asked my opinion as to whether or not they had. It was my opinion that they indeed had and when it was reported in the *Casper Star* the next morning, it created a stir that would not go away during the remainder of my term in office.[144]

Article 3, Section 46 of the Wyoming Constitution states that "A member who has a personal or private interest in any measure or bill proposed or pending before the legislature shall disclose the fact to the house of which he is a member and shall not vote thereon." In spite of this restriction, both the house and senate have adopted rules that allow members to vote on bills that may impact them financially.[145] Often, legislators will declare a conflict of interest and refrain from voting, which is the honorable thing to do. In fact, most states have adopted the Council of State Government's guidelines which provide that even an appearance of a conflict would preclude a member from voting on the issue. Ranchers serving in the legislature who hold state leases feel passionate about state land issues as do their neighbors. In this example, the two

---

144 "Lawmakers may have Violated Constitution, Ferrari Charges Conflict of Interest on State Lands Votes," *Casper Star-Tribune*, Kerry Drake, February, 1997, p.A1.

145 Ibid.

legislators who voted in spite of their obvious financial interests, Senator Bill Barton, R-Upton, and Representative Frank Philp, R-Shoshoni, argued that they were representing more than just their personal interests.[146] "I speak for the entire agriculture industry in the State of Wyoming," said Barton, holder of 2,120 acres of state trust lands in Crook and Weston counties. It wasn't clear how he could be speaking for the roughly 8,000 agriculture operators without state leases, however. Philp, holder of 8,820 acres of state trust land, said that his voting on the state lands bill was no different than a teacher voting on education issues. When House Bill 177a was being considered in the house, Representative Roger Huckfeldt, R-Torrington, was the only member who declared a conflict of interest and did not vote.[147] Other members of the house who also held state leases at that time included, Bruce Burns, R-Sheridan, Jim Hageman, R-Fort Laramie, John Hines, R-Gillette, Tom Rardin, R-Laramie, and Marlene Simons, R-Beulah. Senator Charles Scott, R-Casper whose company, Bates Creek, had leases on nearly 6,000 acres of state lands, declared a conflict of interest on several provisions of the bill and did not vote on those provisions. He did, however, vote on the overall bill. Other lawmakers in the senate who were also state leaseholders included, Vince Picard, R-Laramie, and John Schiffer, R-Kaycee. Still, other lawmakers also held state leases under company names. Other than Senator Scott's, no conflicts were declared.

Liz Fassett, former president of the Wyoming Outdoor Council and a member of the 1996 state lands taskforce, said the items the conference committee (House Bill 177a) dealt with were almost

---

[146] Ibid.

[147] Ibid., p.A10.

exclusively lease provisions.[148] "It is not surprising that the changes the committee made were all in the interests of the grazing lessees and provisions the task force had rejected as against the trust mandate," she said. She also said that the presence of legislators with apparent conflicts of interest on the conference committee, "not only weakens the bill, it also violates the public's trust of our elected officials."[149]

Others expressed similar concerns. Tom Thorpe, a former Oregon state lawmaker and Executive Director of the Wyoming Outdoor Council, said the constitutional issue may have to be resolved through a court challenge. "It may be the only way to force the issue," said Robert Hoskins of the Sierra Club. Thorpe added that in Oregon the statutes clearly prohibited lawmakers from voting on any bill that would impact them financially.[150]

As an outgrowth of these discussions and in response to the on-going controversies surrounding state land management, legislation was passed in 1997. The legislature largely ignored recommendations from the task force and members of the State Land Board. The bill that was approved was designed to discourage the sale of lands. The Legislature adopted what it called "statements of principle" to guide the Board and Land Office in its management.[151] First, the law directed that the "state land trust", consisting of trust lands, trust minerals, and permanent land funds should be managed under a "total asset management policy." Second, it declared that the state land trust is inter-generational and the focus should be on protecting the corpus for the long term. Third, it stated that trust lands should

---

[148] Ibid.

[149] Ibid.

[150] Ibid.

[151] Supreme Court of Wyoming, *Riedel v. Anderson*, Ibid., p.11.

remain a substantial, integral component of the state land trust portfolio, and there is no mandate to sell any lands to maximize revenue in the short term. And, fourth, the lands should be leased to assure a return of at least fair market value after considering risk assumed by the lessee, when this fair market value is determined.

In amending the statutes to reflect these philosophies, the legislature abolished the practice of establishing a minimum-and maximum-rental value which Magagna had successfully advocated earlier. Although none of the changes were designed to generate maximum income from the use of the lands, they did seem to alleviate some of the concerns expressed by the lessees and those who did not want these lands sold. Unfortunately, the legislation failed to address the problems associated with conflicts of interest and it failed to make the statutes conform to the Wyoming Constitution and the Act of Admission. However, the use of such explicit trust language in the 1997 legislation indicated the legislature's intention that the lands be subject to a trust and administered accordingly. This had a profound influence on a 2003 Wyoming Supreme Court decision, which concluded that the school lands in Wyoming were subject to a statutory rather than a constitutional trust and were governed by the statutes, not by common law trust principles.[152] It seemed clear to me that what resulted was a reflection of both Mr. Magagna's and Attorney General Bill Hill's philosophy on how these lands should be managed. In other words, Magagna's *"there is no constitutional mandate to maximize income"* would stand and Hill's *"discretionary clause"* enabling the board to continue to fix grazing rentals *"on as near an equitable basis as possible"* was perfectly legitimate. The State would, in other words, continue the status quo.

---

[152] Ibid., p.14.

Mr. Magagna continued in his position until being terminated by the Governor in late 1997 and being replaced on a temporary basis by Cynthia Lummis,[153] currently Wyoming's lone representative in the United States House of Representatives. He had survived in spite of his conflict and was terminated because of an incident that occurred in his office, not because of his state leases. He was asked to resign after it was determined that someone in his office had deleted a proposed rule on public lands access.[154] The rule was under consideration for adoption when it mysteriously disappeared. Cynthia, like Magagna, was strongly supported by the agriculture industry representatives and lobbyists and as was the case with Mr. Magagna, the new interim director also had state land grazing leases in her family's ranching operations.

In addition to the status quo provisions, the new state lands bill transferred much of the Board's power to the director, giving the director broad authority to manage state land issues.[155] According to the new law, the Land Board would only have the authority to "override any decision made by the director." To some, this provision was also in conflict with the State constitution. In fact, Bill Hill, the Attorney General, advised the lawmakers that the "bill's transfer of many powers from the Board to the Director could be constitutionally challenged."[156]

In spite of the fact that the intent appeared to be to lessen the Board's influence in the decision-making process, there were a

---

153 "Cynthia Lummis Appointed as Interim Land Office Head," *Wyoming Livestock Roundup, Chris Aimone,* December 6, 1997, p.1.

154 Ibid.

155 "House Passes State Lands Bill, *Casper Star-Tribune,* Kerry Drake, February 8, 1997, p.B1.

156 Ibid., p.8.

number of things the Board could do to increase income from our school lands. One issue that came out of the 1997 lands legislation had to do with taxpayer money used to make improvements to state lands. Representative Eli Bebout, R-Riverton, amended the bill to allow that the lessee would be given credit for one hundred percent of the value of any improvement regardless of who paid for it.[157] Improvements, such as the installation of water wells, are often paid for by both the grazing lessee and the government through water development and other grants. Prior to Bebout's amendment, the government's contribution to the project was considered to be property of the state. His amendment meant that even if the lessee hadn't paid for it, the improvement became the property of the lessee. Thus, the benefit was going to the lessee at the expense of the trust beneficiaries. The new law created a problem for the trust that simply didn't exist prior to its passage.

Another area where the beneficiaries appeared to be getting shortchanged was with respect to surface damage payments. Mineral exploration, oil and gas development, and other activities can have a disturbing impact on state lands. Grasses may be destroyed, fences taken down, and temporary roads built, necessitating the movement of cattle and disrupting ranching operations. Since 1969, the State had shared payments made by mineral companies for damages caused to the lands on an equal basis.[158] The lessee received fifty percent and the State received fifty percent. In some cases these payments amounted to thousands of dollars. There were examples of cases where a lessee was paying only a few dollars a year for use of the affected state lands yet was receiving payments of tens of thousands

[157] "Ferrari Seeks to End Surface Damage Split before Leaving Office," *Casper Star-Tribune*, Jason Marsden, December 8, 1998, p.A12.

[158] Ibid., p.A1.

of dollars for surface damages. A few years after I left office, a March 3, 2001 editorial in the *Casper Star* said that in the year 2000 alone, "a handful of lessees paid a combined $28,000 in rent yet received a windfall of roughly half-a-million dollars in surface damage payments." Only one other state, South Dakota, shared surface-damage payments with the lessee. All of the other land grant states in our region kept the damage payments and paid the lessee a refund for any loss of forage that resulted. I proposed that the State should negotiate these payments with the mineral company; and if the lessee loses any forage as a result of the surface damage, the lessee would receive a reduction in the lease rate reflecting this loss of forage. The lessee would also receive compensation for any documented loss sustained due to interruption of the ranching operation. My motion failed on a three-to-two vote. It was decided that the new board which would take office in January of 1999 should make the decision on whether or not the policy should be changed. The *Casper Star* in its editorial[159] on December 8, 1998, entitled, "Payments for surface damages should go to state," said "We're glad that State Auditor Dave Ferrari intends to raise the issue of surface damage payments. . . . There is no good rationale for paying lessees thousands of dollars more in surface damage payments than they pay the state to use our trust lands." The editorial concluded: "We urge the members of the land board to make the policy decision that the Wyoming constitution really demands–to maximize the proceeds from the state trust lands to support our schools and the education of our youth."

---

[159] "Payments for Surface Damages Should Go to State," *Casper Star-Tribune*, Editorial, December 8, 1998.

Dick Sadler, a former State Senator from Casper said in a letter to the editor[160] on August 16, 1995: "There is no known rancher since statehood who has ever lost a state grazing lease even though violating their leases." A few years later when a Meeteetse rancher, Martin Thomas, was convicted of illegally killing nine elk without a license on the 91 Ranch northwest of Meeteese, I questioned if his lease should be cancelled.[161] Wyoming law provides that anyone who does not comply with all of the laws of the state is not eligible to lease state lands. Mr. Thomas' conviction seemed to disqualify him as a lessee, and I asked the Board to cancel his lease on those grounds. The Governor did not indicate whether or not he supported such action, but did ask Attorney General Gay Woodhouse to determine if the Board could legally take such action. My term as State Auditor and a member of the Board concluded before any answer came.

Many of the issues that were troubling didn't get resolved during my years in office, but it's fair to say that the actions taken during that period brought these issues to the forefront. There were eight years of discussions; some arguments we won; most we lost. Actions taken by the Board during our time ultimately did result in the trust question going to the Wyoming Supreme Court.

The opportunity for the Wyoming Supreme Court to hear the case of whether or not the Wyoming Act of Admission, the Wyoming Constitution, or Wyoming statutes establish a trust with respect to our school lands and whether or not the preferential right given to expiring lease holders was a violation of the State's trust responsibilities evolved from a conflict between Craig and

---

160 "Running Roughshod Over Accumulations," Letter to the Editor, Dick Sadler, Casper, *Casper Star-Tribune*, August 16, 1995.

161 "Ferrari Works to Revoke Lease," *Casper Star-Tribune*, Jason Marsden, December 5, 1998, p.A1.

Gail Anderson and their neighbor William H. Riedel in Laramie County.[162] The Andersons held a lease on 640 acres of land which was to expire in December, 1997. They submitted an application to renew the lease and offered an annual lease rate of $4,586.40. There were two other parties that wanted to lease the land and each submitted bids. One offer was less than the $4,586.40 offered by the Andersons and the other, submitted by Mr. Riedel, was more, at $6,000.00 per year. Consistent with Wyoming statute, 36-5-105, the Andersons met Riedel's bid and on January 16, 1998, the Andersons were awarded the lease for a ten-year term at $6,000.00 per year. Riedel contested this decision in an administrative appeal to the Board and after conducting a hearing on May 6, 1998, the Board upheld the decision. Riedel then filed a petition for judicial review in the District Court, but the Court dismissed it on the grounds that the Court lacked jurisdiction to review the constitutionality of a statute based on an administrative action. In June, 1999, six months after I had left office, Mr. Riedel sought a declaratory judgment against the Board. On July 10, 2000, the District Court granted motions to intervene submitted by the Wyoming Stock Growers Association, the Wyoming Wool Growers Association, and the Wyoming Farm Bureau Federation (the Associations). The District Court, on October 29, 2001, concluded that the lands were indeed encumbered by a trust, and the State had a fiduciary duty to manage the lands exclusively for the beneficiaries.[163]

At this point in the deliberations, one thing seemed abundantly clear: Howard Schrinar, while Director of the Land Office was absolutely correct in trying to manage these state lands for the

[162] Supreme Court of Wyoming, Riedel v. Anderson, Ibid.

[163] Ibid., p.3.

maximum benefit of the State's common schools. But, Mr. Schrinar's apparent vindication was only temporary. Following this trust ruling, the court considered whether the right-to-renew statute was in conflict with the trust responsibilities and was therefore unconstitutional. Upon the Association's motion to dismiss, the court dismissed the case on the grounds that Riedel failed to prove that this preferential right to renew violates the State's fiduciary responsibility. Riedel appealed this dismissal to the Wyoming Supreme Court and the Associations cross-appealed the order that the school lands are held in trust.

Riedel's appeal was based on five separate constitutional objections, all of which were rejected. First, he claimed that the preferential right to renew "violates Wyoming's fiduciary trust obligation to receive fair market value . . . ." The Court responded that "we conclude that any trust in Wyoming is a creation of Wyoming statute, that trust does not carry with it the duty to maximize revenues . . . ."[164]

Riedel's second argument was that the preferential right to renew is tantamount to an absolute right of renewal which violates the enabling act's ten-year limit on leasing. However, the court response was that "prior preferential right-to-renew leases are conditional, not absolute . . . the incumbent must re-apply every ten years, must have met prior lease payments, must otherwise maintain eligibility, and most importantly must match any higher bid offered for the same land. The State may still decide to sell the land or not to lease it at all; if it does lease, it does so at the highest rate bid by anyone. We

---

[164] Ibid., p.13.

therefore find that the conditional right to renew does not violate the enabling act's prohibition of leases longer than ten years."[165]

Riedel's third argument was that the preferential right-to-renew statute violates the requirement that the school lands be disposed of by public auction. The court said that "The framers clearly did not consider a lease to be a sale when they granted to the Board of Land Commissioners the 'direction, control, leasing and disposal' of the state lands. . . . We conclude likewise that a lease of state lands as authorized by the constitution is not a disposal of those lands and need not be accomplished by public auction."[166]

The fourth argument advanced by Riedel was that the right-to-renew violates the constitutional prohibition of "granting any privileges to persons who may have settled upon any of the school lands . . . by which the amount to be derived by the sale or other disposition of such lands, shall be diminished directly or indirectly." The court responded by saying that "This argument lacks cogency: the lessees of today are not the original settlers contemplated by the Constitution and . . . the leasing of the lands is not a 'sale or other disposition' of the school lands."[167]

Finally, Riedel's last argument was that the right-to-renew depresses the value of agricultural leases and thus violates the trustees' duty to maximize revenue from the trust lands. His argument assumed the existence of a trust and assumed the trust was governed by common law trust standards rather than by the legislature. But, the court ruled that "the land trust in Wyoming is created by the legislature and hence the management of that trust

[165] Ibid.

[166] Ibid.

[167] Ibid., pp. 13-14.

land and, as specifically authorized by the constitution, the leasing of the trust lands, are governed by the statutes and not by common law trust principles."[168]

The court said that much of Riedel's evidence "was of a historical nature and addressed past management practices of the board without tie-in to the current statute or the lease at issue. To conclude from that evidence that the state is not realizing sufficient income from its trust lands, rising to the level of breach of fiduciary duty, would be sheer speculation and falls far short of Riedel's considerable burden to prove the statutes unconstitutionality. While there may have been problems with earlier versions of the preferential right to renew statute, the current version requires that the renewing leaseholder match any competing bid and therefore approximates market value."

At the end of the deliberations, the Wyoming Supreme Court reached the following conclusion:[169]

> "The lands granted to the State of Wyoming by Congress upon the State's admission were not conveyed subject to a federal trust, nor did the people of Wyoming constitutionally impose a trust on those lands. However, the Legislature has appropriately exercised its authority under the Act of Admission and Constitution to declare those lands subject to a trust. The legislature, concurrently with the establishment of that trust, provided that incumbent leaseholders of the state lands would

168 Ibid., p.14.

169 Ibid.

> have a preference in renewing their lease. Riedel failed to prove that such preference violates any fiduciary or constitutional constraints on the State's management of trust lands, and the district court's grant of defendants' motion to dismiss is therefore affirmed."

There is one fundamental issue that this Court decision failed to consider and that is: "In either the sale or leasing of state lands, how does the process possibly 'approximate market value,' if a qualified bidder is discouraged from submitting a bid because he knows his bid will simply be matched by the existing lessee?" The leaseholder should be required to bid along with everyone else, but the law enables the one person who has the greatest interest in leasing the land to sit idly; he does not need to match any competing bid because no one else will submit one.

I am sure that I'm not the first to disagree with a court decision. I thought then and continue to believe now that the 1997 legislation was deliberately designed to cloud the issue of the Constitution's mandated trust responsibilities. The establishment of a sacred trust occurred in Wyoming in the same manner as it occurred in all of the other land grant states, and that is when the Federal Government granted and the states accepted Sections 16 and 32 for the exclusive benefit of public schools. The 1997 Legislation and subsequent Supreme Court decision discreetly substituted a statutory trust for the Constitutional trust. Unfortunately, the statutory trust can be manipulated for the benefit of others.

Mr. Riedle was represented in this case by former Wyoming State Senator and former Wyoming Attorney General Steve Freudenthal of the firm Freudenthal, Salzburg & Bonds, P.C. Having served in these previous positions for years, Steve was intimately familiar with the Constitution, Act of Admission, and Wyoming statutes. Few in Wyoming are more familiar with the issues involved in these proceedings. Others will have to judge whether or not these deliberations were free from political persuasion. I, for one, think they were not. As one reviews the record, a number of incidents occurred which suggest a strategy was developed to eliminate the constitutional trust responsibility regarding our state lands:

1. January, 1995 - The fact that the school lands were trust lands was disputed only after a new Governor assumed office.
2. July, 1995 - the new Director of State Lands, declared there was no constitutional mandate to maximize revenue.[170]
3. July, 1995 – the new Wyoming Attorney General opines that the Board has "broad discretion to set fees" on "as near an equitable basis as possible."[171]
4. September, 1995 - the Wyoming Livestock Roundup accused the State Auditor of "misunderstanding" the state constitution.[172]
5. May, 1996 – the Wyoming Livestock Roundup accused the State Auditor of having a "highly disputed interpretation of the Wyoming constitution".[173]
6. October, 1998 – State Superintendent of Public Instruction said maximizing income was an "interpretation issue" and

170 "Grazing Fees, Education Linked," *Casper Star-Tribune*, Ibid., p.A1.

171 "Land Board Sets '96 Grazing Fee," Ibid.

172 "Listening to the Western Rangeland Fugue," *Casper Star-Tribune*, Doug Cooper, September 21, 1995.

173 "State Lands Panel Holds First Meeting," Ibid.

"... what I am about is determining long-term policies that are fair to everyone . . . ."[174]

7. October, 2001 - the District Court rules that state lands were indeed encumbered by a trust and the state had a fiduciary duty to manage the lands exclusively for the beneficiaries.[175]
8. June, 2003 – the Wyoming Supreme Court reverses the district court decision and declares that since the trust is created only by statute and not by either the constitution or the Act of Admission, there is no duty to maximize revenues.[176]

In voting on this issue was the Chief Justice simply voting to affirm what he had previously opined when he was the State's Attorney General? Should he have recused himself from these deliberations, given his earlier ruling of the so-called "discretionary clause" and the endorsement of grazing rentals being "fixed on as near an equitable basis as possible"? Should this matter be appealed to the United States Supreme Court? If it isn't, no one will ever know the answer to any of these questions. Sadly, the State will indeed continue the status quo for the benefit of existing leaseholders at the expense of the legitimate beneficiaries. Our in-state farmers and ranchers, who must compete with them, will have to continue to operate at a distinct disadvantage.

Although our efforts to help the small farmers and ranchers in Wyoming met with only limited success, we pressed on for other programs that would benefit the agriculture industry. In 1997, I had

[174] "Making the Most of Grazing Fees," *Casper Star-Tribune*, Deirdre Stoelzle, October 25, 1998, p.A1.

[175] Supreme Court of Wyoming, Riedel v. Anderson, Ibid.

[176] Ibid., p.14.

a bill drafted, entitled the "*Wyoming Agricultural Development Act*" which contained two major provisions.[177] First, it would authorize the State to take advantage of federal tax exempt bonds for beginning farmers or ranchers, enabling them to borrow up to $250,000 at interest rates as low as between 5.25 and 5.75 percent. At that time, agriculture loans were being written at interest rates between 7 and 9 percent. This lower rate would save first-time farmers and ranchers between $5,000 and $7,500 per year in interest expenses. This program[178] was authorized by the federal government in 1980 with the passage of legislation to create pilot programs in Georgia, Alabama, and Iowa. Activity in the program peaked in 1984 when it was widely used in 24 other states. When I proposed this program for Wyoming, the Iowa Agricultural Development Authority was recognized as having the longest continuously operating program with more than $190 million in outstanding loans. The Illinois Farm Development Authority was the next oldest operating program with more than $213 million in outstanding loans. Nonetheless, in spite of this demonstrated success of the program, it had never been authorized by the state legislature in Wyoming.

The second provision in the bill was designed to benefit existing agricultural operators by authorizing taxable bonds at lower interest rates of about 7 percent. At the time[179] there were over twelve hundred farmers and ranchers who were paying between 8 and 10 percent interest on loans totaling over $163 million to the State Farm Loan Office. By refinancing these loans at a lower interest rate of 7

---

[177] "Ferrari Wants Low-Interest Loans for Ag," *Casper Star-Tribune,* Joan Barron, December 7, 1997, p. A1.

[178] David G. Ferrari, Wyoming State Auditor, "Revenue Enhancement Issues," October 15, 1998, p.15.

[179] Ibid., p.18.

percent, the average annual savings for each borrower would have been around $1,300. Over a thirty year loan the total average savings would have amounted to roughly $40,000 and for a twenty year loan, the savings calculated to be approximately $24,000.

This program would benefit not only our ranchers and farmers but also the entire State by releasing the $163 million currently committed to agriculture loans for investment in equities which would yield a greater return to the state treasury. The state treasurer estimated this would amount to around $9 million in additional earnings per year. In order to get a good bond rating and thus a lower interest rate, the State would guarantee the bond payments using the Permanent Mineral Trust Fund. To protect this fund in the event of default, the State would accept farm or ranch real estate as collateral. State Treasurer Stan Smith endorsed the program. "I like it," he said. "I think it might be useful for the State and I endorse it."[180] He said any program that can get low interest loans to agricultural operators is beneficial.

The bill died in the Legislative Agriculture, Public Lands, and Water Resources Committee in the 1998 legislative session. There were a number of reasons for this and none had to do with the bill itself. The various agriculture associations did not voice support for this new financing idea. The Stock Growers, the Wool Growers, and the Farm Bureau Federation, as well as several legislators who were also state land lessees did not support the bill in spite of the fact that it would be a boost to their industry. This seemed to be further evidence that only the large member operators with state land leases were represented by these powerful lobbying groups.

---

[180] "State Treasurer Backs Ferrari's Agriculture Loan Program," *Casper Star-Tribune,* Joan Barron, December 9, 1997, p.A1.

Another problem in gaining support for the bill's passage was that many people who were not involved in agriculture felt that farmers and ranchers were already receiving too many government subsidies and other advantages, and they were opposed to any new program which would make available even further benefits to that industry.

Passage of the agriculture bonding bill was also stifled due in part to my efforts to get ethics legislation through the legislature in each of the previous four sessions. Although supported by most Democrats, many of my fellow Republicans in the legislature thought that Wyoming did not need the ethical guidance contained in the ethics bills. They were offended that anyone would suggest that their behavior might be viewed as anything but honorable. Their resistance to ethics legislation seemed to spill over onto the bonding bill. Still, others didn't understand bonding and thought the issue was too complicated. Failure of the legislature to authorize this program was another lost opportunity for our small farmers and ranchers who would have enjoyed substantial savings in interest costs.

On a more positive note, in 1995, the legislature adopted an early retirement plan for state government workers[181] designed to downsize state government and save money. It involved providing financial incentives for long-term employees to retire, resulting in vacating positions which could then either be eliminated or filled with new hires at a much lower rate of pay. The bill was patterned after a 1987 program[182] that we created while consulting on government efficiency. To be eligible, employees in either the

---

[181] "547 Wyo State Employees Take Early Retirement," *Casper Star-Tribune*, Joan Barron, November 21, 1996, p.A1.

[182] Dave Ferrari, Wyoming State Auditor, "State of Wyoming, 1995 Early Retirement Proposal," November 1, 1994.

executive or legislative branches must be at least 52 years old and had worked at least 18 years. The qualifications included staggered combinations of age and service, up to the age of 55 and over, with at least 15 years of service. The early retirees had to declare their intent to retire during a three-month window, between April 1 and June 30 of 1995. They would receive bonus pay of 20 percent of their current salary until they reached the age of 62 in addition to a monthly payment of $215 for medical insurance until they reached their 65th birthday. The logic was that at age 62 they would qualify for early Social Security benefits and at 65, for Medicare coverage. We had scoured the payrolls of all agencies and determined that over eleven hundred employees would qualify; and if only half participated, the state would save at least $34 million during its first eight years of operation. Another advantage of the program was that it would open opportunities for advancement for many employees who would be promoted to some of the vacated positions. One of the bill's provisions, inserted by the legislature, was that at least 10 percent of the vacated positions must remain vacant.

The bill easily passed the Wyoming House but met with stiffer resistance in the Senate.[183] "There is not an element of fairness in this bill," said Senate President Boyd Eddins, SD16, R-Smoot. He was referring to the fact that employees who were under 52 years of age but with far more than the 18 years of employment would not qualify for the program. Some of his constituents fell into that category. "This is a pretty sweet deal," declared Senator Hank Coe, SD18, R-Cody, suggesting the $215 per month allowed for health insurance was unprecedented. The bill also came under fire by

---

[183] "Early Retirement Bill Survives First Test," *Casper Star-Tribune*, Joan Barron, February 24, 1995, P.A1.

agency supervisors who would not themselves qualify but had people in their departments who would. They were worried that they could not carry on the work load if 10 percent of the vacated positions were to remain empty. They also objected to the creation of what they called a "brain drain" resulting from the departure of the more experienced and seasoned employees. Jerry Fox, the director of the Wyoming Retirement System, also expressed concerns that the early retirees would have a negative impact on the retirement system's actuarial soundness since so many would hit the system all at one time. In spite of these objections, the bill ultimately did pass the senate and become law. It was enthusiastically endorsed, of course, by those employees who would qualify. Ultimately, nearly half of those qualified accepted the incentive; and by the end of the first year, over $10 million was saved through lower payroll costs.[184]

By the time I left office at the end of 1998, the savings from the program had already exceeded the $34 million originally projected. In fact, the latest projections indicated a total savings of $65 million over the life of the program. I wrote an article for the *Government Finance Review* magazine describing Wyoming's program, entitled "Designing and evaluating early retirement programs: the state of Wyoming experience." It appeared in the February, 1999, issue of that national publication.[185] It was also given a "thumbs up" by the *Casper Star Tribune* on November 23, 1996. Since this offering as well as the 1987 version saved the State tens of millions of dollars, I said at the time that the program ought to be offered every seven

---

[184] "Early State Retirements Save Millions," *Wyoming Tribune-Eagle*, Tony Monterastelli, November 21, 1996.

[185] "Designing and Evaluating Early Retirement Programs: The State of Wyoming Experience," David G. Ferrari, Government Finance Review, February, 1999.

years. "Ferrari has the right idea," observed the *Star*.[186] That idea, however, has not been implemented in the last seventeen years.

In the early nineties, state government morale was "at a 15-to-20-year low," according to Phil Kiner, director of the Department of Administration.[187]. He blamed the Wyoming legislature as did members of Governor Sullivan's cabinet. Dennis Smyth, executive director of the Wyoming Public Employees Association, a union representing about 3,000 employees, also said the main reason for low morale was due to "the abuse employees take during the legislative session."[188] These arguments made sense. I recall early in my career, it was common for members of the legislature to proclaim that state employees "were lucky to have a job." This was usually in conjunction with their voting "no" on compensation increases for state workers. Such attitudes were fairly common from both the legislators as well as private sector people who generally considered government employees to be useless and unnecessary. At that time, the state had set up a task force to study employee compensation.[189] It was chaired by Senator Jim Geringer of Wheatland. One member of the study group, Mr. Hal Herron of Riverton, representing the private sector, said that people he talked to in Riverton told him to "get rid of half the state employees." Such negative comments do tend to take a toll on morale. Obviously, you can't get rid of government employees if you want your prisons guarded, clean air to breathe and safe water to drink, highways cleared of snow, hospitals

---

[186] "Saving Taxpayers Money," Thumbs Up, *Casper Star-Tribune*, November 23, 1996.

[187] "State Workers Need Consistent Pay Plan," *Casper Star-Tribune*, Joan Barron, June 17, 1993, p.A1.

[188] Ibid.

[189] Ibid.

staffed, school children taught, home fires extinguished, streets and highways patrolled, and other fairly desirable services to be rendered. Such thoughtless bantering probably makes for good politics, but it does nothing to improve morale or efficiency in government. In response to this problem, I crafted an employee incentive plan, patterned after private sector programs, which was designed to reduce government spending, improve employee efficiency, and increase employee morale and compensation.

The plan was called the *Wyoming Impro-share Plan.*[190] It was tied to employee evaluations and would have enabled employees to earn a bonus of up to $2,600 per year for saving money in their departments but only if they rated a grade three or above in their performance evaluations. State employees at the time were rated on a scale from one, unsatisfactory, to five, outstanding. Any savings or reduced spending resulting from employee suggestions or improvements would be shared on a 50-50 basis. Fifty percent would be saved by the government and fifty percent would be transferred into a pool to be distributed to those in the agency where the savings were generated. In spite of the plan's success in the private sector, it went nowhere in the legislature. Another opportunity lost, but it did exemplify how difficult it is to transform government into a more efficient operation. Not everyone agrees how to get there. I had implemented a similar plan for managers in our restaurant operations that proved effective. I believe that it would have also worked in state government.

In 1996, a Canadian company had asked the State Land Board to approve a 30-year easement across ten miles of state lands for its

---

[190] "Ferrari Proposes Bonus Plan," *Casper Star-Tribune*, Joan Barron, June 17, 1993, p.A1.

pipeline, Express Pipeline, which would run from Hardisty, Alberta to Casper. It would carry up to 172,000 barrels of crude oil per day from Canada.[191] The company was represented by Bill Thomson, a Cheyenne attorney, who assured the Board that the project would generate additional revenues to the state land trust. "There's a lot of money involved," he said. The company originally offered a payment of $70,000 plus an additional $640 per rod for state lands crossed. For the ten-mile line, this calculated to be somewhat over $2,000,000. In addition, the company would pay for all surface damages. Some Wyoming oil producers were adamantly opposed to the project on the grounds that it would negatively impact not only the demand for Wyoming oil but also the state's entire economy. In response to the Board's concerns, Express Pipeline upped its offer to $20 million, with $5 million to be paid in each of the first two years and up to $5 million for the third and fourth years. State Senator Bill Hawks, R-Casper, a Wyoming oil producer, opposed saying the pipeline could reduce mineral severance taxes, ad valorem taxes, and federal mineral royalties.[192] Karen Kennedy, also an independent oil producer, lobbyist, and frequent attendee at State Land Board meetings, was vehemently opposed to the project.[193] She said the pipeline, "literally affects everyone in Wyoming." "I would ask what about the producers and what about the people of Wyoming who work for the oil and gas industry," she said. On the other hand, there were those who supported the pipeline, including Frontier Refinery in Cheyenne. Representatives of that company said they would greatly benefit from the additional supply of crude

191 "Express Offers State $20 Million," *Casper Star-Tribune*, Joan Barron, June 7, 1996, p.A1.

192 Ibid., p.A14.

193 Ibid.

for their operation, and they didn't feel that the pipeline would have a depressing affect on the demand for Wyoming crude. The board ultimately approved the company's easement request. I asked for assurances that Wyoming producers could tie into the pipeline but these assurances did not appease our Wyoming producers, as they continued to express outrage that the Board had voted in favor of the project in spite of their opposition. It wasn't an easy decision, but in reflection, the right one for our state. None of the negative impacts predicted by the local oil producers occurred.

I was never really comfortable with the information received from lobbyists and others who make their living off the state's public lands. As the Express Pipeline discussions demonstrated, there is often less than accurate or helpful input. There was one notable exception, however. The setting of oil and gas royalty rates was always a contentious issue. Oil and gas producers and their hired guns were always arguing for lower rates. They claimed Wyoming's royalties, mineral severance tax rates, and allowable deductions from values were out of line when compared to other states. The consequence, they argued, was that our producers would simply move their efforts to other states where the rates were lower, and leave Wyoming with lower collections of royalties and taxes, fewer industry jobs, less income for our public schools and a damaged economy. In early 1996, the Board was asked to lower the state royalty rate on new oil and gas leases from the existing 16.75 percent to 12.5 percent.[194] All state leases would initially be offered at the higher rate; but if there were no takers, the rate would then be reduced in the hopes of attracting bidders. The argument was that

---

194 "Board Cuts State Oil & Gas Royalty Rates," *Casper Star-Tribune*, Chris Tollefson, March 8, 1996, p.A1.

the reduced rate would make marginal leases more attractive. Casper oil man and former State Senator Tom Stroock said he didn't believe that lower royalty rates would stimulate production. "Price," Stroock said, "is the determining factor in a company's decision to drill."[195] This, of course, was just the opposite of what the local producers and other industry lobbyists had professed in their many appearances before the board. Stroock suggested that the Board reduce the rate down to 10 percent for production from all new leases drilled within one year of the time the lease was auctioned. "People drill because the price justifies the cost. But take it down to 10 percent . . . to give it a fair test so that the results are conclusive," Stroock said. The Board approved the measure based entirely on Stroock's testimony.

I had known Tom Stroock for many years and had worked with him on several issues during my career in government while he was in the State Senate. While serving as Governor Hathaway's Budget Director, I had spent many long days with Tom, who at that time served on the Joint Appropriations Committee. I, along with other members of the budget division staff, presented the state budget to the committee and sat through its meetings with the state agencies while their budgets were presented and defended. Over the years, Senator Stroock and I developed a good working relationship. During the 1981 legislative session, after I had left the budget office and became deputy state auditor, Tom wanted a meeting with me and Jim Griffith, the State Auditor. Tom was concerned that Wyoming wasn't receiving the full amount due from royalties on mineral production on state lands. He was a royalty owner himself and had seen numerous instances where private royalty owners were cheated of royalty income from production

[195] Ibíd.

occurring on their lands. He sensed the same thing was probably happening to the State. There are a number of ways for a company to reduce the amount owed in royalties or taxes on oil and gas. Any overcharging of deductions against the value, such as transportation of the product from the wellhead to market, or under-reporting of actual production, or under-valuing of the fair market price of the product at the wellhead, would result in a reduction in the amount of royalties or taxes owed.

Stroock came down to Griffith's office and the three of us discussed his concerns. He wanted our office to look into the situation and wanted to know what resources and expertise would be required to get it done. Jim told him that it wasn't the state auditor's job to police revenue or tax collections; that was the job of the Wyoming Department of Revenue. He knew that, Tom said, but he wanted the state auditor to do it anyway. He asked me to put together some figures on how much it would cost to hire a couple of auditors and get the program going. He then convinced the legislature to appropriate the necessary funds. We hired a couple of auditors experienced in oil and gas production accounting. One, Steve Wilson, came from the state of New Mexico land office and the second, Randy Fetterolf, from Mobil Oil. Their success was immediate and their audit findings of unpaid royalties and taxes greatly exceeded the cost of the program. It was obvious that the audit effort would pay for itself many times over. It began as an audit of mineral production on State lands, but it soon became clear that the major benefit from such an effort would be from the federal lands within our borders. Because of the state auditor's position on the State Land Commission, and our close relationship with Governor Herschler, we were able to gain access to records in the Land Office, the Department of Revenue, and the Wyoming Oil and

Gas Conservation Commission. Without this access, auditing of the production activity on our State lands would not have been possible. Getting this same authority to audit federal mineral production would be much more difficult, but Griffith had a plan which likely would not have worked anywhere in the world except in Wyoming.

At the time, James G. Watt was Secretary of the Interior. He had been appointed by President Reagan[196]and served in that position from January 23, 1981, until November 8, 1983. As was Griffith, he was born in Lusk, Wyoming, and the two Jims had known each other all of their lives. They weren't close and Griffith hadn't seen Watt for several years. But, on September 11th, some seven months following Watt's assumption as head of Interior, he was to return to Wyoming and along with State Republican Chairman Ed Witzenburger and U.S. Senator Alan Simpson, he and Griffith would fly from Gillette to Worland and then to Casper in a small plane.[197] Griffith would wait his turn to bend Watt's ear on the need for auditing mineral royalties while Simpson appealed to Watt not to allow drilling in the Washakie Wilderness area. Griffith later said that he had only twenty-three minutes to convince Watt to authorize the Department of Interior to enter into a joint audit agreement with the State. That agreement was announced in Casper on that same day and broadcast on the evening news throughout the country. It was not welcomed by the federal bureaucrats who would be affected by it.[198]

The United States Geological Survey is a bureau of the Interior Department. Its headquarters are in Reston, Virginia, with major

---

196 http://en.wikipedia.org/wiki/James_G._Watt.

197 James B. Griffith, *A Funny Thing Happened on the way to the Wyoming Capitol*, 1988, p.82.

198 Ibíd., p.83.

offices in Lakewood, Colorado, and Menlo Park, California.[199] The Lakewood office had field offices located in the federal office building in Casper, and it was there where the records of federal mineral production and royalty accounting resided. The USGS is the sole scientific agency of the Department of Interior with four major science disciplines, including biology, geography, geology, and hydrology. It was created by an act of Congress on March 3, 1879, and was charged with the "classification of public lands, and examination of the geological structure, mineral resources, and products of the national domain."[200] In view of this mission and the scientific focus of the agency, it is understandable why accounting and finances were not a priority in the USGS. The agreement reached between Griffith and Watt was that they would each have two auditors assigned to the joint-audit effort. Working together they were to determine the extent to which federal mineral royalties were accurately collected, accounted for, and paid to the state and federal governments. From the outset, getting access to the federal records and cooperation from the USGS proved difficult. Our federal partners were not enjoying this new partnership. In spite of these difficulties, millions of dollars in underpayments in royalties were indentified and these findings along with years of other questionable incidents in the USGS added to a national concern about the management of the federal mineral royalties program.

Several months before our meeting with Senator Stroock when the audit program was conceived, an incident occurred on the Wind River Indian Reservation which was described in an article written by Howard Kohn. The article, entitled, "The Lawman Who

---

[199] http://en.wikipedia.org/wiki/United_States_Geological_Survey.

[200] Ibid.

Corralled the Oil Rustlers," appeared in *Reader's Digest* in August, 1984.[201] The lawman Mr. Kohn described was Charles Thomas who was an inspector for the USGS. According to the article, one of his responsibilities was to police the oil fields on the Reservation. As he was finishing his day on June 11, 1980, and during his drive home that evening, he met an oil tanker departing the Reservation. Curious, Thomas flashed his headlights and signaled the truck to pull over. The driver indicated he was hauling sludge oil, but when asked for his "run ticket," the driver could not produce one. The run ticket, completed by the purchaser, is used to show who owns the oil being transported; and upon closer inspection, Thomas discovered that high-grade crude oil was being transported.[202] He reported the incident to his superiors at the Interior Department and upon further investigation four men were charged with oil theft and all pleaded guilty.[203] Two were convicted of stealing oil from the Reservation, based in part upon Thomas' investigations where he found other evidence that oil was being stolen. Pipes used to transport oil deliberately by-passed measurement meters and pump seals were missing. Following his report of these findings, according to the article, he began receiving phone threats. In response to these threats, the Interior Department shipped him off to Alaska. However, the Shoshoni Tribe wanted him back so they hired him as an independent contractor. Shortly after his return, a dead snake was placed on his doorstep and a bullet was shot through a window

---

201 "The Lawman Who Corralled the Oil Rustlers," *Reader's Digest*, Howard Kohn, August, 1984.

202 http://www/dickshovel.com/rogue.html, p.8.

203 "*Fiscal Accountability: Nation's Energy Resources*," Commission of Fiscal Accountability of the Nation's Energy Resources, David Linowes, Chairman, January, 1982.

of his house, nearly hitting his wife. Later she was run off the road by a truck, and on the same day he barely avoided a collision with a tanker truck.[204] Coincidents? Perhaps.

There had been a number of issues and problems with the USGS over the years. Oil thieves had been caught and convicted in Oklahoma, New Mexico, and Kern County, California.[205] Some of the oil stolen in these cases was produced on federal lands. Between 1959 and 1981, the GAO had issued six different reports criticizing management of the royalty collection effort. One report suggested that royalty underpayments were amounting to as much as 10 percent. In 1981, as we were getting up and running, criticism of the USGS program was gaining national attention.[206] Three articles appeared in the *Los Angeles Times*; two in the *New York Times*; and one in the *Washington Post*. On April 12th, *60 Minutes* ran a story on the problems as well. The media accused the federal government of mismanaging the program and accused the oil and gas industry of being corrupt and greedy. Calls for reform of the program were coming from the media, the states, the Indians, and many in Congress. This ultimately led to Secretary of the Interior Watt establishing a committee to look into the ongoing allegations. The Linowes Commission was established on

---

204 Op. cit., http://www.dickshovel.com, p.8.

205 Op. cit., David Linowes, "*Fiscal Accountability: Nation's Energy Resources*," p.27.

206 See, e.g., *Los Angeles Times*, Jan. 12, 1981, sec.4, p.1; *Los Angeles Times*, Jan.15, 1981, sec.4, p.1; *Washington Post*, Feb.1, 1981,p.A17; *Los Angeles Times*, Mar. 21, 1981, sec.3, p.18; *New York Times*, Apr. 4,1981,p.7; CBS News, *60 Minutes*, vol. XIII, no.30, April 12,1981; *New York Times*, April 15,1981, p.A26.

July 8, 1981.[207] Named after its chairman, David Linowes, who was a professor of political economy and public policy and senior adviser to the Institute of Government and Public Affairs at the University of Illinois,[208] the Commission issued its report some six months later. The report, "*Fiscal Accountability of the Nation's Energy Resources,*" was issued on January 21, 1982. According to the report, there were severe shortcomings in the USGA royalty management program. The major findings were:[209] "1) the USGS did not verify data reported by companies, 2) the lease account records were so unreliable that the agency often did not know which companies had paid the royalties owed and which had not, 3) late payments were common, 4) lessee's records were seldom audited or critically reviewed, and 5) penalties for underpayment scarcely existed." The report concluded that "because the USGS recordkeeping was in such disarray, the Commission could not determine the exact amount of underpayments.[210] The results of individual audits suggested, however, that hundreds of millions of dollars (7-10 percent of annual obligations) went uncollected every year." These findings reflected some of the information offered to the Commission by Griffith and Fetterolf when they testified before it.

Interior Secretary Watt had been briefed throughout the Commission's proceedings and in response to these briefings and his own conviction that large royalty losses were going undetected, on January 19, 1982, he replaced the USGS Conservation Division with

---

[207] Op. cit., David Linowes, "*Fiscal Accountability: Nation's Energy Resources,*" p.xi.

[208] http://epic.org/privacy/workplace/linowesPR.html.

[209] Op. cit., David Linowes, "*Fiscal Accountability: Nation's Energy Resources*", p.15.

[210] Ibid., p.xv.

the Minerals Management Services (MMS).[211] Recognizing this lack of emphasis on accounting in a scientific organization, he took this action before the Linowes' Commission Report was even released.

The need for an audit of oil and gas royalties in Wyoming and other states had been clearly proven, especially in light of the obvious incompetence of the MMS. The program we put together was the first of its kind in the country and in the years that followed was replicated in all of the mineral producing states with mineral production on federal lands. Our program was also important, along with other national influences, in leading to Secretary Watt creating the controversial and powerful agency in the Federal government–the Minerals Management Services agency within the Department of the Interior.

Griffith and Stroock deserve all of the credit for this very effective effort which has generated hundreds of millions of dollars for Wyoming and the other states; Stroock for the idea and Griffith for carrying it out.

Ambassador Stroock was a true statesman; someone who put the State's and the Country's interests ahead of his own and ahead of his party, which he served as state chairman from 1975 to 1978. He served five terms in the Wyoming Senate and later served as United States Ambassador to Guatemala under President George H. W. Bush. His achievements in life are well documented and his honesty and integrity were beyond question. He was the only spokesman from the mineral industry whom I trusted unequivocally. When he testified before the Land Board, I knew we could take it to the bank. The State lost a great patriot when he died on December 14, 2009.

---

211 http://wikipedia.org/wiki/Bureau_of_Ocean_Energy_Management_

# CHAPTER ELEVEN

# "Trying to Look Ethical"

The need for ethics legislation in Wyoming was obvious not only in regards to state lands issues but also in many other areas of government. For several years since assuming office, I had drafted legislation for Wyoming using the "model legislation" written by the Council of State Legislators.[212] I had found sponsors to introduce the bills, only to see them die, year after year, in the legislature. Wyoming was one of only two of the fifty states without an ethics law.[213] Not all of the other states had adopted the council's recommendations, but all had ethics legislation of some form. There were a number of issues that the ethics legislation would address, but the more important provisions were:

- Defining what a conflict of interest is and when one occurs, how it should be handled.

---

212 *Council on Governmental Ethics Laws (COGEL)*, Council of State Legislatures, September, 1991.

213 "New, Revised Ethics Bill Surfaces in House," *Casper Star-Tribune,* Joan Barron, February 3, 1995, p.B3.

- Prohibiting, for one year, any public sector official or employee in Wyoming from accepting a job or position with a company that the employee or official regulated while employed by the government entity.
- Prohibiting for one year, any public sector official or employee in Wyoming from accepting a job or position with a company with which the employee or official negotiated a contract.
- Prohibiting, for one year, a state legislator from lobbying the legislature after leaving elective office.
- Prohibiting state or local employees from using public facilities, equipment, or other resources for personal gain.
- Prohibiting legislators and other public sector employees from accepting anything of value, other than a cup of coffee, from lobbyists that appear before the legislature or other governing body or from companies that the official or employee regulates.

Over the years, there were a number of outstanding legislators who sponsored the legislation. In 1995, Senator Charles Scott was the main sponsor and he said he wasn't too surprised that the bill went down by a vote of 5-0 in the House Travel, Recreation and Wildlife Committee. "The good old boys in the legislature don't want to see anything changed," he said.[214] The League of Women Voters consistently supported ethics legislation each year, but others were opposed for a variety of reasons: some legitimate, some not. For example, one of the most unbelievable arguments against it was

---

214 "Ethics Bill Affecting Public Employees, Officials Killed," *Casper Star-Tribune*, Joan Barron, January 27, 1995, p.B1.

expressed by the Wyoming Association of Municipalities (WAM). A spokesman for that group, Carl Classen, said the legislation would be a "logistical nightmare," suggesting that public officials would be prohibited from using public libraries, driving on public streets, or using state or national forests for recreation.[215] Representative Cale Case, HD54, R-Lander, one of the bill sponsors, responded, "WAM deliberately overreacted to the bill." Representative Cris Boswell, HD39, D-Green River, was angered by Classen's comments, saying, "WAM apparently found an attorney that was willing to offer outrageous scenarios of what might occur." Representative Wendy Barker, HD45, D-Laramie said the bill was a slap at public employees.[216] "We don't pay them. We don't compensate them. We don't value them," Barker said. "Now we're going to say they're not ethical." Case responded that the employees themselves, "think this is overdue." District Attorney Jon Forward spoke against the bill saying he would need more staff to handle the increased number of prosecutions if the bill passes.

The conflict-of-interest provision was opposed by a number of legislators, but there were many situations where clarification would be helpful. Over the years, there have been examples of doctors voting for or against health care reform that could directly affect their income; truckers voting against raising the gas tax; oil, gas, and other mineral producers voting to cut taxes on minerals; bankers voting on banking regulations; and, the most common, ranchers with grazing leases voting for or against legislation involving state land sales or leasing issues that would directly affect their financial interests. Examples in the executive branch had been just as plentiful.

---

[215] "Panel Dismisses Ethics Measure," *Wyoming Tribune-Eagle*, Brett Martel, January 29, 1996.

[216] Op. cit., "New Revised Ethics Bill Surfaces in House," p.B3.

There was a state inspector who ran a private business which remedied the irregularities he found on his job.[217] The most obvious case was that of the state land director recommending action to the State Land Board which would directly affect the some 9,000 acres of state land he leased. In another case,[218] an agency manager hired a consultant for five consecutive years without allowing any other company to bid on the contract. One year she gave that consultant a bonus of $38,000 even though the contract did not call for it. Finally, one year later she went to work for that contractor. There was another situation where an advisory board conducted contract reviews for several companies doing business with the state.[219] One week prior to the review, one company took the entire board to Denver for a Colorado Rockies game. Wining and dining the board may not have resulted in a contract renewal, but it certainly didn't hurt. It's obvious the company wasn't providing this entertainment simply out of friendship. Though it is surprising how many elected officials and public employees truly believe they are close friends with lobbyists and others who are simply trying to do business with the government. They value the official's friendship because it is valuable.

At that time under Wyoming statutes, none of these legislative or executive examples were a violation of law, but all were improper. It's clear why someone who wants to engage in such behavior would not want legislation identifying it as illegal. One legislator told the Wyoming League of Women Voters he was against any

---

[217] Op., cit., "Ethics Bill Affecting Employees, Officials Killed," p.B1.

[218] "Good Government; State Auditor has Learned to Give and Take," *Wyoming Tribune-Eagle*, Editorial, November 17, 1996, pA10,

[219] "Ferrari Optimistic about New Ethics Bill," *Casper Star-Tribune*, Chris Tollefson, August 27, 1996, p.A8.

ethics legislation.[220] "You cannot legislate ethics," Representative Jim Hageman, R-Ft. Laramie, told them. "If you do, ethics then becomes anything you can get by with." Senator Bill Barton said the bill was an unnecessary intrusion into the lives of elected officials who are private citizens 320 days out of the year.[221] "Here we're being asked to put additional covenants on our behavior just because we're doing what the people in our area elected us to do," he said. Representative Les Bowron, HD57, R-Casper,[222] said the ethics legislation "seems to be a bit heavy-handed." He made an argument similar to that made by Senator Barton, questioning why a legislator who spends only 40 days a year in session should be restricted by the bill. "If I should lose my employment, then I should have to store my experience for a year and not be able to feed my family?" he asked.

Certainly, not all legislators were opposed to the idea of ethics legislation. Some strongly endorsed it, such as Senator Rae Lynn Job, D-12, Rock Springs.[223] She suggested that politicians should follow a higher standard of conduct, even if it is inconvenient, in order to restore the public's trust in government. "History is full of leaders who set the bar of conduct and expectation higher for themselves," she said. Others, such as Representative Cale Case, Senator Carroll Miller, R-Shell, and Senator Charlie Scott, proudly put their names on the line to sponsor such legislation, knowing it would be a tough

---

220 "Ferrari Optimistic on Ethics Bill Passage," *Casper Star-Tribune*, Kerry Drake, November 10, 1996, p.B1.

221 "Panel Dives into Ethics Bill," *Wyoming Tribune-Eagle*, Tony Monterastelli, November, 1996.

222 "Ferrari Pushes Public Ethics Law," *Casper Star-Tribune*, Kerry Drake, June 1, 1995, p.A1.

223 Op. cit., "Panel Dives into Ethics Bill,".

sell and knowing in some cases their colleagues would be angered and take it personally.

During the 1995 legislative session, Joan Barron in her monthly column in the *Casper Star-Tribune* discussed the death of the ethics bill as follows:[224]

> "This was a fairly tough bill and perished unloved like its predecessors. The reaction has been the same every time some brave lawmaker has sponsored a conflict of interest or other type of proposed law dealing with these touchy issues. In the past legislators have fretted over whether they would be penalized for accepting such perks as a free lunch from a lobbyist if a bill passed. As a result, the bill didn't pass. The benefit from these debates has been a heightened sensitivity among lawmakers about the propriety of accepting freebies or voting on bills that could benefit their businesses or themselves."

During the 1996 legislative session, three bills had failed. One involved ethics, another lobbyist disclosure, and the third, conflicts of interest for governmental treasury investors. Failure of these bills caused outrage in the press and among those who had worked long and hard on the issue. On March 26, 1996, the *Wyoming Tribune-Eagle* editorial made several observations:[225]

---

224 "Can't Cope with Ethics Issues," *Casper Star-Tribune*, Joan Barron, March 29, 1995, p.A1.

225 "Good Government; State Lawmakers are Ignoring this Issue," *Wyoming Tribune-Eagle*, Editorial, March 26, 1996.

> "What remains to be seen is whether Ferrari's fellow Republican lawmakers believe as strongly as he does in good government legislation. If this past session is any indication of solons' interest in such legislation, Ferrari has a laborious task ahead of him. . . . Those against the bill claim Wyoming doesn't have an ethics problem. They are mistaken! Our state has its share of questionable activities. . . . Wyoming's population is sparse, but it is not so small that we can operate on a handshake. Placing government on the honor system is naïve.
>
> "State Auditor Dave Ferrari is providing the Wyoming Legislature with much of the groundwork needed to pass a good government bill. It would be inexcusably negligent of lawmakers to refuse to act on Ferrari's proposals. The time has come for a good government bill in Wyoming."

In a later editorial, on November 17 of that same year, the *Tribune-Eagle* said:[226] "Ferrari has a passion for good government; it's unfortunate his fellow Republicans, who have a majority in the Wyoming legislature, don't carry that same torch."

But these pronouncements apparently had no effect. "I think it's a mistake to judge Wyoming compared to other states; I think we're a small enough state," said Senator Bob Grieve R-11, Rawlins. Grieve, Senate President, had let the lobbyist bill die on general file

---

[226] Op. cit., "Good Government; State Auditor has Learned to Give and Take," p.A10.

on the last day. "There are not many secrets in this state, and we try to be public,"[227] he said.

After numerous failed attempts to get an ethics bill passed by our legislature, I decided to try a different approach. The government reorganization bills we successfully guided through the legislature in the early 1990's were crafted by committees after months of study and several public hearings and much public input. Perhaps a task force consisting of legislators, public officials, and private citizens could have similar success with ethics legislation. It was worth a try. Instead of being appointed by the governor, members would be selected and appointed by the state auditor. We had no trouble finding people who wanted to participate.

The task force we put together consisted of representatives from the League of Women Voters; the Wyoming Public Employees Association; Senator Carroll Miller, chairman of the Senate Corporations Committee; Representative Cale Case, chairman of the House Corporations Committee; David Resnik, director of the Center for the Advancement of Ethics at the University of Wyoming; John Fanos, a former state senator and Uinta County Commissioner; Curt Kaiser, Cheyenne investment broker; and Flip McConnaughey, Laramie City Manager. We held public hearings throughout the state and after several months constructed legislation which we thought would satisfy the opponents who had argued against the idea for the last several years. It was called the *Public Employees and Officials Ethics Ac*, and was introduced in the 1997 legislature. The bill was sponsored by the corporations committee of each house. It was a watered-down version of earlier attempts, having been reduced

---

[227] "Government Bills Take a Beating," *Wyoming Tribune-Eagle*, Brett Martel, March 25, 1996.

from 28 pages to only 11. Representative Case dubbed it "ethics light."[228]

The ethics bill died on general file without any discussion or debate.[229] Senate President Bob Grieve, R-Savory, and Majority Floor Leader Jim Twiford, R-Douglas, were opposed to the bill. Twiford said that only a few people wanted it, naming me and the League of Women Voters. No senate member, he said, wanted the ethics bill brought to the floor. Of members who opposed the bill, he said, "They won't speak freely in front of the press. If the senate kills it, the senate gets a black eye," he said. "Right now, I'm the only one who will get the black eye."[230] So, Mr. Twiford let the bill die. His logic seemed absolutely flawed. If it was indeed bad legislation, why would anyone who voted against it get a "black eye"? Why wouldn't Twiford bring it to the floor for discussion? My push for dealing with conflicts of interest was very unpopular among legislators, and any attempt to change the way government operated was met with resistance from those in charge, apparently viewing it as a personal attack. I was surprised there was little respect for the efforts made by members of the task force and for the League of Women Voters itself. The senate leaders knew the League's position on the bill. In fact, in a letter to the editor on January 22, 1997, the League President, Rosemary Shockley of Powell, said the ethics bill "will be one of the most important pieces of legislation considered this year."[231] She

---

228 "Task Force Opts for 'Ethics Light' Bill," *Casper Star-Tribune*, Joan Barron, September 7, 1996, p.A1.

229 "Ethics Bill Dies without Discussion," *Casper Star*-Tribune, Joan Barron and Jason Marsden, February 7, 1997, p.A1.

230 Ibid., pp.A1 and A12.

231 Letter to the Editor, *Casper Star-Tribune*, "The Voting Public will be watching," Rosemary Shockley, President, Wyoming State League of Women Voters, Powell, Wyo., January 22, 1997.

was right. It was indeed important. It was important that it be killed before anyone could discuss it and before it changed the way our leaders in the legislature conduct the public's business.

Following these defeats, it was obvious that we would have no success getting ethics legislation passed through the legislature, so a statewide effort to gather signatures for a ballot initiative was undertaken. In order to get the *Wyoming Ethics in Government Initiative* on the ballot we needed to collect 32,377 signatures, which represented 15 percent of the number of ballots cast in the preceding gubernatorial election.[232] Linda Stoval of Casper headed up the effort and in spite of several months of fundraising and soliciting volunteers to gather signatures, we fell short of gathering a sufficient number of signatures prior to the start of the 1998 legislative session. We received help from hundreds of people throughout the state, including Ambassador Stroock and United States Senator Alan Simpson, who had sent a check for $10,000 to assist in the effort. In spite of these efforts, we failed to qualify the initiative in time for the 1998 Session. However, in response to the initiative, the legislature finally passed its own version of ethics legislation in 1998, *Title 9, Chapter 13*. Critics of this legislation argued it was adopted simply to avoid the more restrictive language contained in the initiative.

The law governing initiatives gives the legislature a chance to pass a law substantially the same as the initiative and if it fails to act, then the initiative goes on the next general election ballot. Passage of the law would render the initiative unnecessary because there would already be an ethics law on the books. It appeared this strategy worked. I asked Attorney General Bill Hill to determine if

232 http://ballotpedia.org/wiki/index.php/Wyoming_Ethics_in_Government_Initiative, 1997.

the law passed was substantially the same as the ballot initiative.[233] Hill refused to make the comparison since our initiative lacked the required number of signatures. "Without the signatures, no petition is filed," he said. "What the Legislature did this time wasn't in response to a successful initiative," he concluded. From a legal standpoint, Hill was no doubt right. But, realistically, the legislature was responding to the initiative. A number of people were concerned the initiative might be successful. At one point during the process, the state auditor's office received a call inquiring about the status of the initiative and questioning whether or not we expected to gather the required signatures. The caller refused to identify herself, and at that time we didn't have "Caller ID," but the "reverse look-up" feature indicated the call originated in Casper at the offices of one of the largest companies in Wyoming and one of the largest contributors to Republican candidates throughout the state running for legislative or statewide public offices.

The governor implemented a *Code of Ethics* on December 3, 1997, for the executive branch of state government through an executive order. Both this *Code* and the new ethics law had some elements contained in the ethics initiative, but neither equaled the model legislation recommended by the Council of State Governments. As a result, the legislature still allows members to vote on issues that affect their personal financial interests; legislators can still immediately begin lobbying the Legislature once they have left elective office; members of the executive branch can still immediately accept employment with any company they had previously regulated; they can still accept employment from companies with whom they

---

233 "Hill says Comparison of Ethics Legislation, Initiative Premature," *Casper Star-Tribune*, Joan Barron, 1998, p.A1.

have negotiated contracts; and, all can continue to be wined and dined by lobbyists, companies and others with whom they do the government's business. But Wyoming is no longer the only state in the nation without legislation governing the behavior of its officials and employees. And these actions by the Governor and legislature do specifically address conflicts of interest and the acceptance of gifts and things of value. The issues are no longer politely ignored as if they didn't exist and that is an improvement for the people of Wyoming.

Although our efforts did not result in particularly effective ethics legislation on the books of Wyoming, it is clear that as a result of our work, greater awareness was brought to questionable activities that had gone on quietly for years. It is never pleasant to highlight the dishonorable actions of a few which directly tarnishes the honorable behavior of others. If anyone gets a "black eye," it isn't because they're trying to do the right thing. It's because they are doing quite the opposite.

The consequences of our policymakers opposition to the Wyoming Public Employees and Officials Ethics Act surfaced some fifteen years later when early in 2012 the Center for Public Integrity, Public Radio International and Global Integrity reported its findings on a new study of all 50 statehouses.[234] Researchers examined a total of 330 "corruption risk indicators" across 14 categories. Sadly, Wyoming was one of only eight states receiving an "F" grade, ranking 48th out of 50 among the states. We earned an "F" for "ethics enforcement agencies," "political financing," "lobbying disclosure," "public access to information," executive accountability,"

[234] http://foxnews.com/politics/2012/03/19study-state-governments-at-high-risk-for-corruption.

and "judicial accountability". We soared to a "D-" in our grade for "legislative accountability."[235] Caitlin Ginley, project manager of the study said, "In every state, there's room to improve the ethics laws, the level of transparency on government proceedings, the disclosure of information, and--most importantly--the oversight of these laws. One of the major findings was that even when ethics laws are passed, they are difficult to enforce and lack meaningful consequences for violators."

I was often criticized throughout my two terms as state auditor by the special interests, including the agricultural, oil and gas, and liquor dealer lobbyists. I figured this probably meant that I was doing something right. I was also criticized by some of my fellow Republicans in the Wyoming legislature. This was a disappointment, but, of course, anyone arguing against good government is probably on the wrong side of the issue. I was generally supported by our two major newspapers, the *Casper Star-Tribune* and the *Wyoming Tribune-Eagle*, and by the League of Women Voters, the Wyoming Public Employees Association, and the Wyoming Education Association. Again, this probably indicates that my positions were largely on the right track. I was a frequent speaker at meetings of the League of Women Voters and was named an honorary lifetime member by the Wyoming Education Association. The greatest honor of course is that bestowed on you by someone who seeks nothing in return and whose opinion you respect. In her Letter to the Editor of the *Casper Star*, Barbara Parsons of Rawlins and a former member of the Public Lands Task Force, on March 1, 1997 opined:[236]

---

[235] http://www.stateintegrity.org/wyoming,wyomingcorruptionrisk reportcard.

[236] Letter to the Editor, *Casper Star-Tribune*, "No Conflict There," Barbara Parsons, Rawlins, Wyo., March 11, 1997.

> "I want to take this opportunity to thank State Auditor Dave Ferrari for his continuing crusade to implement a high standard of ethics in State government. Although I knew of Mr. Ferrari, it wasn't until I was monitoring the state land board meetings a few years ago that I had an opportunity to see him in action. Mr. Ferrari is a rather quiet, unassuming man for a politician. Behind that facade, though, he's waged a long and intense battle for integrity in government. For years he's documented and promoted ways to more efficiently and ethically conduct state business. Wyoming is fortunate to have him as a public servant."

I have labeled this chapter "Trying to look Ethical" in remonstrance of an article which appeared in the December 6, 1997, *Wyoming Livestock Roundup.*[237] The author was lambasting John Jolley of the *Grassroots Advocate*, members of the Land Board, and the *Casper Star-Tribune.* He accused Diana Ohman of "trying to ride the state land controversy into the governor's mansion," the *Star-Tribune* of "wanting to embarrass a republican administration," and he mocked me as "trying to look ethical."

Pushing for ethics in government was never about me. It was really about him and the other lobbyists and special interests who shared his views.

---

[237] "Barbed Wire," *Wyoming Livestock Roundup*, Doug Cooper, December 6, 1997.

# CHAPTER TWELVE

## Time to Go

Early in 1998, a number of Republicans wanted me to challenge for the governor's office. Democrats, too, wanted someone to send Governor Geringer home after his first term, and I considered it for a time. I was discouraged from entering the contest by state party leaders as the last thing they wanted to see was an incumbent challenged in their own party. It was about ten o'clock one Friday night when my home phone rang. On the other end of the line was an official of the state Republican party. "I want to talk to you about the governor's race," she said. "Are you going to run?" I was exploring the possibility, I said, but haven't made any decision yet. "Well, I am just telling you not to do it," she threatened. I knew she was expressing more than her own opinion, as it was clear she spoke for the inner circle of the party and for the state chairman who called most of the shots. I told the message-bearer that I wasn't particularly surprised or concerned that they might not want to see me run.

I had the informal support of the Wyoming Education Association and the Wyoming Public Employees Association, both powerful players in Wyoming politics, but knew if I ran I would be going up against the deep pockets of the various special interests.

They weren't particularly satisfied with the Governor, but they would remain loyal to him. The agriculture leaseholders would never forgive me for advocating state land management reform and the Republican legislators were still steaming from having to deal with the ethics initiative. As I reflected on the possibility of a run for governor, I was reminded of a conversation I had with former Governor Hathaway. "Davey, if you ever want to run for higher office you need to re-think your position on these land issues," he said. "You simply can't win the governor's race without the support of agriculture." At the time I had no thoughts of running for a higher office and although I greatly respected Stan's opinion, I thought he was probably wrong on this one. I figured I had the support of most agriculture families in Wyoming, except those few hundred with state grazing leases.

After giving it some thought, the decision wasn't particularly difficult. I really had no interest in becoming governor. I had worked for and with the last four Wyoming governors and was familiar with the issues they faced and the sacrifices involved in serving in the highest office in the state. The last seven years serving as state auditor had its rewards but it also had its moments of disappointment. The governor's job would be much of the same and then some. So, on February 6, 1998, at a little before eight o'clock that morning I walked down the hall to the governor's office and told Geringer that I would not oppose him in the primary election that year. The decision of whether or not to run for a third term for state auditor had not yet been made.

During the latter weeks of March of that election year there was a lot of speculation about who would be running and for what statewide offices. State Treasurer Stan Smith was retiring after a long and distinguished career; Diana hadn't said if she would seek a second term as Secretary of State; and, I hadn't yet reached my decision to leave state government. Retiring Senate President Bob Grieve had indicated an interest in running for either state treasurer or state auditor, but in a telephone conversation, indicated to me he would not run for auditor if I was going to run again. I told him that in all likelihood I would not be running, but encouraged him to jump in whether I did or not. Former Department of Commerce Director Max Maxfield, who had ran and lost in the Republican primary for Secretary of State four years earlier was anxious to run for Auditor, but he, too, said he would not run against me. I told both Grieve and Maxfield that I would make a decision by the middle of April.

On Tuesday, March 31, 1998, Diana announced that she would not seek re-election to the Secretary of State position.[238] She said she had no specific future plans but thought it was time to move on. In response to a question from the press, she indicated that her disagreements with others on the State Land Board, primarily the Governor, played a small role in her decision. "It's a factor but it's only one of lots of things that a guy thinks about," she said. "There have been a lot of good things; these four years have been fun, so I can't say it's been a negative experience. I just think it's time to move on," Ohman said.

Diana had also been urged to run for governor and said she did give it serious consideration. But, in the end, she was ready to do something else. I was saddened to think about the capitol building without Diana in it, but at the same time knew that I would not be there either. She and I were nearly always on the same side of the

---

238 "Ohman Won't Seek Re-election," *Casper Star-Tribune*, Joan Barron, April 1, 1998, p.A1.

issues regarding our state lands. We remained convinced that the state land board had a constitutional responsibility to get the most income that it possibly could from these lands for the benefit of the trust beneficiaries. It was perhaps due to this conviction that we both left after two terms in office.

Some two weeks later I also made the public announcement that I would not run again.[239] "I think two terms is enough in these offices," I said. When I ran for the second term, some four years prior, I said I would not seek a third. I wanted to stay true to that commitment. By then Wyoming voters had passed an initiative limiting their statewide officials to two terms in office. I was still eligible to serve another because the measure took effect during my second term, but clearly the voters had expressed their will and I wanted to respect it. Like Diana, I also was disappointed in the disagreements that had been pervasive on state land issues, but this was by no means the primary reason for my decision. I was approaching my 55th birthday, was growing tired of politics and of government, and knew there were other opportunities to pursue before my time ran out. So at the end of 1998, my career in state government came to an end. On Sunday, December 27, 1998, the *Casper Star* ran a front page story summing up my time in office, under the banner, "Ferrari's legacy – fiscal common sense." The article was written by Joan Barron and it began like this:[240]

> "State Auditor Dave Ferrari saved the state hundreds of millions of dollars through progressive

---

239 "Ferrari Warns of 'Financial Crisis'; Auditor Won't Run Again," *Casper Star-Tribune*, April, 1998, p.A1.

240 "Ferrari's Legacy – Fiscal Common Sense," *Casper Star-Tribune*, December 27, 1998, Joan Barron, p.A1.

> management and ideas. He also irritated some of his fellow Republicans with his push for strong ethics and financial disclosure legislation and his insistence the state needs to get more money from its management of state lands. The state's policy on state lands is costing $20 million a year in opportunity costs, he said. A former budget officer, public policy specialist, and government watchdog, Ferrari never has been comfortable with the political side of the State Auditor's job."

I was appreciative of Joan's assessment at that time and remain so today. She was always fair to me in her observations and deserves respect for her lifelong commitment to hard work, honest journalism, and sometimes controversial reporting. Not everyone shares her views about my time in office but the people of Wyoming would be largely in the dark about their own government had she not been there for all of these many years.

I still believe the state is losing huge sums in lost income from the management of its lands but that's an issue for others. I had my opportunity. It was a great ride, and I hope in some way government was better after my time than before the people of Wyoming chose me as their State Auditor. I was honored to serve but anxious to depart. I don't remember who, but someone once said, "It is better to have left too soon, than to have stayed too long." I'm not sure if either applies in my case. I chose to leave but would have been happy to continue the fight had I stayed. Supporters were disappointed to see me go. Critics were delighted that I didn't stay. This was perhaps the only time that I agreed completely with the critics.

I never expected to participate in politics again after those years, but some time later once more found myself deeply engaged in the political process.

Kay and I had often discussed what we should do after leaving state government. She was still chairman of the business department at Cheyenne East High School and truly loved teaching, her students, and the people in her department. She wasn't quite ready to give that up. And although we both thought we would like to relocate to Denver to be closer to our kids and grandkids, we knew that would have to wait for awhile. Our oldest son, Brian, a banker in Northglenn, was a single dad raising our first grandson, Marcus, who was only two years old at the time. We were anxious to get down there and give him whatever help he might need. Our youngest son, Justin, and his wife, Cindy, were also in the northern Denver area and they had just brought their son, Payton, into the world. He would be followed by Connor and Brooke some years later. Justin was a computer expert, working for a company called Doubleclick and Cindy was teaching at one of the local grade schools. We figured we would end up there as well, but that didn't happen.

During my last few months in office, we considered a number of different possibilities. At age 55, I certainly was not ready to retire. I'm not a golfer, don't often hunt or fish, and have never turned the TV on before five o'clock in the evening. Watching soaps, CNN or FOX wasn't an option. I had enjoyed the consulting business and a number of other ventures over the years, so I knew I wanted to be in the business world. The question was, which business? Our first venture in the early seventies was the purchase of a very popular pizza restaurant, which had operated in the same location for over thirty years. We bought the business from the owner who was retiring and moving to California. His records indicated that it was a successful business and he assured us at the time that a lot of the restaurant's income was not even reflected on the books. After a few weeks of operating our new business it was obvious that the previous owner told the truth.

We learned that owning a restaurant that is open seven days a week could be very frustrating and time-consuming, even though we had a full-time manager. So, after a couple of years, we sold our share of the restaurant to one of our partners. We made a modest profit in the sale and our partner successfully operated the store for another twenty years before closing it when his manager retired. We later learned that the previous owner lost the fortune he had accumulated in the restaurant. After vacationing in Europe one summer, he returned to his California home to find that his son had broken into his home and emptied his safe which contained nearly all of the cash he had accumulated during the thirty years he owned the store. He was heartbroken. Not just because he lost his fortune, but also because he lost his only son over the incident.

Following our venture in the restaurant business, we partnered with friends, Clyde and Bernice Gerrard, and opened a ladies clothing store in 1973 at the corner of 17th and Capitol Avenue in Cheyenne. This business proved to be quite successful for the next ten years. My only involvement was overseeing the financial issues: bill-paying, payroll, inventory, cash management, etc. Kay and Bernice worked with the store manager and handled all of the management functions, such as buying merchandise, marketing, sales, preparing daily deposits, etc. The operation remained viable until 1983 when a new mall came to town. Its opening completely changed the traffic patterns in Cheyenne. People who shopped downtown for years, stopped. They were attracted to the shiny, new stores in the mall. Within a year, we closed the downtown store and moved it to the mall.

In 1979 we started a fast food franchising company. Our first store proved to be a disappointment, hidden behind some other businesses on a street with only limited traffic. When McDonalds came in down on the corner, our sales tumbled. In less than a year we were incurring sizable losses. Fortunately, we had signed only a one-year lease so when the one year was up, we had the option to either renew or close up shop. We did neither. Instead, we found an existing restaurant with a proven sales history. We bought the site, remodeled the store to accommodate a drive-up window, moved our equipment into the remodeled building, and installed our business name, menu and system. Along with our equipment, we moved our debt and within a couple of years had paid it off. We were very pleased with the new location, as was our banker.

We went on to open thirteen franchised stores and at one time owned five company stores. Over the years, the franchised units became independent operations, and we sold all but one of the company stores. It remains in operation today, after thirty-three years in business. Its success is due largely to its location. It is on a busy corner, located just a mile from the main gates of F.E. Warren Air Force Base, with good egress and ingress and a good traffic count most days of the week. Running this company has not always been easy. In a retail operation with high volume, you have a lot of employees to deal with who are handling a lot of cash. Both can be trouble.

One of our first managers was intelligent and capable; but, unfortunately, he could not resist the temptations of being around all of that cash. We had to let him go when the daily deposits repeatedly failed to reach the bank. He always had an excuse, such as they were lost, temporarily hidden, held back to make change, or he was just too busy to make the deposit. Once he was gone, deposits no longer came up missing; and, ironically, the periodic late-night burglaries stopped as well.

So, while waiting for Kay to retire from teaching, I had a number of experiences and options to choose from. Over the years we had invested in a number of different real estate ventures. We fixed up and sold some of the properties; others we retained for awhile as rentals. Of all of my experiences in business, I came to the conclusion that I enjoyed real estate the most. I also knew from my time serving in elected office that I wanted to be my own boss. As an elected official you don't have the luxury of working for one boss--you have thousands. And, you can't please them all. When you satisfy one person or group, you usually have angered others.

I formed a small real estate limited liability company and began buying properties in Cheyenne. Unlike state land sales, I had to submit the highest bids in order to buy them. This new venture proved successful and over the next dozen years, I bought and sold several million dollars worth of real estate involving several dozen properties. I quickly grew quite fond of ugly, stinky houses. The excitement of buying or selling property is a feeling that is unmatched in any other career that I am familiar with. In over forty years of owning businesses, as a government executive working with governors, senators and legislators, as a consultant on both private endeavors and public affairs, I have never experienced anything as thrilling and exuberating as putting together a real estate deal. Whether it is buying property or selling it, to me, it is fun, exciting, and rewarding. In addition to the financial rewards, it is satisfying in many other ways as well. Anyone who has ever thrown a coat of paint on the wall and then stood back and admired their work knows the kind of reward I am talking about. Those who have been inspired by planting a bush or flower and watching it grow; or who couldn't resist walking barefoot through a room full of newly installed carpet; or, simply is in awe by the sight of a well-manicured, lush, green lawn, knows this feeling. All of us have a vision of the way things should, or could, be. In real estate, you have the chance every day to make this vision a reality. You have that chance to stand back and admire what you did. And, if you're careful, you get rewarded quite well for your efforts.

My first experience buying real estate with the idea of fixing it up and then selling for a quick profit, known as "fix and flip," occurred several years ago in California before the huge explosion in housing prices. My friend, Ken, lived in Los Angeles and was active in real estate. I was living nearly a thousand miles from there, but he thought there was an opportunity to make money in that area. He had found a two-bedroom, two-bath condo in a large complex in Culver City. We spent a few months fixing the place up and sold it for a modest gain. That was pretty good for a short-term period which required very little of my time. Ken hired all of the contractors and oversaw the project. I was more like a silent partner. The venture worked out satisfactorily so we did it again. By this time prices had increased somewhat in the same complex and we had to pay more for the property. We spent more on fix-up costs and had difficulty selling it, even after lowering the price several times. We lost a few dollars on the deal and it kind of chilled any interest I had in buying real estate in California. That was over twenty-five years ago. Those properties are now selling for nearly a million dollars each. Had I known then what I know now, I would have avoided that small loss, became a landlord, hired a property manager, and would likely have ended up in that one percent that the politicians in Washington are arguing about today.

One of the more memorable properties I got involved with after leaving the state began early one Sunday morning, barely after the sun came up when I received a call from my realtor, Larry Shippy. There was an excitement in his voice and I could tell he was up to something. "You got any time this morning?" he asked. "I want to show you something." I grabbed my coffee mug and headed to his office. "I have some property that hasn't even been officially listed yet," he explained as we jumped into his Mercury Mountaineer. "I want you to see it before my office gets wind of it. It will hit multi-list on Tuesday, so if you're interested in any of it, we need to move fast." With that we were off on a two-hour drive around town. There were five properties in all. Four were single-family dwellings; the other was a duplex. The property belonged to an old newspaper reporter who had been in the hospital for weeks, but he hadn't tended to any of his property in years. The tenants quit paying rent months ago and most had moved out after their utilities had been shut off by the power company. Some had even left most of their personal belongings which obviously didn't amount to much. The owner didn't have the energy or the interest to deal with them any longer and wanted out. The properties had been paid off for years, and it was obvious he hadn't put any of the money back in them to keep them up.

When we finally pulled up in front of the last house, Larry shut off his car, turned to me and said, "Well, here it is; the last one. Go on in and see what you think. I'll wait for you out here." "Is it open?" I asked. "Yea, you go on; I'm not going in that dump," he replied. I reluctantly approached the house and slowly entered the front door which was left, or had blown, open a few inches. As I cautiously touched the door I was startled by a shrieking noise as a black critter flashed through my feet and out the open door. The wild cat was frightened even more than me, and I began to understand why Larry stayed in the car. Things quickly got worse and I hadn't even made it past the front entryway. The first thing I noticed was that the wall paper was loose. It was still hanging but had areas where it had pulled away from the wall and it appeared to be moving. Upon further examination, it was moving. The place was literally covered with roaches. They weren't the large ones like you might find in Los Angeles or Las Vegas, but rather ranged in length from about one-eighth to one-half inches long. They were everywhere: under the wall paper, on the walls, in the cupboards, in the sinks, in the sofa, in the shelving, in the beds, and throughout the entire house. I nearly turned around and fled, but thought, *"No, I'm here and I just as well see it all."*

It appeared to be a three-bedroom, two-bath house, but it was hard to tell because there was furniture and clutter everywhere and several of the rooms had two doorways. You had to go through some rooms to get to others. I saw two toilets: one in a room with a tub and the other in a small room no larger than a closet. Both were crusty, the stench was overwhelming and both were full of feces which had not been flushed. I was wrong about the two baths. It turned out that the one stool actually was in a closet with no plumbing. That didn't stop the latest tenant from using it, however.

There were two mice in the bath tub. They had fallen in and couldn't get back out. Both were alive but one was nearly dead, as the other had gnawed off parts of its legs and tail and appeared determined to eat the entire thing. I have never seen anything like it and felt like I had bugs crawling all over me by the time I got out of there. All of the properties were in terrible shape but none were quite as disgusting as this one. I couldn't believe they were even on the market in their present condition. "How much are they?" I asked Larry. "Depends on how many you want," he replied. I couldn't picture myself owning anything as repugnant as these houses, but when Larry said thirty-five thousand would probably buy two of them, I knew I had to seriously consider it. They were within two blocks of each other, close to the state capitol building, close to downtown, close to shopping, close to schools, close to federal government offices, and near the entrance of F.E. Warren AFB. I had them under contract before that Tuesday and was the proud owner of two very ugly houses within a month. These two houses turned out to be a couple of the smarter buys I have ever made.

Looking back over the three dozen or so deals I have done during the past fourteen years, the projects that were the most profitable for me were either bank-owned or government-owned houses. Some were bought through a realtor and others were purchased using a competitive bidding process. I never had the luxury of sitting back and waiting for someone else to bid. No, I had to submit my best bid and then wait to see if someone else was willing to pay more. I didn't always win the bidding war, and it seems to have worked out okay. It's possible that I paid too much for some of these properties, but at least the sellers, whether a bank, a government or a private person, knew they were receiving the maximum amount that anyone was willing to pay. What a concept.

# CHAPTER THIRTEEN

## "Kiss My Ass"

That's probably not the message you want your campaign manager giving to one of the most active Republican lobbyists in the state if you want to be the next Governor of Wyoming.

On January 17, 2002, at the Hitching Post Inn in Cheyenne, my good friend, along with his wife Nancy, announced his candidacy for governor.[241] In his announcement, Dave Freudenthal began: "I am today formally applying for the job of Governor of Wyoming. While Governor of Wyoming is a unique job--it is first and foremost a job. And, you, the citizens of Wyoming, are the employer." He said that the concept of the governor being an "employee' was probably inconsistent with modern politics, but it was "clearly the intent of our forefathers." He said he viewed the campaign ahead as an extended job interview with the citizens of Wyoming. Then, he went on to explain why he wanted to be governor.

Wyoming had just gone through eight years of the Geringer administration and during this period, access to the Governor and

[241] Dave Freudenthal, "Announcement of Gubernatorial Candidacy", January 17, 2002, p.1.

to many areas of state government had been less than satisfying for many of our citizens, whether Republicans or Democrats. This was illustrated by the fact that, for the first time that anyone could remember, the back door to the governor's office was closed and locked. Throughout all of the previous administrations, going back some forty years, that back door, which stood only a few feet from the governor's working office, was left open. Anyone could enter and see the governor. I had walked through that door a hundred times, starting with Governor Hathaway's administration. Under Geringer's policy, nearly everyone, including his top political advisors and cabinet-level appointees, would have to enter through the main entrance and be processed by the receptionist, take a seat in the reception area, and wait to be beckoned by the Governor's personal secretary. This new policy was not popular and Dave wisely made it a campaign issue from the start.

Dave said he wanted to be governor for two very important reasons. "First," he said, "I want the people of Wyoming to be priority number one in the Governor's Office." He said in his administration, people would be welcome in the capitol building and treated with respect; they would be able to reach him on the telephone. He said there would be "no penalty for disagreement, whether it is over taxes, school finance, or the time of day."[242]

Dave's second reason: "I believe the governor and state government should be the people's ally, not their enemy, in building a better life for themselves and their families." He said that one trait all of our citizens share is that "We choose to live in Wyoming." Wyoming is "an unmatched expanse of beautiful, resource-rich

---

[242] "Freudenthal Starts Run for Governor," *Wyoming Tribune-Eagle,* Chris George, January 18, 2002.

land, clean air, and clear water," he declared. He said we work hard to make sure our decision to live in Wyoming remains one of our best decisions. And we want our children to be able to make the same decision for their future. "In this common effort, the governor should be the citizen's ally," Freudenthal said. He went on to identify the reasons he believed the citizens of Wyoming had chosen to live in the state and, as Governor, what he would do to reinforce and strengthen these factors. He pointed to the fact that Wyoming is a safe place to live, citing the character of our citizens and the strength of our law enforcement. Dave had spent the previous seven and one half years as the chief federal prosecutor for Wyoming and based on these experiences he knew there were some bad people in our country and in our state. "As parents, our first priority is our family's safety. As governor, my first duty would be vigilance in the cause of public safety," he said.

Noting that Wyoming was a great place to raise a family, partially due to the State's long-term commitment to education, Dave pointed out that as parents "our greatest concern is for our children to have the best possible preparation for the complex world in which they will live--no matter where they choose to go, whatever they chose to do." Dave said he wanted to work directly with parents, teachers, school boards, and citizens to "refocus our attention on the classroom." In reference to the current Governor's reluctance to meet with litigants on education finance and reform, he would not let lawsuits, whether pending or threatened, keep him from working with these groups, he said in his announcement.

With regard to the environment, the candidate thought that the most common reason folks chose to live in Wyoming was because of the landscape. "Our mountains, the night sky and open spaces capture our spirit and define much of who we are as people and as a community," he said. He thought this appreciation for our natural beauty and wonderful outdoors could be heightened even further by expanding the citizens' access to public lands. As Governor, he said he would work to expand this access but at the same time respect private property rights. This seemed like quite a courageous, but risky, position for a gubernatorial candidate, I thought. Had he not been watching the debates of the State Land Board during the eight years I was there? I wondered if he had not heard Governor Hathaway's advice with regard to the agriculture vote. It is rare, indeed, that any leaseholder of public lands would support expanded public access. They view these lands as their own lands. The last thing they want is for the public to be trampling across them with gun, fishing pole, or four-wheeler in hand. But, today's recreationalists had become more vocal in recent years, calling for their elected officials to help them gain access to these lands. They correctly felt, as taxpayers, they were part-owner of state lands. Dave apparently figured that the 1,500 or so leaseholders and their families could not continue to control our lands at the expense of the thousands of people who were now demanding the opportunity to enjoy them.

In addressing economic development, Freudenthal said he would offer two tests that he would apply to proposals for developing the economy. "First," he said, "what does the proposal add to the existing programs that have evolved from decades of similar concerns? Second, does the proposal actually benefit the people who have chosen to live in Wyoming?"

In wrapping up his announcement, Dave referenced something Harry Truman said while running for President in 1948. He urged the voters, "Don't vote for me, vote for yourself." Dave asked the voters to think about their own reasons for living in Wyoming and to elect a governor who would honor those reasons.

There was never any doubt in my mind that Dave Freudenthal would one day be Governor of Wyoming. It was clear from the time we first met that he had a special sense about public policy. I often thought and frequently told him that one of his purposes in life was to be Governor; he was simply destined. He appeared to have no choice in the matter; his only choice was when, and apparently the time was now.

By the time Dave made his announcement, he had already raised slightly over $50,000 for his gubernatorial campaign. He also had put together a beginning semblance of a campaign team,[243] naming his friend of many years, Phil Noble, Campaign Manager; his daughter, Hillary as Field Coordinator; Cynthia Pomeroy, Campaign Chairman; Kim Floyd, County Coordinator and Union Representative; and Al Minier, one of the smartest people I had ever met, as the person in charge of Opposition Research. Rich Lindsey, a former staffer with Governors Herschler and Sullivan and advisor to several statewide Democrat candidates for years, was named Chief Strategist. Dave Lerner, a former news anchor with Cheyenne's CBS affiliate, Channel Five, was named Press Secretary. He wanted me to be Finance Director and his Campaign Treasurer. He called his committee Folks for Freudenthal and set up offices a couple of blocks from the state capitol building at 419 Randall Avenue in Cheyenne.

Dave always suggested that when he ran for governor he wanted me to publicly endorse him. "I want you out front with me," he said. He explained that having a Republican involved in his campaign, particularly a former statewide elected official, would demonstrate broad appeal, regardless of political party and would

[243] http://www.govdave.com.,Campaign Team, January 17, 2002.

attract like-minded Republican and Independent voters. He knew that gaining support from the GOP would have to be done "one Republican at a time." So, I signed on as treasurer and we began the long process of raising funds and running for office. Kay was dragged into the contest as well when Lindsey talked her into helping run the campaign office. Her main job was to be the scheduler and Rich assured her it would take only a few hours a week. They both knew, at the time, that wasn't the case and ultimately, she assumed all of the office management functions, including serving as receptionist, answering the telephone, keeping the office and everyone in it stocked with supplies, computer graphics, designing the layout for advertising, typing letters and correspondence and, yes, serving as the candidate's scheduler. It was a full-time job for both of us and, after wrapping up the current real estate project, we spent the next year unlocking the office around seven in the morning and locking it up again at five or six each night. Often we would return after dinner to put together some campaign piece or react to some crisis which frequently occurs in every political campaign. Saturdays and Sundays became like every other day of the week. There are no weekends in the middle of a campaign. But, it was fun. We enjoyed the work and thoroughly enjoyed the people we worked with.

We expected that the primary would be a very tough run. There were three Democrat contenders in the race, including construction worker Toby Simpson, businessman Kenneth Casner, and attorney Paul J. Hickey. Dave's most formidable opponent, by far, was the well respected attorney from Cheyenne, Paul Hickey.[244] Hickey was known throughout the State as an experienced trial lawyer in both the state and federal courts. He had tried numerous cases,

[244] http://pview.findlaw.com/view1550584.

involving personal injury, employment law, commercial, and oil and gas matters. He was a member of the Wyoming Bar Foundation and was past president of the Wyoming State Bar. He had served on a number of state boards and commissions, including the Wyoming Water Development Commission and the Wyoming Natural Gas Pipeline Authority. A few of his corporate clients included Qwest Corporation, PacifiCorp, Source Gas, and Rocky Mountain Power. He also was quite familiar with political campaigns.

Paul was perhaps most famous for being the son of Joe and Winifred "Win" Hickey. His dad, J. J. "Joe" Hickey served as Governor and United States Senator. Joe Hickey was elected Governor in 1958 but served only a partial term, between 1959 and 1961. He was probably best known for resigning the governorship and appointing himself United States Senator to replace Republican Keith Thomson, who had died unexpectedly.[245] That decision turned out to be quite unpopular among Wyoming voters, and Hickey paid the price for it when in the special election conducted in 1962 he was beaten by former Republican Governor Milward Simpson for the privilege of filling out Thomson's unexpired term which would conclude on January 3, 1967.

Paul's mother Win served with distinction as Wyoming's First Lady during Governor Hickey's brief term, but she became even more admired and respected as a politician herself following her husband's death in 1970.[246] She was the first woman ever elected Laramie County Commissioner and also was the first woman elected

---

[245] "GOP has Chance to Gain Two Senators from West," *The Harvard Crimson*, October 30, 1962, Joseph M. Russin. http://www.thecrinson.com/article/1962/10/30.

[246] "Win Hickey, former Wyoming First Lady, Dies," *Billings Gazette*, April 7, 2007.

to the State Senate from Laramie County. She served on the Board of Trustees for the University of Wyoming and was also President of the University of Wyoming Foundation. This rich family heritage would serve Paul well in his run for Governor and we knew we had our work cut out for us. There was little doubt that the Hickey name was far better known than our guy's. Both men were well regarded and both appeared to be very qualified to be our next governor. Paul had to be the early favorite. And a lot of people we hoped would help joined the other camp, thinking they knew a sure winner when they saw one. Maybe we were too dumb to know any better, because the thought of losing the race never entered my mind and I don't think it occurred to anyone else in our office either. If it did, no one ever mentioned it.

The early days of the campaign were spent trying to raise money, defining issues, and writing position papers and letters for the candidate. Dave and his daughter Hillary were out around the State trying to meet with as many people as possible. Their presence in the office was rather infrequent, but they stayed in touch with us each day via cell phone. Kay would schedule appointments with television and radio stations, newspaper editors and reporters, mayors, county commissioners, senior citizen centers, volunteers, schools, and other local government entities and officials as they visited each city and town. It wasn't unusual for her to line up a dozen activities in a single day. The candidate would often complain about the pace, but he loved getting out and meeting with people. Knowing this, we had little sympathy when he grumbled about his schedule or how hard he was working. We figured the heavy lifting was really being done in the office, not in some coffee shop, press lounge, or plush board room on Main Street.

Kay's job was to keep the office running and Dave's schedule full. Phil's was to coordinate all of the activities of the campaign, including seeing to it that strategy was developed and implemented in a timely manner, advertising budgets and schedules were on target, volunteers were being directed and supported, and, most importantly, that the candidate had everything he needed. As the manager, Phil had responsibilities for everything involving the campaign. Among many other duties, he also met with media, interest groups, legislators, and volunteers and made sure that the campaign was being managed properly. He had a high-stress position; but, of course, he was one of only a few being paid. The rest of us were volunteers.

My primary duties were to solicit donations, keep track of the money, pay the bills, write letters for Dave's signature, prepare position papers on various issues, and tackle anything else that needed done that others could not or would not do. Having previously run two statewide campaigns ourselves, Kay and I had a pretty good idea of what those things would be. There is so much going on all at the same time that it is very normal and easy for things to slip through the cracks. We tried to help Phil see to it that nothing did.

One of my first efforts, following Dave's announcement, was to try to raise funds from Republicans and from others who had been involved in my political career. This included literally hundreds of people who had contributed to my campaigns or helped me with the statewide ethics initiative. I figured either group would be interested in electing someone who had philosophies or issues similar to my own. If these folks liked my ideas about government, ethics, efficiencies, accountability, accurate reporting, etc., they might also like Dave's vision for the way government ought to be run. They might be willing to help pay for the campaign. So we dusted off the old reports that had been filed with the Secretary of State and put together a large mailing list of potential contributors. On Friday, the day after Dave's announcement, several hundred letters were mailed out.[247] In them, I said:

> "I have known Dave for nearly thirty years and know he will make the kind of Governor you can trust and depend on. I have been a Republican all of my life, and, yes, Dave is a Democrat. But, he is a conservative Democrat. . . . Dave believes in good government, but small government. . . . If we are ever going to have a state government that makes any difference, Dave is exactly the kind of person we need in the Governor's chair."

I had known Rich Lindsey for a number of years leading up to this campaign. He was a good guy and, like the candidate, was pretty astute at public policy, politics, and statewide campaigns. He had experience in a number of statewide campaigns, including serving as campaign manager in Governor Sullivan's successful re-election campaign in 1990 against Mary Mead. The outcome wasn't even close as Sullivan garnered 65 percent of the vote to Mary's 35 percent.[248] The Governor was extremely popular and although Mary was very well liked throughout the Republican party, she was less experienced on the issues and public policy matters and was no match for Sullivan in the debates between the two. I liked both candidates. I worked with Mike during his first term and spent a lot

---

[247] Letter dated January 16, 2002, from David G. Ferrari to potential donors, mailed January 18, 2002.

[248] Op. cit., *Wyoming Blue Book, Volume V.*, p.16.

of time with Mary during the campaign. She was a very thoughtful, adorable lady, but being the daughter of former Wyoming Governor and United States Senator Cliff Hanson wasn't enough to overcome Mike's popularity. I was sad to see her lose but felt at the time the voters had made the right choice. They almost always do. Rich did a good job in that campaign. He had a very good candidate, but all campaigns are tough, involving a lot of risk and an enormous amount of work. Win or lose, if you manage a statewide race and survive, you've earned your keep.

Rich also managed Mike's run for the U.S. Senate in 1994, and although they lost to then-U.S. Representative Craig Thomas, it wasn't due to anything lacking on Rich's part. Rather, it was more likely Mike's friendship with President Clinton coming back to haunt him. There was a Republican wave in the 1994 elections nationwide and most Democrats with close ties to the President were beaten handily. Sullivan lost the election to Thomas, 59% to 39%.[249] It didn't help when Thomas enlisted Defense Secretary Dick Cheney to offer a testimonial on television which ran throughout Wyoming:[250] "Bill Clinton's proposals . . . have been a disaster for our nation. We simply cannot afford to send another friend of Bill Clinton's to Washington," Cheney said. Looking back now, it seems those words couldn't have been more off the mark but Cheney made those comments at the height of his own credibility, long before serving as Vice President. There was little Lindsey or Mike could have done to offset or counter this kind of tactic at the national level. In spite of what the latest poll numbers were, I think even

[249] Ibid., p. 172.

[250] Thomas B. Rosenstiel, "Upbeat Messages Won't Do, Political Candidates Find," *Los Angeles Times*, October 9, 1994, http://articles.latimes.com/1994/10-09/news/mn.

Rich was surprised by the margin of defeat. Rich was very aware of Mike's enormous popularity while Governor. We all were. I think the twenty point defeat shocked even the Republicans.

When we began the campaign, Rich was anxious to get involved. He had been engaged in Democrat party politics for years, interacting with the state party headquarters and members of the Central Committee. He had always helped Democrats in local campaigns, but had rarely been on the winning side in a statewide general election. That is not too surprising given the fact that Democrats are out-numbered by a huge margin (nearly three to one) in Wyoming.[251] The latest figures show that only 23% of registered voters are Democrats, 63%, Republicans, and about 14%, all others. These numbers haven't changed much over the years. Our race or ethnic make-up, or origin, is roughly 89% white, 6% Hispanic, 2% Native American, less than 1% black, and the remaining 2%, is all others, including Asians and Hawaiians.[252]. These numbers simply do not bode well for Democrats running for statewide offices. All too often, the outlook is so bleak that they can't even field a candidate for Auditor or Treasurer and the Republicans run unopposed. But, a number of Democrats in the gubernatorial contest over the years have overcome these odds and won. We thought if we got past the primary election, our candidate would do the same.

We figured at the outset that Hickey probably had better name recognition among Democrats, because of his family history in the party. Rich, Dave's brother Steve, and Dave, developed a strategy to create a local following which would help overcome whatever advantage Paul had as well as strengthen Dave's chances

---

251 http://soswy.state.wy.us/Elections/VRStats.aspx.

252 http://www3.nationaljournal.com/pubs/almanac/2008/states/wy/

in the general election, should we win. They patterned the first several months of the campaign after a plan Rich had earlier developed for the Wyoming Wildlife Federation (WWF).[253] The WWF, created in 1937, became one of the State's largest statewide sportsmen/conservation organizations, with membership of about five thousand people. Its mission statement says the Federation: "works for hunters, anglers, and other wildlife enthusiasts to protect and enhance habitat, to perpetuate quality hunting and fishing, to protect citizens' right to use public lands and waters, and to promote ethical hunting and fishing."

Kim Floyd was the new director of the Federation at the time, following years of membership decline. He believed the organization had lost members because it had strayed too far from its original mission and had placed too much emphasis on "green" issues and environmental concerns. Kim wanted to get the membership up and asked Rich to help him figure out how to do it. They put together a statewide strategy where Kim and other WWF staffers and volunteers would converge on a community, interview with the local press, make guest appearances on talk radio programs, submit guest columns to the local papers, and generate as much attention to themselves and their mission as was possible in a short period of time. In conjunction with these visits, the WWF would also run local radio advertising spots and display ads in the papers trying to attract new members and to entice previous members to re-join the WWF. Immediately following their departure, they would follow up these visits with a direct mail piece and additional media reminding the local people that they had recently visited their community. This strategy proved effective in building the Federation's membership

---

[253] http://www.wyomingwildlife.org/ht/d/sp/i/25194/pid/25194.

and Rich was convinced it could also be used to build a voter base with loyalty to Dave in his campaign for governor.

Working with the state Democrat party office in Casper, Rich obtained statewide printouts of voter precincts in each county. During the early months of the campaign, in analyzing each precinct, he was looking primarily for those areas which had more Democrats than Republicans. Like the famous bank robber, Willie Sutton, when asked why he continued to rob banks, he replied, "because that's where the money is," Rich wanted the candidate to focus on these precincts because that's where the Democrat voters were. The printouts from the Casper office showed each street and house number that Dave and Hillary needed to visit while in the area. Similar to the WWF strategy, while in the community, Dave would be doing radio and newspaper interviews and we would be running local advertising spots. The thought was that after spending several days in the area, by the time Dave and Hillary left, most people would have at least heard his name and hopefully had learned what he was all about. His visit would then be followed up with a mail-back piece, again soliciting support for his candidacy.

We had very little money early in the campaign and, of course, we were on a limited budget. There were no funds to hire media specialists or advertising gurus, so we had to come up with our own stuff. Usually, Rich and I would develop the message to be conveyed in newspaper ads, Kay would lay them out graphically, and after Dave's input I would take them to Jim Angel at the Wyoming Press Association. Jim would outline which papers and during what time period the ads would appear in order to stay within our budget constraints. It wasn't a very elaborate or professional process, but it seemed to work. Our ads were anything but sophisticated and, at least on one occasion, were criticized for being "beneath the dignity" of a gubernatorial campaign. But, they did seem to attract attention and drew a clear distinction between the two Democrat candidates.

The ads were usually 2 columns, by 4 inches and the least sophisticated one appeared in newspapers throughout the state under the bold heading: **I SLOPPED THE HOGS.**

It proclaimed:

> "As your next Governor, you may not ask me to slop the hogs, but you will ask me to work hard to bring higher paying jobs to Wyoming and better opportunities for our young people. **I can handle it.** I learned the value of hard work growing up on the farm in Thermopolis and, as Governor, I will work hard every day to make things better in Wyoming."

No one would confuse this ad as being one from Paul Hickey's campaign. It wasn't clear to me why Paul Hickey was running for Governor, what issues he believed in, or what his agenda would be if elected. What seemed clear, however, was that he was running a fairly traditional campaign. He appeared to be visiting one city or town and then another as events occurred. He didn't seem to be creating too many of his own events. We suspected he was saving his money for a media blitz towards the end of the primary. We, on the other hand, were spending modestly on marketing and media as we went, hoping to elevate Dave's name recognition not only in the primary, but also in the general, in the event we should win.

We never attacked our opponent in our advertising, but did try to point out the kinds of experiences possessed by our candidate that were absent in his opponent. For example, as U.S. Attorney,

Dave had been Wyoming's leading crime fighter. We ran several ads to capitalize on this issue. One, under the bold heading, **CHEATERS**, said:

> "Are you sick of cheaters? Our children are being cheated out of a quality life by drug pushers and child molesters. Our grandparents are being cheated out of their retirement savings by scam artists and stock schemes. Our government is being cheated out of income by greedy corporations using creative accounting. Let's put a stop to all of this cheating! Dave Freudenthal spent the last eight years as U.S. Attorney prosecuting and locking up cheaters. He is the only candidate for Governor who knows how to deal with cheaters."

Another ad, titled, **ATTENTION DRUG PUSHERS**, declared:

> "Time is running out! Wyoming will have a new Governor soon and your days are numbered. As U.S. Attorney, Dave Freudenthal has spent the last eight years locking up people like you. He is the only candidate with law enforcement experience, and he knows how to deal with pushers, pornographers, child molesters, and cheats. He'll protect our way of life and he is ready to go to work for Wyoming."

Dave had articulated why he was in the race and what he wanted to do when governor. As you would expect, both candidates were for economic development, against gun control, for the death penalty, against an income tax, for education, and against crime. One major difference was that Dave was for a "woman's right to choose" and his opponent was "pro-life." Paul's consistent message seemed to stress leadership. A few days before the election he said the central issue in the campaign was leadership.[254] He contended that he was the candidate who had the leadership ability to "take this state forward." He also often talked about the need to keep nuclear waste out of our state[255] and his desire to support economic development at the local level by providing state resources to aid in the effort.[256] In fact, two weeks before the election, he declared that an economic development organization was just as important a component of local government as a fire department. Not everyone agreed with this, but these were good positive messages. What wasn't so positive, however, was the use of an automated phone bank system just two days prior to election day, urging Democrats to vote for him.[257] Wyoming law prohibits the use of autodialing machines in political campaigns. But, in spite of this, Kathy Karpan, former Chief Elections Officer while Secretary of State, and an ardent supporter, apparently unaware of its illegality, urged Hickey to use the device.[258]

Dave's work with local law enforcement while serving as U.S. Attorney enabled him to develop quite a statewide network of local support which would be instrumental in both the primary and general campaigns. Another thing that assisted our campaign was

---

254 http://www.highbeam.com/doc/1P2-15845565.html.

255 http://highbeam.com/doc/1P2-15843657.html.

256 http://highbeam.com/doc/1P2-15845313.html.

257 http://www.highbeam.com/doc/1P2-15845729.html. "Hickey Also Unit Automated System," Wyoming Tribune-Eagle, Jessica Lowell, August 18, 2002.

258 Ibíd.

the endorsement of his candidacy by the *Wyoming Tribune-Eagle.* Although the newspaper wasn't necessarily read or discussed in all corners of the state and in all of the smaller communities in the State, we got its message out statewide by putting together a number of ads using its comments about Dave.

Next to a picture of Dave, we ran the ads under the banner: **FREUDENTHAL ENDORSED**. We started the ad out: **"Here's what the Wyoming Tribune-Eagle Editorial Board had to say:"** We closed each ad with the following quote: **"In the end, the board agreed that Mr. Freudenthal's vision for Wyoming is 20/20. All state residents can share in it—and it can be achieved. That's why we like him in the Democratic primary for Governor."** In between these two statements, quotes from the endorsement about the various issues were highlighted.

We won![259] After seven long months, it was over. The final tally: Freudenthal, 53.6%; Hickey, 37.5%; Simpson, 5.2%; and, Casner, 3.7%. We won every county except three: Carbon, Sublette, and Uinta. Our largest margin of victory was in Natrona County where we won by 1,472 votes. Our smallest margin was in Niobrara County where we beat Hickey by a single vote. We won because we had the best candidate and we had Nancy and Hillary.

Nancy was one of the smartest and most conscientious people I had known and worked with in state government. She was a lawyer with a variety of experiences which made her extremely effective in the campaign. Together, she and Dave made a formidable team. She began her government career by spending eight years in the Wyoming Governor's Office, working both for Governor Herschler and Governor Sullivan, as an attorney for intergovernmental affairs.

---

[259] http://soswy.state.wy.us/Elections/Docs/2002/2002PrimaryResults.aspx.

Six years were spent with the Wyoming Tax Commission where she served as Chair. She was also Chair of the Wyoming Board of Equalization. "Nancy Freudenthal has spent much of her legal career working on energy and environmental issues. In 1995, she took a job as an associate at the Cheyenne, Wyoming, law firm of Davis & Cannon. In 1998, she became a partner and held that post until her nomination as a federal judge."[260] Clearly, these experiences were invaluable to Dave and the campaign as they developed public policy positions that were instrumental in the win.

And then there was Hillary. Hillary was not only Dave's daughter, she was his best friend. She was his driver; his road manager; his advisor. She was a people person. She was supportive. She kept him moving. He trusted her. She had good judgment. He trusted her judgment. When he wanted to quit and head home, she made him do one more stop; one more speech; one more house; one more mile; one more handshake; one more interview; one more yard sign; one more brochure; one more event. They liked each other. They enjoyed being on the road together. They were having fun. And, they were winning. Could they do it again in the general election against the Republican Speaker of the House and against overwhelming odds?

Representative Eli Bebout won the Republican Primary over his four challengers by a wide margin.[261] It was Bebout, 49%; Hunkins, 28.0%; Sniffin, 15%; Watt, 6.3%; and Self, 1.7%. Bebout garnered more Republican votes (44,417) than all of the Democrat votes cast for Governor combined (36,799). We knew we had our work cut out for us. There were 241,200 registered voters in Wyoming[262]

---

[260] http://en.wikipedia.org/wiki/Nancy_D._Freudenthal

[261] Ibid.

[262] Op. cit., http://soswy.state.wy.us/Elections/VRStats.aspx.

and only 65,775 were Democrats, or just 27%. The Republican voters totaled 148,925, or 61%; nearly 2 and ½ times that of the Democrats. There were also some 26,500 registered voters who were neither Republicans nor Democrats. Voter registration rolls had always favored the Republicans, but it was never as lop-sided as it was going into the 2002 general election.[263] There were a few positive signs, though. Since statehood nine of the twenty-three people who served as Governor were Democrats and they occupied the Governor's chair during fifty of those years. The longest serving Governor was Democrat Ed Herschler, who served for twelve years, between 1975 and 1987. In fact, in twenty of the last twenty-eight years a Democrat served as Wyoming's chief executive.[264]

Bebout was elected to the Wyoming House of Representatives in 1986.[265] He served as House Minority Whip while a Democrat, but in May of 1994, he switched parties to join the Republican majority.[266] This flip-flop allowed him to serve as Majority Floor Leader in 1997 and 1998 and later as Speaker in 1999-2000. Unfortunately for Mr. Bebout, however, this switch apparently didn't do much to help his campaign for Governor as it only added to his negatives which already seemed quite high. Throughout the campaign we were told by a number of people that there were several incidents that made voters feel uncertain about this candidate, stemming back to his college days. They were reminded of the cheating scandal at the Air Force Academy which occurred at about the same time that Eli left the Academy. We could never find any documentation that he was

---

263 Ibid.

264 Op. cit., *Wyoming Blue Book,* Volume V, pp.21-22.

265 http://vote-wy.org/intro.aspx?state=wy&id=wybebouteli.

266 Ibíd.

involved, but in an election year, there was plenty of speculation. The matter had surfaced earlier during the Republican primary. Some people were also uncomfortable with the rumor that, while in the legislature, he sat on the board of a company that wanted to build a temporary storage facility to store spent nuclear rods in Wyoming.[267] This accusation was lodged at him by one of his opponents in his primary race. He was also, while in the legislature, associated with a company that had allegedly received over $20 million in Abandoned Mine Land (AML) funds. It was alleged that he failed to disclose his interests in the company receiving the government contracts. These were character questions raised by his opponents in the primary, that we thought, when contrasted with Dave's positive policy issues, would persuade many Republican and Independent voters to support our candidate.

Bebout declared throughout the campaign that there were "huge differences" between him and Freudenthal.[268] He seemed to be running as much against President Clinton as against Dave, when he suggested that one of Dave's biggest negatives was the fact that he was President Clinton's appointee as U. S. Attorney. His dislike for the President was also expressed by his friend, Republican National Committeeman Diemer True, in an article entitled, Ex-Democrat in Cheney-land, written by John Gizzi on October 14, 2002.[269] "And the reason for changing parties really says something about Eli--he changed because he couldn't stand Bill Clinton," Diemer said. Eight years earlier, the Republican strategy of "Clinton bashing" seemed

267 http://www.3.nationaljournal.com/scripts/printpage.cgi?/pubs/almanac/2008.

268 Ibid.

269 John Gizzi, "Ex-Democrat in Cheney-land," October 14, 2002, http://findarticles.com/p/articles/mi_903827/is_200210/ai_9121924.

to be a pretty good tactic, not only in Wyoming politics, but also throughout the country. It didn't seem to be nearly as effective now that Clinton was out of Office and Bush and Cheney were in.

Bebout said on a number of occasions that he wanted to be a part of the "President's Team." This seemed to indicate a misreading of the Governor's role and the relationship between the Governor and the federal bureaucracy. The Governor is not a member of the "President's Team;" rather, people in Wyoming, especially in the Republican party it seems, want their Governor to oppose the federal agenda as an intrusion into the affairs of the State. They want the Governor to stand up to Washington and not let the feds further restrict the use of public lands in our borders. They love to bash the federal government; to oppose the federal agenda, whatever it might be, and criticize any federal presence in the State. If you are a candidate for Governor of Wyoming, the last thing you want to be is close to the feds.

Having just gone through eight years of Republican Jim Geringer's administration, we believed that the people of Wyoming were probably ready for a kinder and gentler chief executive. Bebout seemed to extend a kind of abrasiveness during his primary campaign. His use of negative tactics against his fellow Republicans in that race outraged many Republicans. Voters were offended when he paid for attack ads, featuring Senator Al Simpson. Conversely, during his primary, Dave had put forth a kinder image when he talked about why people chose to live in Wyoming and how to make it easier for people to earn a living. He wanted them to be able to continue enjoying Wyoming's unique quality of life. He laid out several plans which he thought advanced this idea. He wanted to create "business friendly" communities to attract economic development in those localities that wanted it. He wanted to strengthen consumer advocacy in the Public Service Commission in an attempt to keep utility rates fair for small businesses and citizens. He supported coal bed methane development but with safeguards to protect our environment and our people. He talked about improving citizen access to public lands, but with respect for private property rights. He wanted to increase auditing on oil and gas to generate millions of dollars in additional revenues. Dave said that "character" really does matter, and talked about his security clearance from the FBI. He also stressed his ties to former Governors Herschler and Sullivan, two of the most popular Governors in our state's history. And, he didn't run away from his association with President Clinton.

Dave was concerned about our state and our people. His genuine concern for people was perhaps best evidenced during one of the earlier debates. He was saying in a speech that "people matter." He made a passionate, convincing, argument that "people really do matter." This was caught on video by Liz Storer, and when later viewed by Rich and Liz, both thought they had discovered a major theme that could be used effectively in the campaign: "People Matter." We set out to develop this idea into a defining difference between the two candidates. Ours began to take shape as a sort of "populous" campaign. Our opponent's was anything but.

Dave had the right message. He had an incredible way of saying things that had great appeal to the voters. He was extremely intelligent. He was very aware of how people thought about things. He was articulate, knowledgeable, warm, friendly, and witty. He was down-to-earth; a common man who related well to people. But, he was also blessed with one of the best writers I have ever known. Al Minier had a talent for condensing a very complex issue or subject down to a very understandable topic, no matter how complicated it might be. He had a wonderful way of editing or re-writing letters or position papers, transforming them into simple, understandable messages. We drafted individual letters to every teacher in Wyoming, to every mayor, county commissioner, and all other local government officials. We prepared individual letters to every constituency group we could identify, including doctors, nurses, social workers, hunters, fishermen, labor union members, and others. The messages, after Al's touch, struck to the heart of the matter, often persuading the recipient to vote for Dave or in some way help in his run for Office. One of the most effective letters which showed great insight into the problems facing educators was sent to every teacher, school official, and administrator and it started like this:

> "Thank you for educating our kids. I am aware of the many, many hours teachers, administrators, and staff put in each day and I appreciate the difficult challenges you face every day trying to teach our children; many of whom have problems learning, or even focusing on the subject, for a variety of reasons.
>
> "Those of us outside of the classroom take for granted the freedoms we enjoy in our jobs which are simply unavailable or impractical for educators with a room full of children. Running brief errands, visiting with co-workers, taking phone calls, or even going to the bathroom are privileges most of us enjoy in our work which are rarely afforded to you in yours."

Al's wife, Muffy Moore, progeny of the Benjamin Moore Paint family, also had a keen eye for correctness and was a great asset in developing materials, such as brochures, handouts, letters and press releases. But, most of the credit goes to the candidate himself. He had put together a great primary campaign with the right approach, the right people, and the right message and he needed to do it again in the general.

For different reasons, everyone in the campaign office wanted to beat Eli Bebout. Most of the workers and volunteers were registered Democrats and most resented that he abandoned the Democrat party. Some were Republicans who felt they had been badly treated by Geringer and Republican members of the state legislature. For me, it had nothing to do with party politics. I had worked with Eli during the second phase of government reorganization in 1989 when he was a member of the Joint Reorganization Council, some five years before he switched parties. He was an effective council member, along with Representatives Bill Rohrbach and Cynthia Lummis, and Senators Perry, Prevedel and Geringer. Our studies that year covered the Departments of Administration, Health, Family Services, Transportation, and Revenue. As a result of our work, all five agencies were created and Eli, along with the other legislative members, successfully guided the various reorganization bills through their respective houses of the legislature. I liked him and felt that we had worked well together during the entire four-year reorganization project. It wasn't until later, when I was in my second term as State Auditor and he was a new Republican in the Wyoming House of Representatives that a difference developed between us. It was the same issue that began to separate me from a number of other Republicans: ethics. Since changing sides of the isle, he apparently became opposed to ethics legislation. It was during the 1995 Session that he and several other Republican members of both the House and Senate made a visit to my office to explain to me why Wyoming did not need an ethics bill. The meeting was cordial; everyone was polite and respectful; but, there was an irreconcilable difference of opinion between what I thought was good government and what they did. I was especially disappointed in Eli because I knew that he knew better. As Republicans, we had an opportunity and a responsibility to make government, at all levels, better. As Eli ascended to leadership positions over the next few years, he became steadfastly opposed to good government bills such as ethics, lobbyist disclosure, and conflict of interest legislation. He along with his Republican colleagues in the legislature became champions of the status quo. It was as if they had to oppose any reforms in order to demonstrate that their previous arguments had validity and that their actions had been honorable all along. So, I was anxious to help our candidate defeat Eli, not because he was an ex-Democrat but because he was a member of my own party who had opposed the very issues that I believed would have made government in Wyoming better. I doubted that, as Governor, his actions or judgments would be any better. I certainly didn't want to find out.

We began the campaign with a review of the things we did in the primary. For a short period, Dave thought a complete shake-up might be in order so he solicited the advice of a political consultant who had some prior experiences in Republican campaigns. There was very little from the primary campaign that this new guru liked and she immediately suggested that we throw everything out and begin anew. She suggested changing the logo, colors, slogans and messages; everything. Having just pulled off a major upset using these very attributes, naturally everyone who had anything to do with it was surprised; perhaps, shocked is a better description. Why would you abandon everything that was successful and start over, we wondered? Why would Dave even suggest such a thing? Our surprise and shock quickly turned into collective outrage. Here was this stranger who was supposedly an expert whom we'd never even heard of, coming into our offices, criticizing our performance, and challenging our judgment. It was a very unpleasant situation. Everyone wanted to quit. And, most said they would quit rather than work with her. If anyone had any problems with any other member of the staff, they quickly got over it. The problems suddenly involved only her. Everything else was manageable. She unified this staff like nothing I had ever seen. Following a discussion with the candidate about what a disruptive force he had interjected into his own campaign, Dave decided maybe he didn't need new blood, a new direction, or new ideas. Maybe the old blood and ideas that helped him get through the primary would also help get him through the general. That was the last we heard from the strange consultant, but it wasn't the last we heard from Dave on the subject. He explained that he knew all along he wasn't going to use her in the campaign, but he merely brought her in as a tool to get his staff to work better together. It certainly had that effect, but we doubted that it was planned.

So, we kept the old logo, the old colors, the old slogans, and the old people and began the new run against that old Democrat who apparently was now a Republican. Rich again called on the state Democrat headquarters and began a new analysis of voter precincts. This time he was looking for targets which contained swing voters; Republicans and Independents who had previously shown a tendency to switch over and vote for a Democrat. The central party office, under the chairmanship of Linda Stovall was far more helpful than Rich had ever seen it before. Linda and her small staff and capable volunteers helped by providing money, postage, and labor for direct mailings. The party didn't have a lot of money, but it did have a lot of enthusiasm for Dave's candidacy and Linda saw to it that whatever help she could find would be applied.

As the days went by, the money started to roll in from every corner of the state; from small towns and big towns alike; from traditional Democrat areas, but also surprisingly from Republican strongholds. Ranchers and oil and gas producers were sending big checks. Agriculture operators concerned about coal bed methane development and ground water contamination were eager to climb on board. Every day, the mail box was jammed with letters and campaign contributions. It was incredible. Rich would call in every day with his usual question, "How much did we get in today?" "Tens of thousands of dollars," was usually my reply. It was nearly a full-time job just keeping track of the money. We had taken in a little over $250,000 for the primary. Between the primary and the general election, a period of roughly eighty days, receipts totaled over $533,000, an average of nearly $45,000 per week. There were large checks for $1,000, but there were hundreds of smaller individual contributions, ranging from $1 to $1,000 and everywhere in between. Our Statement of Receipts and Expenditures Report[270] filed with the Secretary of State at the end of the campaign consisted of over 70 pages, containing the names of over two thousand individuals who had contributed.

We built on the "People Matter" theme that Dave had expressed in one of the earlier Primary debates, but this wasn't enough. We had to tie it into the various issues that he had advanced throughout the past several months. They had clearly resonated during his bout with Hickey and they would be even more effective in the race

---

[270] Statement of Receipts and Expenditures, Folks for Freudenthal, General Report, November 15, 2002.

against the Republican contender. We continued to operate under a tight budget; cheap offices, small newspaper ads, thirty-second radio spots, unpaid staff, and practically no outside expertise, until late in the campaign. We continued the same approach with our advertising dollars. We would create the newspaper ads, run them by Dave, Hillary, Phil, and Al and then deliver the revised idea to the Wyoming Press Association. The quality of the ads had improved only marginally since the primary and would have to compete with the slick material generated by the well-funded opposition and its seemingly unlimited budget and continuous flow of outside consultants and paid political experts.

We expanded our newspaper ads to displays of 4-column by 3-inch blocks with a picture of Dave and a group of his constituents in the upper left-hand corner. Below the picture was a quote from the candidate and below that was his name within the mountain logo. Running through the middle of the display was a black banner with bold white letters announcing the issue, including the following: Lower Utility Bills Matter!; Public Access Matters!; Lower Taxes Matter!; Agriculture Matters!; Jobs Matter!;Seniors Matter!; Women Matter!; Freedom Matters!; Children Matter!; and, Character Matters!. Underneath the banner was a repeat of the issue, followed by "People Matter, You Matter!" Above the banner was a sentence or two describing how Dave would address the issue, when elected. Because of the pictures, the ads were warm and fuzzy. The wordage was brief, direct and to the point. They conveyed the message that people really do matter; that, you, the reader, matter. We spent over $40,000 getting that message out.

In the latter stages of the campaign, Dave brought in professionals to outline and create his radio and television advertising program. The media consultants were hired during the last week of September and they worked with Phil, Liz Storer, and Dave to develop the media blitz that would run during the month of October and through Election Day in November. The Washington DC firm, McWilliams, Robinson, developed the spots and placed the buys in the radio and television media and nearly $350,000 was expended during the last five weeks. It was apparently just enough, as when the votes were counted, we had 3,789 more votes than Bebout.[271] It was Freudenthal with 92,662 votes to Bebout's 88,873 votes; a 49.96% to 47.92% victory. Bebout won in sixteen of the twenty-three counties, but we won in most of those areas with the larger number of voters. We won Albany by 2,368 votes; Laramie, by 7,076; Natrona by 3,350; and, Sweetwater by 2,783. As expected, Bebout won in his home county, Fremont, by a margin of 2,608 votes. The third party candidate, Dave Dawson, garnered a total of 3,924 votes statewide. In total, 185,459 votes were cast for Governor in the general election.

It was a particularly sweet victory, given the odds. Forty-nine of the sixty-six Wyoming Republican legislators had supported our opponent.[272] The national Republican Party brought in the big guns in an attempt to defeat us and it nearly worked. Vice President Dick Cheney and his wife, Lynne, were featured attractions at Republican Party rallies throughout the State and on November 4, 2002, Cheney spoke to a crowd of several hundred people at the Cheyenne Civic Center.[273] According to the *New York Times,*

---

271 http://soswy.state.wy.us/Elections/Docs/2002/02Results/02General/02_General%20Election_SW.candidates.

272 "Republican Legislators Support Bebout," *Wyoming Tribune-Eagle*, Lara Azar, July 9, 2002.

273 "The 2002 Campaign: The Vice President; On Friendly Turf in Wyoming, Cheney Tries to Help Keep Top Jobs in G.O.P. Hands," *The New York Times*, Michael Janofsky, November 4, 2002.

he urged the voters to keep their highest elected positions in the hands of Republicans, as they now were. "In his 25-minute speech to a cheering crowd of several hundred . . . . Mr. Cheney talked little of the candidates sharing the stage with him. Instead, he stuck closely to a stump speech in which he emphasized the importance of supporting Bush administration strategies against Iraq and the terrorists of Al Qaeda," the *Times* said. The article went on to say: "As he had in previous stops, Mr. Cheney delivered his words slowly, his style a somber contrast to the other Republican speakers here, who tried to fire up the crowd with exhortations to defeat the Democrats on Election Day."[274]

John Gizzi of another national publication, *Human Events Publishing*, said in his October 14, 2002, publication,[275]that "winning the governorship in Dick Cheney's Wyoming would be a major blow to Republicans--one that national Democrats would love to deliver." The article said it would be like taking the governorship in George W. Bush's Texas. Gizzy, noting Bebout's "pro-life and . . . conservative stands on other cultural issues," referenced Bebout's televised endorsement from "none other than former Sen. (1978-98) Alan Simpson (R-Wyo), who is widely known for his pro-abortion stance, his support of the pro-homosexual Republican Unity Coalition, and his acidic remarks about the Christian Coalition and like-minded groups." As a friend and admirer of Al Simpson, it bothered me that Gizzy snidely referred to the Senator with such contempt, but Gizzy was absolutely right about the national Democrats wanting to win in Wyoming and offering to help. However, Dave didn't accept their help. He didn't want to be associated with the national Democrats

[274] Ibid.

[275] Op. cit., John Gizzi.

in any way. He won without any input or financial help from the national party. That party had absolutely nothing to do with the election results.

We won, but we didn't win without making a few mistakes or blunders along the way. Early in the race, we engaged a national pollster to analyze, not only Dave's positioning in the contest; the typical right direction/wrong direction assessment; both candidates favorability numbers and negatives and the usual things a statewide poll would measure. The pollster concluded that the number one concern among Wyoming voters was elementary and secondary education. Education had always been one of Dave's major issues, but we hadn't considered it to be the top concern and it turned out that it wasn't; economic development was actually number one. "It's the economy, stupid," remained the hot button issue. Luckily, Dave's "business ready" community program addressed those concerns and our shifting emphasis late in the contest did not alter the outcome. The pollster got it wrong and we nearly did, too.

Another blunder in our campaign involved a lobbying group and our campaign manager. "Kiss my ass," Phil shouted into his telephone early one Monday morning. He was talking to an official of the Wyoming Heritage Foundation. The organization,[276] established in 1979, was created to promote the State's economy and initially focused on opposing state taxes and fighting with the federal government (Bureau of Land Management) over federal land issues which were thought to interfere with many of Wyoming's industries, including oil and gas, ranching, timbering, and tourism. It later turned its attention to economic diversification and around 1990, began an aggressive lobbying effort of the Wyoming legislature.

[276] http://www/wyomingbusinessalliance.com/

The organization claims that its members and partners "represent over 80,000 individuals and employees who share a commitment to Wyoming's economy."[277] The group further declares that the Foundation is "Wyoming's largest, most diversified business advocate." Assuming these claims are true, it is obvious that any conflict with such a powerful organization ought to be avoided. But, this didn't concern Phil. He said what many of us had thought at one time or another over the years. He was responding to a demand that Dave attend one of the Heritage Foundation's forums to discuss its ideas on economic development. The candidate had no interest in attending and ultimately was able to fix the damage resulting from Phil's rather insensitive outburst.

We narrowly escaped making another mistake and that was the hiring of the Republican consultant immediately following the primary. She was on board for a short time and she nearly cost us all of our full-time volunteers. Had we followed her advice the outcome would likely have turned out differently.

It was a great victory; a great upset and Dave went on to be one of the great Governors in Wyoming history. He was re-elected in 2006 by the greatest percentage in the State's history and when he left office at the end of his second term, he had the highest approval rating of any Governor in the Country, at over 80%.[278] He left his successor, Republican Matt Mead, with a balanced budget and over a billion dollar surplus.

---

277 http://www.wyomingbusinessalliance.com/jantoday.html.

278 http://www.crowell.com/professionals/Dave-Freudenthal

# CHAPTER FOURTEEN

## Think About Living

On Saturday, July 12, 2008, Tony Snow died. I admired Tony for his work at Fox News and then as press secretary to the President and felt deep compassion for him and his family in their battle with cancer. His picture, along with President George W. Bush, was in the newspaper and on the internet that morning. He looked tired and worn out, reflective of the long struggle he'd been through. His hair was thin, grey, and kind of disheveled--evidence of the chemo treatments he endured but which failed to save his life. This is the mark cancer leaves on its victims, and, sadly, it is often the last impression that remains.

The emptiness that I felt that morning was not only because of Tony Snow's passing, but was also related to my own challenge which began some six weeks earlier. I was surprised one morning to see a few drops of blood in the toilet. The sight of blood was, of course, a concern but was not overly alarming inasmuch as I had experienced something similar a few years earlier. I figured, or perhaps hoped, the blood was somehow related to or was due to a minor infection in the urinary tract. Having just completed blood tests at the local Health Fair and getting good results on the

PSA exam and all other lab work, the idea of cancer was only a fleeting thought. Nonetheless, I did call Dr. Lugg's Office and was scheduled to see him on May 29th, some six weeks before reading about Tony. The initial encounter with the nurse that Thursday morning resulted in a urine sample and it was quickly confirmed that, although invisible to the eye, there was indeed hematuria, or blood in the urine.

Dr. Lugg explained that any number of things might be to blame and it could be nothing serious, but we needed to figure out what was causing it. Several tests were scheduled and a number of abnormalities were revealed. I had a cyst on each kidney and a lesion that showed up in the bladder. The cysts were not a concern and did not need to be treated, but surgery was necessary to remove the lesion in the bladder. On June 23rd the tumor was removed and, during the procedure, two additional tumors were discovered. Dr Lugg thought he had removed the cancer completely and that it had not penetrated the bladder wall. To be sure, a second surgery would be necessary.

Being an ex-smoker, I had always feared getting cancer. I fully expected, however, it would be cancer of the lungs. And, it still may be. But, cancer of the bladder was never a concern. And, even if it turned out to be curable, it was very traumatic to learn that I had cancer. I didn't know what the outcome of the cancer treatments would be. Perhaps it would be similar to Tony's, or numerous others I have known. I had always heard and believed that cancer was a very painful disease and from the looks of some of its victims, it obviously is, but, so far, in my case, it had not been physically painful. There was another kind of pain, though, that surprised me. It was the pain of feeling alone with this sickness. All of my life, both personally and professionally, I had been a member of a group, a family, a team. It had always been "we," "us," "our." Any success I had ever enjoyed had largely been influenced by the efforts of others. Any failure or hardship had been shared by that team. The team I had always been a part of would be replaced by a medical team who would no doubt do their best to get rid of that awful growth that I didn't even know was there.

The second surgery was performed on Monday, July 14th, three weeks following that initial visit to the operating room. It was similar to the first. I awoke in the care of a gentle young angel who seemed very concerned about my comfort. She stayed by my side for the next hour and when my vital signs stabilized, we made the trip back to the room where I would spend the next twenty four hours. Dr. Lugg was there shortly to announce that everything went well, and we would know very little more until the pathology report was received, which would not occur for several days. If more cancer was found, he said, we would be looking at additional surgery. It might be necessary to remove the bladder and replace it with a rebuilt from my intestines. I was, of course, horrified at the prospect of going through that kind of procedure. The simple one I had just endured was plenty bad enough, including the insertion of a catheter which seemed to endlessly bleed, rub, pull and tug at me with a level of discomfort that I suspect only a man with a vivid imagination can understand.

The idea of going through life with less than an original bladder, which would require that a drain hose be attached to it, was a thought that I simply couldn't escape. There was an endless flow of blood through the catheter and as the hours passed, the stream became clearer and clearer. Kathy, my caring and compassionate nurse, became increasingly excited as the red dye in the liquid began to fade. But, even her enthusiasm couldn't erase the mounting fear of the possibility that a bag would be strapped to my leg for the rest of my life. I knew I was feeling some stress, but had no idea how much until the blood pressure readings went off the chart. As it reached its peak, Kathy's enthusiasm turned to concern as she ushered my doctor back into the room. He explained that the outcome was no longer in my hands, but instead was "in the hands of God." "You need to talk to him about this," he explained. "You need to turn this over to the Lord and then have the strength and courage to deal with whatever comes." I had hoped for a more positive medical assessment of the situation, but the closest he could come to that was when he said, "You have an excellent surgeon; put this in my hands. Let me do the worrying. Between God and me, we'll take care of you." Shortly following this discussion, the blood pressure readings returned to normal.

The catheter was removed a couple of days later, at which time the physician's assistance announced that the pathology report was negative. This news brought a level of excitement and relief that is indescribable, but I managed to contain my enthusiasm until the information could be confirmed and further explained by the surgeon several days later. Dr. Lugg entered the room with a huge smile on his face and relief in his voice. "All of the news is good news," he said. "There is no more cancer." "If you have to have what you have, this is the best news I could possibly give you." He explained that we would begin six consecutive weeks of BCG instillations. These are painless treatments in which medicine is instilled into the bladder through a catheter. Following these treatments we would need to perform a cystoscopy every three months for several years to monitor the bladder to make sure if the cancer returns it is found and treated quickly. "You won't die of bladder cancer," the doctor assured me. As he got up from his chair to leave the room, I reached out to shake his hand and to thank him for saving me from cancer.

He ignored my hand shake and instead wrapped his arms around me for a hug. I'm pretty sure we both needed that.

I was told to take the next six months off. "I don't want you lifting anything heavier than a pillow for the next several months," advised Dr. Lugg. For someone who had been busy his entire life, this was a prescription that I thought would be hard to follow, but I tried. The surgery left me weak and ten pounds lighter. I really didn't feel like doing much. A lot of time was spent reading, mostly out on the back patio at my home on West 6th Avenue. In fact, among other books, I read the New Testament twice during that six-month period. The second time through, I highlighted all of the writings that seemed especially meaningful, contradictory, or controversial. Then, I went back and reviewed all of the highlighted areas. I don't know what was gained from this experience, but, for years, it was something I wanted to do, and until then, had kept putting it off. I had always been spiritual, or at least frequently talked with God, but had not been active with a church since my days growing up in Veteran. In some cases, reading the scriptures only led to additional confusion, not clarity. But, the entire experience; the surgery, the fear, the readings, the endless hours of inactivity, gave me a lot of time to think. All of this combined to bring me closer to God. I made some deals with him over this incident; commitments I should have made years ago, but didn't. These deals weren't agreements or sacrifices in exchange for freeing me from cancer; rather, they were an acknowledgement, a renewed appreciation of the truly important things and people in my life, and a commitment to always put these things and people first.

As promised by Dr. Lugg, the BCG treatment, which involves inserting a straw-like tube through the male organ, extending about six inches into the bladder, is not painful. The initial insertion is the worst part, but lasts only a few seconds. Once the five ounces of BCG medicine is inserted, which takes roughly three minutes, the catheter is slowly and painlessly removed. Initially, this activity was embarrassing but after a while became less traumatic.

Following the initial six weeks of BCG treatments, the first cystoscopy was conducted. The results were good. I had feared the cancer would put up a bigger fight, refusing to be removed from its new home. But, so far, Dr. Lugg and his staff had prevailed. There was no trace of the cancer, but as a preventive measure, additional BCG treatments were to be a part of my life for the next couple of years, followed by a cystoscopy every six months. I could certainly live with that.

I would have eight more cystoscopies since that fateful diagnosis in 2008 and some fifteen BCG treatments. I feel indeed fortunate to have escaped so far. Too many people have not. But, I still think about cancer almost every day because I know it can return at any moment, or show up somewhere else without warning. What I had gone through and was going through was simply nothing compared to what others have endured. On Friday, May 22, 2010, I watched "Farah's Story," the documentary put together by Farah Fawset about her battle with cancer, which eventually spread to the pancreas. It was very depressing to watch this beautiful, talented lady suffer with this fatal disease and to think that someday soon, we would be without her. Her story had an impact, perhaps because I didn't know how my own story would end. Sadly, Farah's story ended on June 25, 2010, when she died from the dreadful disease. I had hoped that somehow she would be the miracle patient who would survive despite the desperate condition she was in. Farah, Tony Snow, Patrick Swazy, Elizabeth Edwards, Steve Jobs, to name a few, were all given the cancer death sentence. But, their cancers were not of the bladder. So far, I have escaped and, ironically, it is comforting to think that I will die of something else.

I don't know that I ever worried about dying of bladder cancer. Rather, I was fearful of living with it. I was reminded of Tony Snow's comments as he left his job as Press Secretary to President Bush. "Don't think about dying," he said, "think about living." I have taken both Dr. Lugg's and Tony's advice. I don't think about dying. I think about living and appreciating life, people, and the other things that I had taken for granted all of my life. Since surviving this disease, I have shared with other bladder cancer victims the things I learned during those terrifying few months. I have tried to provide encouragement to others by sharing my own success story. If I can survive, so can they. Yes, it is in God's hands. But, I think God expects us to help.

My mother was always a worrier. She worried about everything; her home, her car, her work, her children, her mother, her sisters, how many children Kay and I would have, when we would give her a girl–everything, including cancer. She had survived the disease herself, but often wondered if it would return. I could relate to this, with regard to cancer, but I try to remember the advice given by Dr. Lugg and Tony Snow. I let the doctors worry about treating cancer should it return. I worry about the things I can control. I try to stay out of the sun, eat the right foods, avoid abusing alcohol or tobacco, and get plenty of exercise; and, I do think about living. Cancer is, as are all things, in God's hands. Somehow I dodged a bullet. In the meantime, I will try to keep everything in perspective, being thankful for all that I have and not worrying much about all that I don't.

# Epilogue

Neither of my parents was involved in politics, but they never failed to vote and they cast their ballots very carefully. They loved their Country and they paid attention to the actions of their elected officials. They liked FDR, President Kennedy, and Governor Hathaway, and didn't care much for Nixon. I don't know if they would be outraged by the actions of our politicians today, but they would certainly be disappointed and disgusted. Their lives were not defined by politics, and neither was mine. Some things are far more important.

I never really knew my grandparents. Grandma Ferrari was dead before I came along, as was Grandpa Bailey. She died in 1933 at the age of 54. I never knew when Grandpa passed on and to this day, I don't know anything about him. Grandma Belle, his wife, was married to Cal Woolen when I first met her. She lasted until she was ninety-two years old. She lived in a small apartment not far from my parent's home, while I was growing up. My mother usually had Grandma over for Sunday dinner so I did spend a little time with her at the dinner table and then later as she relaxed in my dad's rocking chair in the living room. I remember her as a very pleasant lady, usually smiling and always happy. But, I never really knew her.

Grandpa Ferrari lived in Portland and I saw him only once, when I was 12 years old. He lived in a one-room shack with no running water and a dirt floor. Liuge Guiseppi Ferrari died on August 22, 1963. He now resides in Grave No. 1; Lot No. E ½ - 222; Section P, in Rose City Cemetery, in Portland. I suspect his quarters are a lot like that one-room shack I visited over fifty years ago, but, of course much smaller. My Aunt Linda thought I ought to have the cemetery papers along with my grandfather's immigration documents. Certificate of Naturalization No.1890507 was issued by the Court of Common Pleas in Edensburg, Pennsylvania, Cambria County on January 2, 1924. The document said he was 46 years old at the time, stood 5 feet, 4 inches, and had six children. He was a "Subject of Italy" and lived in Dysart, PA. He couldn't read or write, as evidenced by the check-mark, rather than signature by his name. The signature line was apparently completed by Mr. Walter Williams, the Court Notary, inasmuch as his and my grandfather's names were written in similar style, and both were obviously completed by the same black-inked calligraphic pen.

Grandpa's certificate came to me in a leather case, housed in a container made of heavy paper, which was then wrapped in a large sheet of waxed paper. All were worn nearly to extinction which my Aunt said reflected the pride of citizenship he felt and the hundreds of times he had taken the document out to show it off. I would have liked to have been there on at least one occasion to witness this patriotic gesture but that wasn't to be. I'm pretty sure he didn't march in the streets or protest for immigrant rights nor fly or wave the Italian flag after arriving in this Country. I am told because of his pride in his new homeland, he would speak only English, not the language of his birthplace. But, he did apply for and receive a social security number and card which was included in the envelope containing his burial and citizenship papers. I haven't figured out for sure what to do with these documents but will probably pass them on to one of the sons or grandsons with the surname Ferrari.

Prior to that trip to Portland with my parents when I was twelve, my father hadn't seen his own father in over 25 years. I guess that's how it was back then, especially for families with worn out vehicles and limited means. I always felt bad for both of them because I'm pretty sure neither wanted so much time and distance between them. How do you know someone that you only see every twenty-five years or so? I could never imagine not seeing my own parents for over two decades and I guess that's probably why Kay and I never got very far from our childhood homes.

Ours began on May 29, 1966, in the Presbyterian Church on North Main Street in Torrington. We had just finished our studies at the University; she earlier that month, and me, in January of that year. We had found a place in Cheyenne where she would eventually begin her teaching career and I, my own in business and government, after finishing active duty with the Air National Guard. Kay was always a happy, bubbly, vivacious girl who was adored completely by my parents, and especially by my dad. They were elated when we first told them they were to be grandparents in 1967. Brian was born on the 15th of July that summer and it wasn't long after that that my mother began nagging us that she wanted a granddaughter. We managed to ignore her for over five years, but on September 10, 1972, our second child was born. Justin wasn't the gender my mom had requested, but he was certainly the right one for me. I preferred to have boys. I didn't gain an appreciation for daughters until after watching my two sisters dote over both of their parents for most of the last twenty-five years. Having daughters seems now like it would have been a pretty good idea. I should have probably listened more to my mother. I doubt that either of my sons will be particularly good at changing my underwear or bed sheets and giving sponge baths, if it should come to that. But, I'm pretty sure they will give it a try.

I have been very blessed with a great family, going both directions. My parents were always there for me. My folks provided a very supportive and loving environment with strong values, and encouragement to pursue any challenge. They never pushed, but they always guided. In spite of my mother's frequent outbursts and my dad's silence, there was never a question of whether or not they loved their children. But, it wasn't until they could see their own ends coming that they spoke of their love. I, myself, have neglected to express these same emotions to family and friends far too many times for far too long.

Few have experienced the level of sibling kindness and caring that I have enjoyed my entire life. One probably does not begin to appreciate these virtues until the latter stages. Having watched a number of families battle over the remnants of their parent's estates, it is indeed a blessing never to have had the same experience. The personal belongings left behind by my mother were chosen by my sisters for their loving memories, not for their monetary values. Most of the things of value had been used up long ago for assisted living and nursing home expenses. The items claimed from my dad when he departed some twenty years earlier were likewise important remnants of his presence while he was here. Although both of my parents had, neither one needed, a will at the end. That is one of the advantages of going out of this world in the same shape as when you entered. Even if there had been anything worth fighting over, a fight would never have occurred. Neither my sisters nor brother would have engaged in this kind of family destruction for any amount of financial gain.

My children have displayed these same instincts, remaining close to their mother and me over the years. We have five grand children, three boys and two girls, ranging in ages from five to eighteen. The boys are all good athletes, involved in, soccer, football, basketball, tennis and water sports, so we get plenty of opportunities to enjoy watching them participate. They, so far, are equally good kids, showing the desire to succeed in school as well as showing kindness to those around them. Like all young people, I guess, occasionally one or more of the three boys will disappoint. So far, however, they have always returned to their roots.

Brian, our oldest son is now forty-six and for more than sixteen years has been a single dad. He and Marcus, who is eighteen, live within a few miles of our home. His little girl, Kaylan, lives with her mom but we see her often. Brian and I were in business together for about five years, reconstructing houses for resale. Neither of us possessed the skills that my dad had for carpentry and I often regret that I didn't have the good sense to learn as much from him as I could when I had the chance. There seemed to always be other things that were more important at the time. Brian was much smarter, taking full advantage of, not only what little I knew, but also learning all that he could from the private contractors we hired. There is little that he didn't learn during those times. I count those years as some of the most rewarding in my working life, and I'm pretty sure he does as well. Ironically, he now spends his professional career as an auditor of minerals, for the State of Wyoming, in one of the programs that I had helped create so many years earlier.

Our other son, Justin is now 41. He is a manager at a computer company in Broomfield. He puts in very long hours, often 70 to 80 a week, but seems to enjoy it. He and Cindy have three children. They live in Denver along with their boys, Payton and Connor, and daughter Brooke. The boys are sixteen and fourteen. Both also play sports and in fact their parents coach their teams; Justin, soccer and Cindy, basketball. Cindy is a beautiful blond athlete herself who played college basketball and was an all-state high school player. Her teams are very well coached and all players know they have to give it their best effort or they'll be sitting on the bench. She is a grade school teacher so obviously knows how to communicate with the youngsters. Granddaughter, Brooke, is nine, and, a handful. She is a gymnast, spunky, creative and always on the go. She is little for her age and is very blond, like her mother. She pretty much runs their household, which took the boys a while to get used to. She is obviously fond of her grandma and the feeling is mutual. They have a lot of fun together.

If he were alive today, Grandpa Liuge no doubt would be proud of what he started here in America. Although there were a lot of decedents, my dad was the only of his offspring to extend the family name. Between my brother and me, and our three sons, there are now six young Ferrari boys running around. Ken and Lynda have ten grandchildren; six carry grandpa's last name. Like his son, Grandpa Liuge would be especially impressed with Kay who has been a rock over the past forty-seven years. I'm not sure about her, but I made a very good choice. I never expected to have anything but a lifetime of wonderful happy years when we came together that day in May forty-seven years ago. But, this has turned out to be even better than I could have imagined.

Dad has been gone now for over twenty-five years and mom for over four. I never did get used to the idea. There are few days that they don't cross my mind. If my presence, while it lasted, has the same lingering impression, then this journey, through politics and back can be said to have taken the right course. And, in the end, that really is the only thing that matters.